University Teaching

University Teaching

A Reference Guide
for Graduate Students and Faculty

SECOND EDITION

Edited by

Stacey Lane Tice, Nicholas Jackson,
Leo M. Lambert, *and* Peter Englot

With a Foreword by Jerry G. Gaff

SYRACUSE UNIVERSITY PRESS

Library of Congress Cataloging-in-Publication Data
University teaching : a reference guide for graduate students and
faculty / edited by Stacey Lane Tice . . . [et al.] ; with a foreword by
Jerry G. Gaff.— 2nd ed.
       p. cm.
     Includes bibliographical references and index.
       ISBN 0-8156-3079-4 (pbk. : alk. paper)
     1. College teaching—United States.   I. Tice, Stacey Lane.
LB2331.U757 2005
378.1'25—dc22   2005002851

Manufactured in the United States of America

Contents

Foreword

Jerry G. Gaff

THIS BOOK IS A VALUABLE REFERENCE for anyone trying to understand what Parker Palmer calls the "maddening mysteries" of teaching. I have always viewed teaching as one of the helping professions and thought that for teachers to be effective, they need a rich panoply of "people skills." Unfortunately, the academy often neglects to cultivate such skills among graduate students and faculty. The essays that follow are thoughtful efforts by experienced teachers—many of whom have been involved with the national Preparing Future Faculty program—to explore various ways of engaging, encouraging, and stimulating students to learn.

This book contains everything you always wanted to know about teaching—but were afraid to ask. The twenty-five chapters cover everything from traditional topics—lecturing, leading discussions, and designing laboratory and studio courses—to present challenges—teaching for diversity, using technology, assessing student learning, and service learning, to name just a few. But they also venture beyond the classical and perennial issues of teaching and learning to deal with such timely topics as the adjunct instructor, nontraditional students, ethical issues in teaching, and the balancing of multiple responsibilities.

One of the reasons this book is so useful is that it is written *for* teachers *by* teachers. Filled with personal reflections and examples, this collection of essays provides vivid pictures of teachers thinking their way through the process of facilitating student learning—a process that necessarily involves both understanding various sources of student passivity and indifference, and identifying techniques that may overcome them.

The book's audience of graduate students and new faculty members will find plenty of information that may quickly be applied. The content will be especially useful in developing teaching assistants, preparing future faculty, and helping to orient new faculty. But its utility goes well beyond these formal programs; it will prove useful to individuals seeking to broaden their repertoire of approaches to teaching and learning or, indeed, hoping to gain fresh perspectives on their own teaching.

This guide builds upon the success of an earlier book published a few years ago. New and revised chapters venture beyond the content of that earlier volume and include discussion and analysis of cutting-edge topics in teaching and learning in higher education. Collectively, these essays constitute an excellent example of "reflective practice." (There is, in fact, a whole chapter devoted to that subject.) Drs. Tice and Lambert have rendered a valuable service to the academic profession by assembling these useful essays about many aspects of effective teaching and learning across the landscape of contemporary higher education.

Preface

NOW IS A TIME of high expectation and demand for colleges and universities. Ours is a world of rapid technological transformation and globalization, pressing issues of diversity, increasingly rigorous standards of accountability, and hectic current events that leave no one unaffected. This changing world constitutes a great challenge to those in institutions of higher learning, whether they are students, faculty, or administrators.

Many institutions are trying to meet the challenge by strengthening and refining the development of graduate students and new faculty as instructors. In the late 1980s and early 1990s, many institutions began offering university-wide teaching assistant development programs. In the mid 1990s, with funding from such grant agencies as the Fund for the Improvement of Postsecondary Education (FIPSE) and the Pew Charitable Trusts, several universities established future faculty development programs. One example of this type of program is the American Association of Colleges and Universities (AAC&U) and the Council of Graduate Schools (CGS) Preparing Future Faculty program (PFF). Another initiative, created by the University of New Hampshire, is the Partnership for Academic Programs in College Teaching (PACT). Both participant institutions of PFF-PACT and many others have developed programs (such as university-teaching certification) to respond to the need for faculty who are prepared to succeed in all aspects of life in the academy. In particular, this text focuses on resources and strategies that will be useful to graduate student instructors and new faculty.

As an outgrowth of PFF this book is a compilation of insights provided by faculty, postdoctorate fellows, graduate students, and administrators, all of whom have distinguished themselves as scholars and teachers. The authors of the twenty-five chapters represent many different disciplines and fields and several different colleges and universities. Their range of experiences and diversity of perspective will be obvious to any reader, and they give the book a valuable breadth and depth.

The editors are particularly grateful to Enid Bogle and Harry Richards, who provided feedback on our plan for the book and suggested authors with whom they were collaborating as the PFF directors of their respective institutions, Howard University and the University of New Hampshire. They are tremendous colleagues who have made numerous contributions to university teaching, both at their home institutions and across the nation, for at least a decade. Drawing on their experience and wisdom, we decided to feature chapters that would encourage reflective practice and to focus on strategies to enhance learning for all students—strategies for assessing student learning, teaching, and mentoring. We also included suggestions on how to foster "deep learning"—learning that will have an impact on society—and material to assist new instructors in balancing multiple responsibilities, considering institutional context, and selecting employment that appropriately matches their strengths and interests.

Through the exceptional PFF leadership of Jerry Gaff and Anne Pruitt-Logan, we have been fortunate to collaborate with graduate school deans, faculty, and graduate students from many different types of institutions across the country in developing practices that will help faculty succeed in a changing environment with many competing demands.

We would be remiss if we failed to mention Bry Pollack's thoughtful comments and editorial guidance; she provided valuable wisdom and advice to both the first edition and this version.

We must also recognize the efforts of our colleagues at Elon University and in the Professional Development Programs of the Graduate School at Syracuse University, who have enabled us to spend time working on this project.

Finally, we must acknowledge the exceptional work of the faculty and graduate students who took the time to envision their chapters and write them with the broad perspective of the entire collection of essays in mind. They have worked vigorously and painstakingly throughout, and we are fortunate to have had the opportunity to collaborate with such fine scholars and teachers.

Stacey Lane Tice
Syracuse University

Contributors

Kristi Andersen, professor of political science in the Maxwell School, has been on the Syracuse University faculty since 1984, where she has served as director of graduate studies and chair of the department. She has been active since 1992 in SU's Future Professoriate Project.

Christine L. Bean is professor of medical laboratory science in the Department of Animal, Nutritional, and Medical Laboratory Science at the University of New Hampshire. She received the School of Health and Human Services Teaching Excellence Award in 1997.

Enid Bogle served as the director of the Graduate Expository Writing Program and the Preparing Future Faculty program at Howard University. Dr. Bogle recently spent two summers training high school teachers of English in Addis Ababa and Makele (Ethiopia).

Steve Braye is an associate professor of English and director of the General Studies Program at Elon University.

Joanne D. Burke is the educational program coordinator for the university system of New Hampshire's College for Lifelong Learning, Portsmouth, New Hampshire. Dr. Burke is also an adjunct nutrition instructor at Boston College in the James A. Woods, S.J., College of Advancing Studies. Her research has examined the role of carotenoids in the diet and eye health.

Heather Frasier Chabot is assistant professor of psychology at New England College in Henniker, New Hampshire. She earned a Ph.D. in social psychology from the University of New Hampshire in 1999, an M.A. in sports studies from Miami University, and a B.A. in biology. As a result of her diverse background, she has had the opportunity to teach a wide variety of courses.

Marvin Druger is professor of biology and science education and chair of the Department of Science Teaching at Syracuse University. He has received numerous awards for science teaching and has been president of three national science teaching organizations: the National Science Teachers Association (NSTA), the Association for the Education of Teachers of Science (AETS), and the Society for College Science Teachers (SCST). He is a Meredith Professor for Teaching Excellence at Syracuse University.

Kimarie Engerman is a Preparing Future Faculty Postdoctoral Fellow in the Department of Human Development and Psychoeducational Studies at Howard University. She was the recipient of the Bennetta B. Washington Memorial Dissertation Award and the Center for Drug Abuse Research Teaching Award.

Anne Schaper Englot is professor of architecture in the Department of Engineering Technologies at the State University of New York, Morrisville. She is a past presenter at the Ubiquitous Computing Conference (2000) and will be published in the forthcoming "Ubiquitous Computing: The Universal Use of Computers on College Campuses" (Bolton, Mass.: Anker). She successfully defended her dissertation in the humanities at Syracuse University in spring 2005.

Peter Englot is director of recruitment for the Graduate Enrollment Management Center of Syracuse University and a doctoral student in Cultural Foundations of Education. He has worked in many areas of graduate affairs at Syracuse over his sixteen-year professional career. His academic interests center on the philosophy of higher education.

Jerry Evensky taught junior high social studies for six years in Webster Groves, Missouri, before joining the Economics Department at Syracuse University. At Syracuse, Dr. Evensky teaches a one-semester introductory economics survey course for which he wrote the book and developed an interactive CD. He has also taught the history of economic thought, current issues in the United States, understanding Rosie the Riveter, and labor economics. His research focuses on Adam Smith's moral philosophy, on the relationship between social systems (in particular ethical systems) and economic processes, and on systems for dynamic assessment of student performance. In 1996 he was honored as a Laura J. and L. Douglas Meredith Professor for Teaching Excellence.

Patricia Featherstone lives in the Baltics, where she is professor of English at Concordia International University in Estonia. In addition to teaching graduate and undergraduate composition, speech, and literature courses, Dr. Featherstone is a member of the university's Academic Council and is the chair of the Professional Development Committee. In 2000 she won the outstanding teaching award.

Michael Flusche earned his Ph.D. in history from Johns Hopkins University and has published a number of articles on southern history and literature. He began his career at Syracuse University in 1970 as a faculty member in the History Department. He currently serves as associate vice-chancellor for academic affairs. In this capacity Dr. Flusche has been responsible for establishing such programs as the Department Chairs Leadership Development Program, the New Faculty Orientation Program, the Meredith Professorships for Excellence in Teaching, and the Chancellor's Citation program. He also teaches Freshman Forum and serves as an academic adviser.

Jerry G. Gaff, who received his Ph.D. in psychology from Syracuse University in 1965, has become over his forty-year career a leading figure in the movement to improve undergraduate education. Beginning in the 1960s as a teacher in the experimental Raymond College at the University of the Pacific, he has contributed to progress in a variety of educational arenas, notably general education, preparing future faculty, faculty development, academic leadership, and strategies for organizational change. He is now senior scholar at the Association of American Colleges and Universities (AAC&U).

Peter J. Gray earned his Ph.D. in educational psychology from the University of Oregon in 1979. As director of academic assessment he is responsible for developing and maintaining a broad program of academic assessment at the U.S. Naval Academy. This job includes supporting and coordinating assessment activities of institution-wide efforts as well as those of programs, departments, and individual faculty members. Dr. Gray is the lead author of "Assessment of Student Learning: Options and Resources," the handbook of the Middle States Association Commission on Higher Education. He also recently wrote "Roots of Assessment: Tensions, Solutions, and Research Directions," a chapter in *Building a Scholarship of Assessment,* edited by T. W. Banta (San Francisco: Jossey-Bass, 2002).

Hilton Hallock, former associate director of the Professional Development Programs in the Graduate School of Syracuse University, recently received her Ph.D. in Cultural Foundations of Education at Syracuse University. Dr. Hallock's teaching experience includes courses in service learning, academic programs, student affairs administration, and legal issues in higher education. She is currently a faculty member in the Graduate School of Education at the University of Pennsylvania.

Jane Hendler earned her doctoral degree in English from Syracuse University in 1998. She is the author of *Best-Sellers and Their Film Adaptations in Postwar America: From Here to Eternity, Sayonara, Giant, Auntie Mame, Peyton Place* (2001). Currently Dr. Hendler is teaching part-time in the English Department at Monroe Community College, Rochester, New York.

Sandra Hurd is professor and chair of law and public policy in the School of Management and also serves as Syracuse University's faculty coordinator for learning communities. She was named a Master Teacher by the Academy of Legal Studies in Business, is a member of the Syracuse University Gateway Fellowship, received the School of Management Award for Excellence in Teaching, and was awarded a Chancellor's Citation for Outstanding Contributions to the University's Academic Programs. She is currently serving as interim dean of the School of Management.

Nicholas Jackson is a doctoral candidate in history at the Maxwell School of Citizenship and Public Affairs of Syracuse University, where he has served for four years as a teaching assistant for courses in European history. He is a university fellow and specializes in seventeenth-century English political and intellectual history.

W. Brad Johnson is an assistant professor of psychology in the Department of Leadership, Ethics, and Law at the U.S. Naval Academy. Dr. Johnson is also a faculty associate in the Graduate School of Business and Education at Johns Hopkins University.

Leo M. Lambert is the president of Elon University. He founded the Future Professoriate Project at Syracuse University, where he also directed the Teaching Assistant Program in the Graduate School. In 1998 *Change* magazine listed him among forty young leaders of the academy, and in 2002 his alma mater, SUNY Geneseo, awarded him an honorary doctorate of humane letters in recognition of his contributions to higher education.

Michael Lee is associate director of the Center for Teaching Excellence at the University of New Hampshire and program coordinator of the Partnership for Academic Programs in College Teaching. He holds a Ph.D. in American literature and has taught in the UNH English Department for fifteen years.

Yoram Lubling is associate professor of philosophy at Elon University. His previous published work includes articles on the classical tradition in American philosophy, Martin Buber, post-Holocaust philosophy, aesthetics, philosophy of education, and Jewish philosophy. Dr. Lubling is currently spending a sabbatical writing a book about the philosophical and psychological process of "overcoming."

Bonnie McClellan, director of disability support services at the Catholic University of America, Washington, D.C., has served as a learning specialist and disability consultant to students and faculty at the postsecondary level for more than twenty-three years. She is a frequent presenter at faculty-development workshops and has presented at local and national disability conferences on issues related to learning disabilities and attention-deficit disorder.

Le'Ann Milinder is the New Hampshire state clinical director at the Institute of Professional Practice, a human services agency that supports people with disabilities. She also serves on the faculty for the joint graduate program in education offered by the Institute and Johnson State College in Vermont. She earned her Ph.D. in psychology and M.S.T. in college teaching from the University of New Hampshire in 2002.

Mark Monmonier is distinguished professor of geography at Syracuse University's Maxwell School. His awards include a Guggenheim Fellowship (1984–85), a Chancellor's Citation for Exceptional Academic Achievement (1993), and the American Geographical Society's O. M. Miller Medal for "for outstanding contributions in the field of cartography" (2001).

Diane Lyden Murphy is director of the Women's Studies Program in the College of Arts and Sciences and a tenured faculty member in the School of Social Work, College of Human Services and Health Professions. Her research interests and teaching include feminist social policy; mental health and developmental disability law; and the intersectionality of race, gender, ethnicity, class, and different abilities.

Alison K. Paglia is an assistant professor of psychology at the University of New Hampshire, Manchester. Dr. Paglia's teaching and research interests include health psychology, HIV/AIDS, adult development, and service-learning. In addition to her teaching, Dr. Paglia has served in several capacities for the McNair Program at Texas Tech University and the University of New Hampshire.

Lisa T. Parsons earned her M.A. in social psychology at the University of New Hampshire. She has taught introductory psychology and statistics in psychology to traditional and nontraditional students in a variety of settings. Currently she is writing and editing for a local publication in Manchester, New Hampshire.

Ryan Petersen is assistant professor of political science at College of the Redwoods in Eureka, California. He earned his M.A. in political science at Syracuse University and is currently completing his doctoral dissertation.

Buffy Quinn is a Ph.D. candidate in the Geography Department in the Maxwell School at Syracuse University. She received an Outstanding Teaching Associate award and served as a teaching fellow for Syracuse University's Graduate School.

Ruth A. Reilly, Ph.D., R.D., is an instructor in the Department of Animal, Nutritional, and Medical Laboratory Sciences at the University of New Hampshire. Her research interests involve women's health issues and college teaching. Dr. Reilly teaches both graduate and undergraduate courses in human nutrition and college teaching. Dr. Reilly is a registered dietitian with clinical, community, and public health experience in dietetics.

Harry Richards is dean of the graduate school and associate professor of education at the University of New Hampshire. He has codirected FIPSE-funded efforts to develop and disseminate the Academic Program in College Teaching. He was director of a Preparing Future Faculty project sponsored by the Association of American Colleges and Universities and the Council of Graduate Schools (funding provided by the Pew Charitable Trusts). He coordinates the university's academic programs in college teaching.

Robin L. Riley is assistant professor in the Women's Studies Program at SUNY Plattsburgh. For three years she was the associate director of women's studies at Syracuse University. Dr. Riley is interested in gender, militarism, and war, and is an activist who has taught women's studies classes to women in prison.

Emily Rocque is a study-skills tutor and learning specialist working both in private practice and for The Catholic University of America. She taught learning strategies to LD/ADHD students at American University for ten years and is a former director of Georgetown University's College Prep summer program.

Merylann J. Schuttloffel is associate professor of educational administration and policy studies at the Catholic University of America, where she directs the Catholic Leadership Programs. Dr. Schuttloffel has served as a consultant to numerous organizations, including the National Institutes of Health, the National Association of Secondary School Principals, and the National Catholic Educational Association. Her research interests include reflective practice in leadership, innovation and school change, the transformation of educational beliefs and practice, and Catholic identity issues.

Lee Seidel is professor of health management and policy and director of the Teaching Excellence Program at the University of New Hampshire. In collaboration with the Graduate School, this program offers graduate-level courses and programs in college teaching for students and faculty. In 2002, Academic Programs in College Teaching received a Hesburgh Certificate of Merit.

Chad Sisson was a graduate student in zoology at the University of New Hampshire, Durham, where he participated in the Preparing Future Faculty Program. Dr. Sisson is currently an adjunct instructor in biology at Grand Rapids Community College in Michigan.

Ruth V. Small is a professor in Syracuse University's School of Information Studies and director of its school media program. She was named Professor of the Year by the graduate students in her school in 1996 and Faculty Technology Associate by Faculty Computing and Media Services at Syracuse University. Her research on designing motivating information-literacy instruction earned her the Highsmith Innovative Research Award by the American Association of School Librarians and the Carroll Preston Baber Research Award by the American Library Association.

Ken A. Smith currently serves as president of Geneva College. Prior to this appointment, he was an associate professor and chair of the Strategy and Human Resources Department in the Whitman School of Management at Syracuse University, where he taught business strategy in the undergraduate, masters, doctoral, and executive programs. Smith was a recipient of the Outstanding Faculty Award from the MBA Student Association and remains committed to excellence in the classroom at his new institution.

David Smukler is a Ph.D. candidate in the School of Education at Syracuse University. Currently a University Fellow, he was a Burton Blatt Fellow in 1987–88 and won the Graduate School All-University Master's Prize in 1988. Since 1998 he has team-taught courses on topics in special education and disability studies.

Anne W. Stork earned her Ph.D. in ecology and evolutionary biology from Cornell University. She then conducted her postdoctoral work, funded by the National Science Foundation's Science, Mathematics, Engineering, and Technology Education Postdoctoral Fellowship, at the University of New

Hampshire. At UNH she worked with the Writing Across the Curriculum staff and biology faculty and graduate students in helping promote the use of writing to teach and learn biology.

Orlando L. Taylor, dean of Howard University's Graduate School and professor in the School of Communications, is a nationally recognized scholar and leader in graduate education and within the fields of communication and communication sciences and disorders. Dr. Taylor is a pioneer of new initiatives and concepts in his field, winning major grants that have addressed national priorities in higher education and science. His efforts have helped to catapult Howard University into a highly visible position as a research university and the nation's largest on-campus producer of African American Ph.D. recipients.

Stacey Lane Tice is an assistant dean of the Graduate School and director of the TA Program and Future Professoriate Project at Syracuse University. She is coeditor of *Preparing Graduate Students to Teach* and *University Teaching: A Guide for Graduate Students,* as well as of several articles related to preparing graduate students for faculty positions.

Patricia P. Tinto is associate professor of mathematics education and associate chair of the Teaching and Leadership Program for Field Relations. She works with the Living SchoolBook as an adviser for the Dialogue Project. Her research interests focus on reformed instructional practice and teacher change. The Dialogue Project has supported her exploration of innovative learning spaces for teacher development.

Barbara Walter is professor of metalsmithing and interim director and associate dean of the School of Art and Design at Syracuse University. She has taught courses at every level, from freshman to graduate, over a period of twenty-five years. Her work may be viewed in many permanent collections, including the Victoria and Albert Museum in London and the Renwick Gallery of the Smithsonian Institution in Washington, D.C.

Dara H. Wexler is a research associate for the Education Development Center—Center for Children and Technology. She received her Ph.D. in the cultural foundations of education from Syracuse University, and taught in the Department of Teaching and Leadership as part of the Future Professoriate Program. Between 1995 and 2000, Dr. Wexler worked with the Living SchoolBook, a research and development project intended to help teachers integrate technology into the curriculum. In addition, between 1998 and 2000, she was a member of the team that designed the Dialogue Project and put it into practice. Her research interests combine media, technology, education, and popular culture.

University Teaching

1

Advice for Teaching
at the University Level

Marvin Druger

YOUR FIRST FEW CLASSES are especially important because this is when an instructor sets the stage for the rest of the semester. Many students feel insecure in the first class session. They wonder: What is the class all about? What sort of person is the instructor? What does he expect of me? Is she sympathetic to my needs and interests? Does he realize that I want to learn but that I am no genius? Is this class going to be boring? How well will I relate to her? Will there be many assignments? How will I be evaluated? What type of exams will he give? How well does she know the subject matter? Can he explain the material well and answer my questions? If I need it, can I get extra help from her?

Because most students have questions such as these at the beginning of the course, you should be prepared at the first session to provide answers to at least some of them and to establish a good learning atmosphere. To this end, I offer some strategies and tips that I have found useful during my fifty years of teaching at the college level.

Tips You'll Find Useful

Expect to be worried or nervous

Feeling some tension can help motivate you to put extra effort into your teaching and do a more effective job. But remember, your students probably feel more insecure and uncomfortable than you do, and it is not unusual for the first class session to be a silent, tense occasion as students anxiously await the answers to their questions. You have the advantage of being in command of the situation. Set the direction and take the initiative to establish expectations and a good learning atmosphere.

Prepare thoroughly

It is particularly important that you know the subject matter you will be dealing with during your first couple of class meetings. Write yourself an outline specifying objectives, key concepts, and questions to ask the students. Especially plan in detail the strategy you will use for teaching that first class session. Students can sense an instructor's insecurity and lack of preparation. They will probably test you during the first few class sessions to establish for themselves whether or not you know the material. Make them confident in your subject matter competency and you will have taken a major step forward in establishing a positive learning environment.

Tell the students who you are

Write your name on the board and tell the students something about your background and special interests. A complete autobiography is unnecessary, but you do want students to know you are a real person, not just a talking statue.

Tell the students as much as you can about the course objectives and how you will conduct the class

Tell them about assignments, exams, grading, class procedures, and your expectations of them as learners. Allow for flexibility in your organization of the course. Let students know you are receptive to suggestions and criticisms, and that you are willing to change course procedures when changes seem reasonable. The essence of your approach should be to make your students aware that your procedures are intended to facilitate their learning.

Inform students about any special rules or policies

Be clear about your attendance policy, the rules about handing in late assignments and making up missed exams, and other procedures. Stating your expectations clearly and early in the course usually will bring about the behavior you desire.

When you establish a policy or a special procedure, explain its rationale

Explain to the students how the policy or procedure will help facilitate their learning. Students usually will be more reasonable in their thinking than you might imagine.

Explain exams, grading, and other evaluation procedures very clearly

Grades are obviously of great interest to students. Tell them exactly how their final grade will be decided. Then keep the students informed at all times during the semester about their progress and grade status.

Design your exams and assignments to be consistent with your objectives

Students will study according to how you test them. If you tell students that your tests will require certain kinds of thinking and problem solving, they will study accordingly. However, if you test, instead, for recall and memory, they will study by memorizing the material.

Be professional in your manner

Demonstrate to your students that you expect to do work in class. Treat students with respect and they will react in the same manner

Assign some work to be handed in at the next class session

Get the students involved in the course immediately. This assignment is an indication that you mean business and that you want the students to learn as much as possible. Grade that first assignment with special care and thoroughness and return it at the next class meeting, offering feedback that will allow for improvement in the next assignment. Use the opportunity to set the tone for future assignments. The students will know what your expectations are and that you take the time to carefully review their work. This is also a good time to reinforce the policy that you expect assignments to be handed in on time and that you will read and return them promptly.

Be cautious of dismissing your class early

Students are entitled to a full class session. Prepare extra material for each session in case you have a few minutes left at the end of the class. It is important to let your students know there is much interesting material for them to learn and that you will provide the opportunity for them to interact with that material for the full class period. Students will quickly come to expect a full period each time.

Plan a motivating beginning, a middle core, and an ending for each class session

Try to introduce the subject matter by relating it to the students' experiences and backgrounds. Why would they want to know about this topic? What does it mean to them? Next, deal with the core material by lecture, discussion, demonstration, or question-and-answer. Finally, summarize the main points to tie the whole session into an integrated whole. What are the few essential "nuggets" that you want students to take with them from this class session? These nuggets should transcend the details of the class and serve instead as organizers to help the students recall details. For each class, try to convey at least one idea that students "never thought about that way before."

Learn the names of your students as soon as possible

One helpful procedure is to have your students fill out index cards, describing their backgrounds, interests, career goals, and any other information that will help you get to know them as learners. In class, refer to the students by name and you will be surprised at the good rapport that results.

Be available to students

The usual approach of "drop in any time" or "see me during office hours" rarely brings to your office the students who need assistance or who would like to chat. A more effective approach is to have "open office hours." Students should know that you are available any time a question or problem arises. Nowadays, communication by e-mail is quick, efficient, and effective. When you think you are too busy to deal with student problems, remind yourself that "students are our business."

Vary your teaching strategies

Do not spend the entire class session lecturing. Sometimes lecturing is appropriate and effective, but it is an approach that should be used sparingly. If you always lecture, students will fall into the pattern of being completely passive in class. They will sit like lumps, simply writing down what you say without thinking; then, just before exams, a frantic search will begin to find out "What did the instructor mean by this sentence?"

Student comprehension involves brain reactions from them, and their brain reactions can be stimulated by their oral participation in class. So stop frequently and ask questions. Then be patient. Wait at least seven to ten seconds for the students to respond; the longer you wait, the better quality response you are likely to receive. Try to draw answers from a variety of students, to maximize discussion and interaction. If you get students involved in questions and discussion during your first few class sessions, they will come to expect and enjoy this pattern of involvement. Later in the course you can use lecturing more often, without losing your students' active involvement and interest. Remember, students are not empty vessels to be filled with information. Instead, your task is to stimulate their effective learning.

Do not feel that you have to know all the answers

If you overprepare your lessons and master an excellent grasp of the subject matter, it is likely that you will be able to answer most questions students come up with. However, students need to realize that you are human and that you do not have all the answers. Sometimes you might just forget an answer; other times you simply might not know. When this is the case, if you hedge your response, it will soon become painfully obvious to your students that you do not know what you are talking about, and their faith in you will decline rapidly. There are a variety of ways such a situation can be effectively confronted. You could admit you don't know, or suggest a reference, or ask a student to look up the answer, or volunteer to look up the answer yourself, or refer the question back to the class. Saying "I don't know" is perfectly appropriate and realistic, but you should not say it so frequently that students become convinced that you really do not have a good command of the subject matter. Extra preparation and a good command of your subject matter is key.

Be encouraging to students

Sometimes it takes courage for a student to offer a comment during class. If you sneer at an answer or make a sarcastic remark, that student might never again participate in class. Students are especially sensitive to your words, actions, and responses to their behavior. Your sarcastic remark could be perceived as a personal affront. So, think twice when responding to a student, and be sensitive. Your positive response will encourage a positive counterresponse. Praise good work. Think and act in a positive manner. An occasional "nice work," "great idea," or "good question" can bring out the best in students. A comment such as "that's a dumb question" has no place in the learning environment.

It is especially important to be encouraging during the first few class sessions, when students are trying to establish a rapport with you. You want them to become comfortable asking questions and actively participating in class proceedings. Frequently, a student will have a question in mind but will not ask it for fear of appearing stupid; then someone else will ask that very question. The same "stupid" question might very well be in the minds of other students in the class, too. Perhaps it reflects a shared misunderstanding, or a step that you skipped, or an inadequate explanation. Oftentimes, a "stupid" question will be an indicator of how well you are teaching. So, you should handle all questions in a professional manner. If you feel that the question really should not be answered at the time it is asked—because of time constraints or its appropriateness—ask the student politely to see you after class, and move on.

Laugh a lot

Teaching should not be a grim encounter between you and your students. Laughing at your own mistakes emphasizes your human qualities, and students respond positively. A bit of humor does not destroy the seriousness of your lesson.

Don't expect every day of teaching to be filled with sunshine and roses

All you can do is your best, and sometimes that is a disaster. The reasons for disaster are not always clear. You might have been in a bad mood, the students might have been distracted preparing for an important exam in another course, the weather might be hot and humid. All these factors, and many others, can contribute to a disappointing class session. Everyone has bad days. Try to put them behind you and look to the future. The sun will soon reappear.

Teach for the future

After completing your course, the students should have a positive attitude about the course and the subject matter, a feeling of accomplishment, an awareness of the scope of the subject, knowledge about how to learn more about it, and a set of experiences that contribute to their personal growth. You can add more objectives to that list, but the ultimate effect of your teaching and your course will be manifested many years after its completion and details of its content are long forgotten. Teach with these long-term, future effects in mind.

The large questions

The preceding tips have been practical. Now I would like to pose some questions that merit your thoughtful consideration. Why do we teach the content we teach? Why do we lecture so much? Why don't more instructors think about teaching from a learner's perspective? Why don't we try to learn more about our own strengths and weaknesses as instructors? What are the most important outcomes of a college education? What will students gain from their college education? What do we as instructors do to build students' self-confidence, a positive attitude toward learning, motivation to learn more, sufficient background to know how to learn more in the field, and practical skills that will transfer to their everyday lives?

These are some of the big questions I ask myself periodically. Despite years of experimentation with teaching strategies and continual revision of my course materials, I still find these questions to be the ones that cause me to reflect on my current practice and, inevitably, to make changes. Ideally, you will clarify and learn from your current practice. As we reflect on our practices, we are very likely to be more successful in encouraging student learning.

2

The Lecture

Jerry Evensky

General Thoughts on Lecturing

DEFINING TERMS: UNDERSTANDING VERSUS LEARNING

I BEGIN BY DEFINING TERMS because communication, be it on paper or in a lecture hall, depends on a common language and a common understanding about what words mean. I will use the terms *understand* and *learn* as I explain my view of lecturing. Given that we might not share common meanings, it is imperative that you know what I mean by these terms.

By *understand,* I mean to appreciate correctly the meaning of a concept (a term or an idea) or the logic of a weave of concepts when presented. By *learn,* I mean to master a concept or the logic of a weave of concepts so that you can independently call upon and successfully apply it as needed. As I define these terms, then, understanding is a prerequisite for learning. You can watch and listen to a lesson on bike riding and understand how to ride a bike, but that understanding won't be sufficient to get you down the block and back on your new ten-speed. Moving from understanding to learning

---

This chapter is dedicated to the memory of my very dear friend and role model Tom Franey. Tom was one of the finest people and finest teachers I have had the privilege to know. He combined courage, conviction, tenderness, and love with creativity and a liberal dose of insanity to create an atmosphere that challenged and nurtured his students. In the environment he created, his students grew in all dimensions of their humanness. His gravestone bears the words of the Tin Man from *The Wizard of Oz:* "A heart is not judged by how much you love, but by how much you are loved by others." By that standard, Tom had a heart as big as all outdoors. Tom became ill and died during the period I was writing this piece. I loved him, and I miss him very much.

requires that you take what you understand and practice, practice, practice with it.

When I lecture about how a change in European real interest rates can affect the strength of the dollar relative to the euro, I want my students to understand the terms involved and the weave of logic that ties those terms into a story about interest rates, international capital flows, and exchange rates. I want my students to understand, but I do not expect them to learn this logic in the course of my lecture. To take their understanding and make it learning, they must practice. They must do homework that requires them to apply the terms and ideas they understand to some contrived or real events I present. They must read the newspaper and apply what they understand to analyze the flow of real events. They must prepare for my exams on which they know I will ask them to analyze real or contrived events.

I tell my students about this distinction—understanding versus learning—the first day of every semester because I want them to recognize our respective responsibilities. My primary job is to ensure that they understand the material. I tell them, "If the thread of the story I'm telling breaks, I need to know so that I don't go on without you."

Their job is to learn the material. That requires them to do two things: ask if they don't understand, and practice, practice, practice. I assist them in their job by trying to create a classroom atmosphere that encourages questions and by providing practice tools (e.g., homework) and incentives (e.g., graded assignments). But I also try to make it clear that if they are to learn, we must *both* do our jobs well.

THE VALUE OF LEARNING

The lecture format allows you to exercise tight control over the teaching environment. You can talk as much or as little as you please. With this control you can maintain the continuity of your presentation as it unfolds and keep the focus of the students on the flow of the logic you seek to convey. Given this control, the great strength or value of the lecture is that it allows you to convey efficiently and effectively a weave of terms and ideas. The terms and ideas are the pieces you work with, and the story into which you weave them is the whole you create.

As with the terms *understanding* and *learning,* I spend time on the first day of every course explaining my view of the relationship between the *pieces* and the *whole*. A metaphor I use to make this point is a puzzle. In a puzzle box are many pieces of information about the image printed on the box top. But that image only unfolds from all the pieces as those pieces take their places in relation to one another. So too the pieces in your lecture course. Every piece of information is part of an image you want to create in each student's mind's eye. The logic that unfolds in your lectures should make that image clear.

Many students are used to approaching their education as an exercise in the assimilation of pieces of information by rote memory. But if they only learn the pieces as pieces, the full image will never unfold for them. You have to work hard to keep them conscious of the big picture, so that they will see the pieces as parts of a whole image. Only then will they be able to consistently take what they understand about the pieces and place them appropriately into a larger frame—that mind's eye image, that vision you want to share in the course. Whether the content of the course is your vision of how to approach a text or of how to analyze a capitalist economy or of how to appreciate the nature of chaos, a lecture format can be a very powerful medium for communicating complex images efficiently and effectively.

Rote memorization is the lowest order of thinking. The beauty of a lecture is that it offers you the opportunity to show your students how all the pieces can be arranged to produce a level of understanding and subsequently learning, which represents a high order of thinking about a rich vision that fascinates you.

The Micro and Macro of a Lecture:
Class Culture and Individual Diversity

If there are 100 students in your lecture, then there are 102 personalities in the room. There are those 100 students who walk in bringing 100 different persons to this new setting, there is you and the person you are, and there is the class. Anyone who has taught for any length of time knows that the class, the wholeness of the 101 persons in the room, takes on an identity of its own. It develops a personality, a culture. As the leader of the class, you have a responsibility to be sensitive to the fact that each person in your class is unique, and you have an obligation to shape the culture of the class such that it is a constructive educational environment for every student in it.

CREATING A CONSTRUCTIVE CLASS CULTURE

Respect

Your students expect and deserve to be treated with respect. And so do you.

Treat them with respect, and insist that they treat you and all their fellow students likewise. Remember, however, that there are levels of respect. Being treated with the basic respect that one is due as a human being, whether teacher or student, should be automatic. But respect as a good person, as a good teacher, or as a good student is not and should not be automatic. This latter dimension of respect must be earned by the quality of one's performance.

Basic human respect is the foundation of all constructive human interactions, and thus it is a prerequisite, a foundation, for developing that earned respect that comes with a quality performance. If you want to nurture those performances, you must create that foundation. And if you make an effort to create that foundation, you will have the valuable and significant power of student peer pressure on your side. The vast majority of students want to function in a respectful environment and will support your efforts to create it. But they look to you for leadership, and you must take the lead. A specific way to establish an atmosphere of respect is to establish community standards for classroom courtesy.

Courtesy

Your students expect and deserve to be treated with courtesy. And so do you.

In a lecture setting, the close proximity of so many people trying to hear and follow your presentation makes everyone vulnerable to the discourtesies of any one person among them. The vast majority of students understand this and act responsibly. However, a few do not understand, a few do not care, and some have lapses of understanding or caring.

If the lecture hall is going to be a constructive educational environment for all participants, it is important that you establish simple, clear community standards of behavior early, and that you make clear your expectation that everyone will honor those standards. In the Notes section of my intro-

ductory lecture course syllabus, for example, I set forth the following standards for class courtesy:

• Late arrival—this should be an exception. When necessary, sit on entering side; do not disturb class.

• Early departure—this too should be an exception, occurring only in
an emergency or with prior consultation.

• Early preparations for departure—please don't.

• Talking—please do it with everyone or with no one.

On the first day of class, I explain these standards and why I think they
are important. I ask that they be honored. I find that the vast majority of the
students not only happily honor the standards, but also appreciate them. In
most cases, social pressure from the students themselves serves as enough of
a sanction to enforce the standards.

On those rare occasions when social pressure is insufficient to enforce
the standards, I do so. Initially I try subtle pressure—a look that makes eye
contact but is not intended to embarrass. (I always avoid embarrassing
someone. Doing so can affect the sense of security other students have about
asking questions.) If that look does not get the student's attention, I will try
a more direct one, or even a closer physical presence, until the student realizes I want the offending behavior to stop. Those methods usually work; but
failing that, I stop the student after class and discuss the issue of community
standards and being welcome in the class.

In cases where the lapse in courtesy is general (e.g., shuffling papers for
early departure), I stop and let the silence speak. And if the silence is not
loud enough, I briefly review the community standard of courtesy. That usually works very well.

Expect an appropriate level of maturity from your students

Adhering to a set of community standards on courtesy is one way in
which you set a standard for maturity in your lecture course. Another way is
embodied in the standards that are implicit in the way you talk and act with
your students. If you talk and act with them as mature people of their age,
they are more likely to respond to you as a mature person of their age would.
Do not underestimate your students' capacity for maturity.

Believe in your students

A necessary condition for success in a lecture class (or any class) is that you believe that your students can succeed, want to succeed, and are willing to work for success.

Contrary to what some cynics would suggest, the vast majority of students do not object to hard work—which is not to say they like it. What they object to is busywork—especially hard busywork. Homework with no feedback, readings that never connect to the flow of the logic presented in the lecture, or lectures with no logic—these conditions make students wonder, "Why am I doing this?" If the class progresses and that "Why" is never resolved, then their "Why" becomes "Why should I bother?"

The vast majority of students value their education as much as anything else in life.[1] Most students really do prefer a challenging class that teaches them something rather than a "blow-off" class that does not, even if the latter offers an easier grade. So, be demanding. Expect much of your students. Then show them you care by making the class worthwhile and by helping them to succeed.[2]

---

1. How do I know this to be true? I do a "discovery" exercise early in the class session on decision rules (the algorithms we follow to make choices). The exercise involves a list of twenty-six characteristics students can choose to have (e.g., strength, beauty, charm, intelligence, wit, courage). I tell the students that each unit of every characteristic costs a dollar (obviously they have to conceptualize the units themselves), and I give them a $100 "budget" to spend. I tell them that when they are finished spending their budget they are to write "Optimal" at the top of the column to certify that this is the best they can do with the funds they have, and then check the two items on which they spent the most units. The first time I did this, as a lark, I went down the list asking who spent the most on this or that. The students and I were struck that the overwhelming majority of the class had purchased more "intelligence" than anything else. In subsequent semesters, I repeated the query, and the results were very consistent. Now I use this empirical result to demonstrate the predictive power of empirical analysis. After they are done allocating, I predict the result. I have a perfect prediction record to date.

2. The last year I taught junior high school, my colleague Tom Franey and I tried an experiment. We took all the students entering the seventh grade who read at below a second-grade level and put them into a two-hour block (social studies and English). We worked those students very hard. They complained constantly. But we believed they could learn to read and we kept telling them so. We challenged them to do it, and they did. The gain was, on average, more than two reading levels. The result was not magic. Instead of being labeled "stupid" and facing low expectations, we called them "capable" and maintained high expectations, and we worked them very hard. When it was all over, there was a sense of pride in our class and in each of those

When students enter your class, their education becomes your and their shared responsibility. You should want to do the best you can to ensure that they leave with something worth the effort you expect of them. Expect them to make that effort. If they do, they deserve a benefit. I believe that is what most students expect and want—a worthwhile challenge.

DIVERSITY: A CHALLENGE AND AN OPPORTUNITY

Every student is unique, but you will be lecturing to many at once. That fact presents you with significant challenges and opportunities.

Diversity as a challenge

One challenge of diversity lies in the fact that a lecture course can only be effective if all its students have in common the skill base that is essential for understanding the content of your course. In the lexicon of pedagogy, the skills you are going to assume everyone shares are called the "prerequisite" skills. In most classes, these skills relate to language— defining "language" broadly to include mathematics and to include the socially constructed understandings that are built into language.

You are going to speak a language, and if the students are going to "get it"—that is, if they are going to understand what you lecture, the story you tell—then they must understand the terms of the language you use and what those terms mean to you. If these prerequisite skills are not in place, your students will hear your words but they will not understand your lecture. For example, it would be pointless to teach in Greek to a class of students who only speak English.

If you have any doubt about your students' ability to "speak your language," you must address this potential problem at the very beginning of your course—before students get lost in your class and locked into their course schedule. A solution begins with identifying the skills you consider prerequisites for understanding the presentation you plan to give (e.g., do they need to know basic geometry?). Then ask yourself the following questions: Is it safe to assume that these skills are in place? Do I know the audi-

---

students that I have never seen in any other class since. They did not like the hard work, but they did appreciate it. They were proud.

ence well enough to answer this? If in doubt on either issue, err on the side of caution. If you are not sure if your students have the prerequisite skills for your course, a rough-and-ready (efficient but effective) quick assessment can usually help.[3] Do not disregard a potential problem just because addressing it will cost you time. The cost of ignoring it may prove much higher to you and your students.

If you believe or determine that there is a significant prerequisite skill problem, you have two choices in addressing it. You can change your presentation to avoid the problem skills, or you can do some kind of readiness activity to bring your students up to speed. A skills review at the beginning of a course is a good solution if the problem is broad (involving many students) but not deep (the skills are easily acquired). If the problem is small in scope (a few students) but deep, you can try to bring these students up to speed with out-of-class activities (e.g., a skill review workbook) or you can redirect them to a more appropriate course.

Another challenge of diversity involves differences in the tacit knowledge, that is, cultural understandings that are taken as fact, without reflection. For example, a notion such as "daddies work and mommies stay home" may be brought, unthinkingly, into the classroom by you and some of your students. The more culturally heterogeneous your class, the more significantly differences in tacit knowledge can affect your ability to communicate and relate your subject to your students. If you draw your examples and language from your formative years in Kenya, then your students whose cultural understandings were formed in Iceland might not always understand you. Conversely, if you grew up in Iceland . . .

You cannot know the unique cultural understandings of every student in your class, but being aware of your students' cultural diversity will prompt you to remember that diversity as you try to think of ways in which to communicate and relate the material to each of them.

Diversity as an opportunity

The opportunity of cultural diversity lies in the fact that it can be a source of creative engagement with your students. When I teach about how social

3. For example, I use a short graph-skills assessment test in my Introductory Economics course.

and political advantages affect market outcomes, I use examples such as so-cial definitions of market roles ("daddies work and mommies stay home") or "good old boy" networks, or apartheid. Doing this makes diversity an asset, because it relates the content of the course to a range of tacit "knowledges" and social experiences.

The diversity of culturally constructed tacit knowledge among my stu-dents can also be a source of intriguing differences among them, allowing me to play with different ways of motivating their mastery of the concepts I teach. For instance, in the process of developing a model of personal choice, I ask my students to jot down on a piece of paper their perception of the probability of getting AIDS from one unsafe sexual encounter with a stranger. Then I rattle off successively higher probabilities and ask them to raise their hand when I get to the number they wrote down. Not surprisingly, the probabilities they choose vary significantly. I use this fact to drive home the role of the variation of individuals' risk perceptions, which in turn helps explain the variation of individuals' choices in apparently similar circum-stances. Thus, the diversity of perspectives from which they see the world be-comes a tool for teaching the concepts of the course.

Another twist on the issue of diversity is that while there is diversity within your class, your students often have some things in common that, as a group, set them apart from other groups in society. For example, most of them share in common the aspects of life that go with being socially active young adults. By tapping into these issues, you can relate the material more closely to the lives your students lead. I do this in my own class by relating the concepts I am dealing with to social exploration—such as the risk and choice example cited above. This puts my subject into the heart of their world.

The Lecture as an Active-Learning Environment

ACTIVE LEARNING AND SELF-ASSESSMENT

The value of the lecture format is the continuity of presentation that it af-fords. As you give a lecture, the weave of your logic (your story) should un-fold for your students. If that story is new and complex, as well as compelling and understandable, most of your students will want to "get it." If your stu-dents are prepared and engaged, if you explain any new terms so that the language never becomes an obstacle, and if the thread of your logic is drawn through the presentation with care so that the students can follow it, then all of your students can "get it."

This is the ideal. The product of this ideal is a new dimension or domain of understanding and learning for your students: a valuable and valued education.

Unfortunately we do not live in an ideal world. In the last section I made the point that you cannot assume that your students are ready: you have to be proactive about ensuring your students' readiness. But being ready is not sufficient to ensure success. If students are going to understand and learn, they must also be engaged in the learning process as it unfolds. Engaged learning is active learning.

An effective lecture is an active learning experience. It continually engages the minds of students—building and weaving ideas, but also encouraging them to reflect on and assess their understanding as the lecture unfolds because they need to be sure they are "with you" if they are going to "get it."

Inevitably, you will use a term that some students don't know, or you will explain a term thoroughly but some students still will not get it, or the thread of your logic will break for some students.[4] If any one of these things occurs, the students who are left behind are lost for the rest of that topic and for all future topics that depend on it.

To avoid this waste and frustration (and path to failure), your students need to constantly self-assess their understanding of what you are presenting; and when they are confused, they need to ask for clarification. This, in turn, requires that your students recognize when they do not know what's going on,[5] and feel safe in asking a clarifying question.

If your students do not understand and do not ask a clarifying question, you might well be *lecturing* but you are not *communicating* or *teaching*. So if your lecture is to succeed, your students must be actively engaged in the learning process. What follows are some suggestions on how to stimulate and encourage active learning in a lecture setting.

---

4. One reason this can occur is that there is indeed a gap in the logic you are presenting. The best, engaged students will point out flaws in your logic. This is a compliment to them and a service to you.

5. When I was a junior high student, our principal always used to tell us, "An intelligent man is one who knows what he doesn't know."

STIMULATING ACTIVE LEARNING

The "get your money's worth" technique

I pose questions to my class to get them to think about the concepts and logic I am presenting. Immediately afterward I pose a question, but before I call on someone, I tell them,

> Now, whether you intend to raise your hand or not, think about how you would answer this question. Once you've thought about your answer, listen to the answer of the person I call on, and then to my response to that person. Doing this will help you see whether you're "getting it." If you just sit there passively and listen to the process unfold, you really can't know whether you "get it." You want your money's worth out of this class. You're going to be sitting here anyway during this exchange. Invest yourself in the process, be active with your mind, and test yourself.

Obviously, after going through this whole speech (or a variation) many times, I begin to give an abbreviated version; but I always remind students to be active, to be engaged—do more than just watch. Then I pause long enough before I call on someone[6] to ensure that they have sufficient time to reflect on the question.[7]

6. A note on calling on students: You need not call on the first person that raises his or her hand. If that student is a very active participant and others have not been, it's perfectly legitimate to look elsewhere and even wait for other hands to come up. I do this often. I usually look at the person I'm going to pass up and say something along the lines of, "I appreciate your participation, but let me try to get someone else involved" (I never do this unless I've already called on that person at least once before). Then I turn to the rest of the class and say something like, "Now, I know you're out there, let's see a hand from someone who hasn't participated yet." It doesn't always work, but it often does; and the person I passed up is generally ready to participate the next time, so being passed up doesn't seem to offend him or her.

7. An alternate way to stimulate the same active engagement is to follow probing questions with a pregnant pause, and then call on specific students randomly. If students know they are at risk of being called on, that is an incentive for them to stay on top of the situation. Indeed, it is also an incentive for a student to make a preemptive strike by asking a clarifying question when they are confused. I personally don't use this method, because it doesn't suit my style or the class atmosphere I want to create; but if done with skill and sensitivity, it can be a very effective technique.

The "try this" technique

Sometimes I direct everyone to take out a piece of paper and pencil and to write down their answer to a question I pose. This "try this" technique is especially helpful for graphical cases and any particularly crucial and complicated issue. When students put their response down on paper it is a more concrete commitment to an answer (there it is in black and white), and thus it is much harder for them to fool themselves about the correctness of their understanding (i.e., for them to think, "Yeah, that's what I would have answered").

The ten-second count

I encourage students to reflect on their understanding of what I have just presented when I ask, "Are there any questions?" Then I *wait* ten seconds. The important part of this method is not so much the question as the wait. This is a lesson I learned from videotape of myself teaching.[8] In the videotape critique session, one of my colleagues pointed out that the time between my query "Are there any questions?" and the next word out of my mouth was hardly enough for students to raise a hand, much less to reflect on whether they had a question. So, armed with that insight, I started counting to ten whenever I asked "Any questions?" I have been struck by how often a response does not come until I get to a count of seven or eight. "Any questions?" is an invitation to your students to reflect on what they do and don't understand. That self-assessment process is undermined if you do not wait. If you do, it encourages reflection. As an extra benefit, waiting sends a signal to your students that you really do care to hear their questions. I have told my students about the ten-count discipline I try to impose on myself, and I joke about it if, in my enthusiasm, I go roaring off too hastily, only realizing too late.

All three techniques are very efficient (they take very little time) and very effective (students get immediate in-context feedback on their understanding). But, their knowing they do not understand is only the first step:

8. In the professional jargon, being videotaped while teaching and subsequently participating in a critique is called "micro-teaching." I highly recommend that kind of self-observation. It is very valuable to see yourself as others see you.

students also need to formulate and ask clarifying questions if they are going to "get it."

CREATING A CLASSROOM CULTURE
THAT ENCOURAGES ACTIVE LEARNING

Your students are only going to be independently engaged in reflecting on their understanding of your lecture if they think that any confusion they identify will be addressed constructively. This means they must be able to form and must feel secure enough to ask clarifying questions. If you take care to create an atmosphere that ensures the safety of asking questions, the iterative process of query and response will help them develop their ability to form the questions.[9]

So how do you create such an atmosphere? I try to accomplish this by taking questions at any time and by treating all questions and questioners with respect.

I take questions any time because I want to identify and address confusion as soon as possible. But while I take all questions, I do not necessarily take them immediately or answer them when I get them. If I want to delay a question, I just offer a hand signal to communicate that "I see your hand, but I'm not ready yet because I want to finish my train of thought." If I take a question but don't want to answer it at that time, I might say, "That question takes us in a direction I don't want to pursue as a class, but I would be happy to talk about it after class." Or maybe I will explain, "We don't have the tools in place yet to address that question as maturely as we will in two weeks, so hold on to it and ask again." Or maybe I will say, "I don't know the answer, but I'll try to find out."

On the first day of class, I talk about questions. I tell my students that I want them to feel safe enough about asking questions so that by the end of the course they all will have raised their hand at least once. In a class of more

---

9. One of the advantages of ensuring that students see the pieces (concepts) as a part of a whole (logic) is that their conceptualizing the content of the lecture course in this way helps students form their clarifying questions. As the image unfolds, your students can begin independently to locate points of confusion (the essence of self-assessment), i.e., missing pieces, or pieces that don't seem to fit anywhere. Furthermore, they can begin to intuit for themselves those pieces you may have missed, based on the context of the gap.

than one hundred students, raising your hand can be intimidating; but I want to send them a signal that I am going to make it as safe as possible and I will do everything I can to encourage all to participate.

I do not see questions as slowing me down. On occasion, taking questions has indeed put me behind the place where I had hoped to be. But I see no point in "getting done" if I get there alone, and I can usually catch up to my original time line by doing a little less embellishing along the way. Sure, there is the occasional student who gets perpetually carried away and can slow down the group, but in that special case I begin to defer more and more of that person's questions to after class. The rest of the students see what's going on, so they do not take it as a sign that my philosophy toward questions in general is less welcoming.

But that is my style. Yours may certainly be different. What matters is that you find a style that works for you by:

• offering your students some means to ask clarifying questions in fairly short order—before the unfolding logic goes too far beyond their point of confusion, because confusion tends to snowball; and

• nurturing the sense among your students that clarifying questions are welcome, will be addressed seriously, and will be treated with respect.

The quickest way to shut down questions is to demean someone for asking one. It not only intimidates the questioner, but it sends a message to all who watched the interaction, "Yes, you too can be embarrassed—just ask a question." Treating clarifying questions with respect is necessary but not sufficient to encourage them. It is also important that you answer such questions effectively. When a student asks a question and you are unsure what is being asked, repeat it back for clarification. Once you have completed your answer, check in with the questioner by asking, "Did I answer your question?"[10] It is easy to presume your answer made sense—after all, it made

---

10. An aside on language and communication: Several years ago, I mentored a Korean teaching assistant who had a very strong accent. His students complained. We did a quick in-course evaluation, and identified two areas of greatest concern: He was hard to understand, and he was not answering their questions effectively. So we experimented. I asked him to repeat every question back to the student who asked it, followed by the query "Is this your question?" Then I asked him to follow his answer with the "Did I answer your question?" line. The effect was dramatic. This TA, whose student ratings had been abysmal, was soon among the highly ranked. The problem was never language; it was communication. Once the communication was carefully attended to, the problem disappeared.

sense to you as you gave it. But you cannot be sure unless you ask. Asking also sends the signal to your students[11] that "I not only want to hear your questions, I want to respond to them effectively." If you ask and the student says no, then you can either try again (if I am going to do that, I usually ask the student to rephrase the question) or you can use the line, "Let me follow up on this with you after class."

Questions are an opportunity, but you have to make them work for you. If you sense that a student's question reflects deep confusion that is peculiar to that individual (a judgment that becomes keener as you get to know the questioner and the class), that's an opportune time to use the "let's talk after class" response. If, however, you sense that the question is representative of a more general confusion within the class (when in doubt, I err on the side of this presumption), the process of working through what has been asked usually helps clear up this confusion. And then there are the questions that reflect not confusion but divergent thinking. These are questions that explore in a creative way the concepts or ideas you are presenting. If such a question takes you in a direction the class can benefit from, play with it. If not, use the "Let's talk after class" response.

YOU TOO NEED TO BE AN ACTIVE LEARNER

Even as your students are actively engaged in trying to understand the material, you need to be actively engaged in gauging their understanding of that material. You can probe for such understanding with the techniques for encouraging active learning I offered above. But the most important source of feedback is the student-initiated communication. If you are successful in creating a safe environment, students will feel free to initiate communication—the most common form of this is the clarifying question just discussed. Clarifying questions are extremely valuable because they are very important forms of assessment of your performance, providing feedback on what the students are and are not getting. Other kinds of student-initiated communication that are invaluable for assessing your own

11. Such signals are very important ways to assure my students that I am committed to doing my job: helping them understand. If they feel that way, it gives them more of an incentive to do their job: the grunt work (practice, practice, practice) necessary to learn what they understand.

performance are those divergent student questions. Clearly, when a student can ask a question that correctly extrapolates or can make a statement that effectively synthesizes, that is a good indication that at least someone is "getting it." The same kind of culture that encourages clarifying questions will encourage these kinds of communication by your students. And they can help you assess how you are doing.

Preparing for a Lecture: Some General Thoughts

"WHAT AM I GOING TO COVER?" — CHOOSING YOUR CONTENT

In deciding what concepts, principles, practices, procedures, and logic you want to present, ask yourself, "What is it I want my students to be able to do when they've mastered what I am going to present?" In the jargon of education, this is defining your "behavioral objectives." Such objectives can range in intellectual sophistication from very low order—"I want them to be able to define *margin*"—to very high order—"I want them to be able to critique the assertion of some famous economists, to wit, that the construction of social ethics can ultimately be derived from an analysis of individual utility maximization." Whatever your behavioral objectives, being explicit about them helps you determine what your content must be, and it makes the next step—organizing—much easier.

Once you have determined the content, you must organize the concepts, principles, practices, and procedures into a thought process that the students will perceive to be coherent. In other words, you must draw the thread through the logic that connects all these elements. If your students can follow the thread of your logic, they are more likely to move beyond simple memorization to more complex, higher-order understanding.

Choose an organizational structure that suits your style and objectives. Various (not mutually exclusive) structures are available: compare/contrast, concrete-to-abstract, simple-to-complex, classification hierarchy, familiar-to-unfamiliar. In most cases it is valuable if you build in a "review the last lecture, preview this lecture, lecture, review-the-lecture" process for each class session. This enhances the sense of a flow in your logic, because the initial review contextualizes, the preview orients, and the final review again contextualizes. These reviews and previews can be very brief—writing an outline on the blackboard provides a simple preview.

GETTING READY TO LECTURE

As you plan, decide what props are necessary or helpful (e.g., colored chalk, handouts, overhead projector, computer), and be sure to arrange for them. Many great lecture plans fizzle in practice when some essential prop fails ("Oh my God, the overhead bulb is out!" or "Whadaya mean there's no Internet link in this room?!").

REHEARSE YOUR LECTURE

Your rehearsal need only be as formal as is useful. I find that the first time I present a lecture on any topic, a formal, out-loud rehearsal is useful. I try to do it in a mirror so I can see that I am keeping my eyes on my audience. If I have lectured on something many times, I just mentally walk through my presentation to tune up.

Rehearsal will help you locate any snags in the flow of your logic. It is also an opportunity to practice your examples to ensure that they work properly and that you can present them easily. In economics classes many is the graph that did not come out as planned because it was not rehearsed.

Rehearsal adds polish. It bolsters your confidence. It is a good time to ensure that the props you will bring with you are arranged in a way that is consistent with your presentation (e.g., are overheads in the right order?) and to think about how you might arrange the blackboard if you will be using it.

When you arrive to present your lecture, check things out. Are the props you will need there (e.g., chalk, eraser, overhead, computer)? Do they work (e.g., bulb in the overhead)? Is the physical environment amenable to attention (e.g., temperature, noise, glare)? If not, can you make it better (open/close window, pull a shade, suggest avoiding some seats, close a door)?

THE GOAL OF PREPARATION

Your goal as you prepare is to feel as ready as possible and to avoid the paralysis of nervousness. At the beginning of any new lecture experience (a new topic or a new audience or both), you will probably feel some nervousness. I have taught the same introductory course for fifteen years. I wrote the book for the course. I know this course. And yet I still start every semester feeling a bit nervous because I don't know this class yet, they don't know me, and I know I will be trying new things. Feeling nervous is okay, even normal, as you close the preparation stage and are poised to begin the presentation. The crucial thing is to prepare as well as you can so that you are confident that you have done your homework. That confidence will get you started, and the fruits of your efforts will allow that confidence to build. Expect to be nervous sometimes, but prepare to be confident.

Presenting a Lecture: Some General Thoughts

ESTABLISH AND MAINTAIN YOUR LINES OF COMMUNICATION

There are a number of means of communication with your students. The most important one in a lecture setting is your voice. Thus, the first and foremost concern you should have about maintaining lines of communication is "Can they hear me?" On the first day of a course and anytime thereafter when you have any reason to be in doubt, ask the students, "Can you hear me?"

Another important form of communication is eye contact. If you want the students to feel that you and they are in the same class, look at them. Scan, regularly making eye contact with as many people as you can, so that they know you know they are there. Students appreciate feeling that they exist (wouldn't you?); and while it is hard to give individual attention in a lecture format, you can at least communicate *that* much.

Then of course there are the technologies you can use to communicate. These range from very low-tech (the blackboard) to medium-tech (copied handouts, overhead projector, film), to much more high-tech (computer links to students at their desks). So what, if any, level of technology should you use? As you consider, keep in mind that technology is a means to an end, not an end in itself.[12] One of my colleagues in the Department of Instructional Design, Development, and Evaluation wears a button that reads, "TECHNOLOGY IS THE ANSWER!" then in small print below it, "But what's the question?"

For technology to be of value it must be appropriate to the setting and the objective. Each technology has its relative strengths and weaknesses. For ex-

---

12. Innovation and technology are not an identity. Most of the most creative, effective innovations in classrooms are very low- or no-tech.

ample, if you are telling a story with graphs, the blackboard allows students to see that story unfold slowly for development of a point. In contrast, an over-head projector allows you to face your students while you show them how things unfold and allows you to predraw particularly difficult graphs[13]—but it has limited space. A computer can show very rich images that do lots of cool things, but it could become "the show" to the detriment of the ideas.

For each technology, there are tricks of the trade for using them effectively. For example, when using the blackboard:

- start at the top;
- write legibly and large enough to be seen (Ask, "Can you see this?");
- turn to the class to talk; do not talk to the blackboard;
- ask whether students have completed their notes before erasing;
- label clearly any graphic material (e.g., graphs or charts);
- use different colors to enhance clarity;
- separate different material with dividing lines;
- erase previous material completely to reduce distractions; and
- put up tedious stuff before class or prepare a handout.

PACING A LECTURE

Pacing a lecture is an iterative process. Start at a pace that is comfortable for you, and see how it seems to the students. Find out by doing a quick survey at the end of the fifth day of class: "On a scratch piece of paper, tell me what you think about the pace of my lectures." If most students score you "about right," with a few scoring "too fast" and some "too slow," then you are probably doing just fine. If the feedback is skewed one way or the other, decide whether there is a constructive adjustment you can (or need to) make.

ENERGIZING YOUR LECTURE

The energy in your lecture hall begins with you. There will be no life in your lecture class if you do not bring it into the room. Your students want to be engaged, but they are depending on you to give them a reason to be. You must provide the catalyst that energizes the students and encourages them

---

13. If the graphs are so difficult as to need predrawing, you should probably also provide them to students in handout form.

to invest in the endeavor. Such a catalyst can take many forms, but I think the most essential and the most dependable is your own enthusiasm for the subject. That enthusiasm might be reflected in the joy that the students see in you as you exhibit a feeling for its beauty. It might be reflected in the fascination you display for the ways in which the subject can be applied to our day-to-day existence. Or it might come from a combination of these, or from some other signal you send explicitly or implicitly that demonstrates that you really believe this stuff is worth the effort of learning.

Whatever its source, some catalyst that energizes the room is necessary. Without it, the life of the mind dies about five minutes into your lecture.

BE YOURSELF — A REAL PERSON

Be a person, not a disembodied intellect. Allow the students to see that you are a human being with an imagination and fascination, concerns and visions, and a sense of humor. While maintaining your authority and expecting appropriate respect for the power you have (respect deriving from the students' belief that you will use it appropriately and fairly), let them relate to you as a person as well as a lecturer. Doing so makes communication easier because it diminishes the awe that some students feel in the presence of the person in front of the room, without in any way affecting the respect they should have for the position.

YOU NEED NOT ONLY LECTURE IN A LECTURE

Obviously, you lecture in a lecture class, but you need not *only* lecture in a lecture. The smaller the class and the more flexible the room (do the chairs move? is there suitable space for group activity?), the more you can do with nonlecture methods in what is a lecture course context. Choose the combination of tools that suits the needs of your students and your objectives for them. A lecture is a very valuable and effective method of teaching, but it can often benefit from being complemented by other methods.

INNOVATE — DON'T BE AFRAID TO MAKE MISTAKES

On this point I share a pearl of wisdom I received from Lew Hoffman, my supervising teacher when I was a student-teacher preparing for secondary

certification in the Webster Groves (Missouri) School District. After a particularly bad and depressing class day, I walked dejectedly into his room. I
briefly described the debacle I had just left behind, and I speculated on
other career options. His response was, "Evensky, remember the standard:
You're doin' pretty good if you have more good days than bad days."

At the time, that was not a particularly comforting remark. I thought,
"What a dismal standard: 'more good days than bad days.' Can I really be
happy in a career where it's a pretty good job when you do it well only a little
more than half the time?" Well, I persevered, and slowly but surely in the
course of my career the Hoffman wisdom has become clearer to me. There
are reasons for bad days that have nothing to do with you as an instructor,
and there are good reasons for having bad days. A reason for bad days that
has nothing to do with you could be the "rush" parties the night before, or
the chemistry exam that most of your class has in two hours, or news of a
campus tragedy, or anything else that might impair or distract your students.
The good reason for a bad day is an experiment in teaching that blows up in
your face. But if you don't experiment with your course content, your style,
or both, you can't grow. A failed experiment costs a day; a successful experiment pays off for a lifetime. Take some chances, and grow.

Find Your Own Voice

THE BEST STYLE FOR YOUR LECTURE

The best style for your lecture is the style that suits you best. In short,
be yourself. When I first started teaching, at Hixson Junior High School in
Webster Groves, I team-taught a class with a person who became a lifelong
friend, Tom Franey. I really admired the way Tom related to the kids, so in
many ways I deferred to him in defining the culture of our classroom. When
Tom moved on to another assignment, I was panic-stricken. I didn't have
much confidence in myself, and I certainly didn't have a "style" of my own.
So I tried to mimic the style of my dear friend Tom. An aide who had worked
with Tom and me together, and now worked with me alone, recognized my
struggle. One day she sat me down and reflected on what she saw. She con-
cluded with some words that have always meant a lot to me. She said, "Jerry,
you aren't and never will be a very good Tom, but you can be a very good
Jerry. Why don't you try being Jerry?" It took me a while to be comfortable

with being just me, but I did find that I was a much better teacher as me than I was as Tom. Not only much better: much happier.

I have colleagues who capture their classes with their humor or their theatrics or their booming voice. I have none of these assets. I am not even sure how I would describe my own style. It's certainly pretty low-key. I just know the style is mine, it's me, and most students seem to respond to it. Ultimately, that is all that matters.

BEING SUCCESSFUL, BEING CONFIDENT

Along the way, your confidence will come from feeling that you are doing a good job. But where does it come from before you start? It comes from preparing to do a good job. Good, careful preparation helps you move with self-assurance. If you also ensure that your students are ready and if you keep yourself and them actively engaged in the process of the lecture, you are going to be okay. You will learn to be ever more successful, and with every success will come more confidence.

Believe in Yourself

Learning to lecture is like learning anything else. First you have to understand, then you learn. I hope I have contributed something to your understanding. Understanding gives you the tools to learn, but the learning comes with practice, practice, practice.

One last thought: Do for yourself as you should for your students. Believe in yourself.

3

About Motivation

Ruth V. Small

"I WAS NEVER SURE I HAD A CHANCE for success." "The vocabulary was way over my head." "Class sessions seemed unprepared and disorganized." "Expectations were vague and inconsistent." "I never got any positive feedback." "The lectures were boring and monotonous." "There were no real-life applications." "There was never any interaction." "I didn't feel challenged."

These are the actual comments of a group of graduate students asked to reflect on past educational experiences they found demotivating (Small, Dodge, and Jiang 1996). In spite of their negative experiences, these motivated learners persevered in pursuit of their personal learning goals. But, unfortunately, many less-motivated students in similar situations will alter their educational aspirations—or worse, drop out altogether. What would your students say about your course's motivation quotient?

This chapter presents an organized structure for creating a positive learning atmosphere in which student motivation can develop and thrive. It begins with a definition of *motivation,* followed by presentation of two models for designing motivating instruction. It concludes with a framework that demonstrates how the two models might be integrated and identifies a variety of related instructional strategies for facilitating the motivation to learn.

Defining Motivation

Most of us believe we know when our students are motivated. We watch for certain physical signs (e.g., eye contact, smile, nodding head) as evidence. We might interpret certain outward behaviors such as question asking or class participation as demonstrating motivation. Or perhaps we judge how motivated students are by the quality and/or quantity of their output (e.g., longer term papers, higher grades on tests, more time spent on projects).

Research on human motivation acknowledges these and other outward behaviors as manifestations of a broad measure of motivation that includes both *attention* and *effort* (Brophy 1998). Attention encompasses *interest* and *curiosity*. In educational terms, attention relates to a student's interest in and epistemic curiosity toward learning, that is, a quest for knowledge (Small and Arnone 1998/1999). Effort requires that a person *value* the task and *expect to succeed* at it; this is "expectancy-value" theory (Vroom 1964). In learning terms, a student must value the learning goal and believe she or he can successfully accomplish that goal. These are the prerequisites to student motivation. As instructors, we can have an impact on these motivation requirements through thoughtful and systematic instructional planning.

Although most of the early research on motivation was conducted in the context of the workplace (i.e., what motivates workers to produce more and faster), within the past twenty years some educational theorists have turned their attention to the classroom, exploring what factors influence a student's desire to learn (Brophy 1998; Keller 1983; Wlodkowski 1993). An effective instructor capitalizes on students' existing motivation to learn and provides a learning environment that continues to develop that motivation (Brophy 1998).

Models for Designing Motivating Instruction

Two models have emerged in the quest to design and facilitate motivating learning experiences for students. In the first model, Wlodkowski (1993) views learning motivation in terms of temporal stages. The "Time Continuum" model specifies that students *begin* the learning process with certain pre-formed attitudes and needs related to learning in general and the specific learning event they are entering. For example, a student who has repeatedly experienced failure in math-related activities in high school likely will enter a college algebra class feeling anxious, lacking confidence, and needing encouragement and extra attention. Because students are involved in the learning process *during* the instruction, they need continuing stimulation and emotional experiences to remain motivated. Our math student, therefore, might be motivated by activities such as computer-based practice, periodic reviews, and group work. As the learning process concludes and the instruction *ends,* students expect to attain competence and receive reinforcement for that competence. That would mean supportive praise for effort and achievement for our math student. Wlodkowski's model provides a *descriptive* framework for organizing motivating instruction.

The second motivation model, which is more *prescriptive* than the Time Continuum model, offers a framework for selecting appropriate instructional strategies to motivate student learning. Based largely on expectancy-value theory and encompassing the research on curiosity (see Berlyne 1960; Day 1982) and several other motivation theories, Keller's "ARCS Model of Motivational Design" (1983, 1987) identifies four major motivational factors (*a*ttention, *r*elevance, *c*onfidence, and *s*atisfaction), all of which must be considered when planning an instructional event.

Consider the following real-life examples related to each of the four ARCS components, collected for a research study in which undergraduate and graduate students were asked to recall an interesting and a boring personal learning experience. Each of the examples illustrates what can happen when motivation is *not* part of the instructional-planning process:

ATTENTION

I was sitting in class. . . . Though I know I needed to understand the material and to pay attention, I just could not. Every week, I would sit in that class bored to sleepiness. The teacher would give incredibly boring, dry lectures—straight out of the readings. Hardly any other comments were given. Once in a blue moon he would write something cryptic on the board or use the overhead. By the end of the semester, weekly attendance was down to a hard core ten from about sixteen originally.

The attention factor is concerned with identifying instructional strategies that capture student curiosity and interest early in the instruction and maintain that attention even beyond the end of the learning episode.

RELEVANCE

Last summer I was enrolled in an extension class. The class was supposed to teach me how to mainstream special education students into my regular classroom. The instructor . . . lectured for two weeks on the definition and implementation of behavior modification. I was joined in my agony by thirty other teachers—all satisfying a newly imposed state requirement. We never did learn anything practical concerning mainstreaming.

Providing a more meaningful instructional context helps students understand the importance of the learning. Relevance strategies help students link the instructional content and methods to their learning needs and interests. This fosters student involvement in the learning process.

CONFIDENCE

The class was supposed to be a Friday morning seminar class in elementary education in which students would participate in discussion of problems and issues directly related to student teaching. . . . Roll was called precisely at 8 A.M., with tardy marks given to those not present (all students were in fifth-year college work). The content of the class was a step-by-step demonstration of how to make a pocket chart. Students were required to follow each step and perform the task. Negative remarks were directed at individual students by the instructor if they did not have the right materials or if they did not follow the exact directions. I was told to do one procedure over because I had taken a short cut.

Creating a positive climate for learning helps students develop competence and self-confidence. Strategies must be incorporated that establish, increase, and reinforce confidence. With particularly difficult, complex, unfamiliar, or abstract subject matter, students can lack confidence in their ability to learn.

SATISFACTION

I was in an undergraduate class in Victorian poetry. . . . It was a strictly lecture course and the prof sat at a table with a typing stand propped before him, reading lecture notes from old, yellowed, curling sheets of note paper. The professor's monotone voice, lack of eye contact, lack of humor [made the course boring]. The class diminished from forty-plus to thirteen.

When students see connections between what is presented in class and what they are expected to learn, and they feel they have achieved learning success due to their ability and effort, then they are likely to experience learning satisfaction. This often results in a desire to continue learning.

The degree to which each of the ARCS factors must be addressed when planning an instructional event depends on (1) students' needs, interests, and abilities; (2) the difficulty and complexity of the subject matter; (3) the level of learning objectives; and (4) the limitations and constraints of the learning environment (e.g., available resources, space, and technology).

An Integrating Framework

While Wlodkowski's Time Continuum model and Keller's ARCS Model of Motivational Design are individually useful, an integration of the two models provides a powerful approach to designing motivating instruction at the college level. The following framework takes a range of motivational strategies across the ARCS components and places them within a sequence across the Time Continuum.

While the following list of strategies is not exhaustive, it provides general guidelines that you can apply to the design of a complete course or a single class session. Which areas to emphasize and how many motivational strategies you choose will depend on your learning situation and your students. (Where possible, I have included specific illustrations of motivational strategies used by various instructors at Syracuse University.)

BEGINNING THE INSTRUCTION

Gain attention

Strategy: Provide novelty or mystery. Students react to unpredictable, perplexing, or incongruous stimuli in their environment. Such stimuli create interest and arouse curiosity. Try using novel teaching methods or personal anecdotes to capture your students' attention (Keller 1987). For example, here is a strategy one instructor used to capture the attention of undergraduate students in a course on information presentation. In the first class session, the instructor entered the classroom wearing hair curlers and an old wrinkled shirt, dropped her notes on the floor, projected overhead transparencies that were unreadable, and spoke in a voice at times too soft to be heard. Her performance quickly captured the students' attention. While

	Attention	Relevance	Confidence	Satisfaction
Beginning	**Gain attention.** • Introduce novelty/mystery • Generate high-level inquiry/thought	**Demonstrate relevance.** • Show learning is worthwhile • Relate new content to previous/future learning • Design/revise goals	**Establish confidence.** • Set moderately challenging, attainable goals • Specify learning requirements • Set mutually determined goals	
During	**Sustain attention.** • Direct attention to important content • Vary methods, media, materials • Use memory enhancement techniques • Encourage participation/active learning • Foster ongoing inquiry • Use humor	**Maintain relevance.** • Relate to real world • Model desired behaviors • Allow opportunities to apply learning	**Increase confidence.** • Describe unfamiliar/difficult concepts in concrete ways • Progress from basic to more complex content • Allow thinking/reflecting time • Assess learning at various points • Provide timely, regular feedback • Allow learning control • Provide sincere praise	
Concluding			**Reinforce confidence.** • Set new goals	**Promote satisfaction.** • Use fair/consistent assessment methods • Reward achievement • Provide opportunities to use/apply new knowledge/skills

TIME SEQUENCE

some caught on almost immediately, most of the students sat mesmerized by this seemingly disorganized and inept professor. After about two minutes of this, the instructor projected a list of "Top Ten Worst Presentation Behaviors," all of which she had just demonstrated. It got the course off to a great start, while teaching students several important concepts upon which the course was based.

Strategy: Generate high-level inquiry and thought. Begin with a thought-provoking statement or question that draws on what students already know but requires them to take their knowledge to a higher level. This strategy uses a constructivist approach (i.e., views learning as a dynamic process for supporting learner-construction rather than teacher-communication of knowledge) that helps each student create a customized structure for the information presented throughout the course (Small and Arnone 2000). This is an ideal strategy for a problem-based learning environment in which the course is based on one or more relevant issues or problems. For example, in an introductory graduate-level course on library and information science, the professor began the course by writing the following statement on the board: "With the development of the Internet, there will be no need for librarians in the twenty-first century." After students recovered from their initial shock, they began the process of disproving this statement, an ongoing task throughout the semester. Students scrutinized guest speakers, readings, and other information sources in relation to that statement.

Demonstrate relevance

Strategy: Show how the specific content to be learned is worthwhile. Students like to learn things that will offer them benefits or a real advantage (Wlodkowski 1993). Well-known motivation researcher Mihalyi Csikszentmihalyi (1997) states, "It is not the knowledge or prestige of teachers that I remember, or the correctness of their methods. It is, rather, the conviction they conveyed that what they were doing was worth doing, that it was intrinsically valuable" (79). As instructors, we clearly recognize the importance of what we teach; but for many of our students, it is not always obvious. Furthermore, although some learning tasks are themselves intrinsically motivating, most people (even adults) seek out learning experiences in which the knowledge or skills to be learned have some type of personal utility (Zemke and Zemke 1981). Describing the usefulness and/or importance of the learning task from the very beginning of the course or class session requires that you understand your learners' world and the context in which they might apply their learning, now or in the future. For example, in a course that required undergraduate students to produce a newsletter, the instructor allowed students to complete the assignment for a personal context, such as a fraternity, sorority, dorm, organization, or place of work.

Strategy: Relate new content to previous or future learning. Making content relevant was one of the most important factors cited by college students for preventing learning boredom (Small, Dodge, and Jiang, 1996). Making connections between existing and future knowledge is a critical strategy for motivating student learning. In your first class session and in your course syllabus, specify the relevance of what students will learn. At the very beginning of his course, one instructor likes to ask each student to think about how the course will be personally useful and to share this information with the class. This not only clarifies the usefulness of the course in each student's mind but also provides additional connections for the other students.

Strategy: Design, and when necessary revise, learning goals to be compatible with student needs, values, and abilities. Determine early where your students are in the learning process and where they expect to be at the end of the course. One technique for accomplishing this is to administer a student questionnaire in the first class session that gathers information about each student, including why each is taking the course, what each expects to learn, and the like. This technique also allows you to quickly correct any misconceptions or inaccurate assumptions about what the course will be and to adjust the course to meet student expectations. It also lets students know whether they have selected the appropriate course for their needs and interests. In a graduate course on media services, an instructor had all students complete a "student profile" questionnaire when they first arrived. Some of the questions were marked for sharing with the class. One student described why she was taking the course, and the instructor immediately realized she was in the wrong course. The instructor was then able to immediately counsel the student out of that course and into the appropriate one before the first week of classes was over.

Establish confidence

Strategy: Set moderately challenging but attainable learning goals. Put simply, if instruction is too easy, students get bored; if it is too difficult, they become anxious. Most learners prefer instruction that presents at least a moderate, "just within reach," learning challenge (Wlodkowski 1993). Attaining this goal requires you to know something about the knowledge and skill backgrounds of your students in relation to what they will be learning and to use that information to tailor (as much as possible) your instruction to meet their needs. In courses that require technical skills, students often come to class possessing a range of skills and experience. A pretest can determine how you might group students for labs and other exercises. Some instructors allow some students to "test out" of a lab or activity, while others place students in expert-novice teams in which the expert student serves as tutor to the novice partner.

Strategy: Specify learning requirements as clearly and thoroughly as possible. On the first day of class, describe the scope of content to be learned and clearly articulate your learning expectations. Reinforce this information by providing students with a comprehensive course syllabus that includes goals and expectations, scope of content, and criteria for evaluating learning. Further clarify the requirements of assignments and criteria for successful completion of those assignments; where possible, show students exemplary models of assignments or projects completed in the past by students like themselves. Bandura (1982) states that these types of models convey "information about the nature and predictability of environmental events," describing their impact in this way: "Seeing similar others perform successfully can raise efficacy expectations in observers, who then judge that they too possess the capabilities to master comparable activities" (126–27). There are many ways you can accomplish this, such as bringing a few exemplary papers or projects to class for students to review, putting some on reserve at the campus library, and posting examples to the class website.

Strategy: Set mutually determined learning goals. When students have some control over their own learning, such as having an opportunity to help set their own learning goals, they feel empowered (Deci 1995). Providing a list of potential topics for an assignment or a selection of possible methods for completing an assignment (e.g., PowerPoint presentation, project, test), allowing students to work on an assignment independently or in small groups, and letting students contribute ideas for evaluation criteria for their assignments are just some ways students can make decisions that affect their learning destiny without your straying from your intended instructional goals (Keller 1987; Wlodkowski 1993). For example, throughout one undergraduate course on information presentation, the instructor and the class jointly developed a rubric that the instructor used to evaluate the students' final presentations. In courses that have exams, some instructors invite students to contribute exam questions and then include at least some of those items on the exam. (The students' questions are almost always more difficult than the instructor's!)

DURING THE INSTRUCTION

Sustain attention

Strategy: Vary presentation methods, media, and materials. People tend to pay more attention to things that are changing than to things that are static (Wlodkowski 1993). Spice up your lectures with new presentation methods such as computer-based presentations, audiovisual materials, and handouts in order to stimulate higher levels of interest. Sometimes you might even have an individual or small group of students present all or part of a class session's topic to the class.

Strategy: Use memory-enhancement techniques. You can help students learn required facts or concepts through mnemonic devices (e.g., rhymes, acronyms), visual representations (e.g., drawings, diagrams), or other associative learning techniques. For example, the instructor of a course on information literacy had the students develop and share mnemonic devices to help them remember his six-factor information problem-solving model.

Strategy: Encourage active learning. As the ancient proverb reminds us, "Tell me, I forget. Show me, I remember. Involve me, I understand." While lecture is one of the oldest and most common teaching techniques used in college classrooms, research indicates that when used alone, lecture is not always a very effective means of facilitating learning and can often become a source of student boredom. Most students prefer activities that allow them to interact and become actively involved in their learning (Brophy 1987). Techniques that increase learner participation will result in increased learner effort, ownership, and achievement (Young 1982). Build into each class session some type of activity that requires students to apply what they are learning, such as small-group discussions, brainstorming sessions, simulation exercises, lab experiences, debate, problem-solving case studies, or role-playing exercises. For example, in a course on information technologies, for a class session on the impact of telecommunications policies on education, one instructor used a "town meeting" format and invited a distinguished panel of experts that included a politician, a school district administrator, and frontline educators. Students in the course were required to develop questions for the panel, and the session was open to the entire college.

Strategy: Foster ongoing inquiry. Encourage students to ask questions during each class session. These questions allow you to clarify content that is not well understood, correct misconceptions, and elaborate on points of interest. One instructor requires students to write a one-sentence question or comment at the end of each class session, to which he responds on the course website the following week. You can vary this strategy in many ways, such as allowing students to submit questions at the beginning of class every day or once a week and then answering them before you start the day's class session, or having students post their questions to the course website.

Strategy: Use humor where appropriate. Whether used spontaneously or deliberately through such strategies as humorous anecdotes or cartoons, humor can help calm students' learning anxiety and establish a friendlier, more comfortable learning environment. For example, one instructor used a political cartoon each week to start off his graduate-level political science class. These cartoons not only created a friendly atmosphere but they also contributed content through humorous visual commentaries on issues to be studied.

Maintain relevance

Strategy: Relate content to familiar, real-world experiences. In addition to encouraging students to draw on their own knowledge and experiences and relate them to the content you are teaching, you can bring in practitioners from the field or students who have previously taken the course to offer testimonials about its usefulness and importance. Some instructors who feel they don't have time in class to do this can use a class website or online listserv to accomplish it. These real-life stories and testimonials provide excellent "triggers" for online or class discussions.

Strategy: Model desired behaviors. In a review of the research, Sherman and associates (1987) found certain behaviors to be strong indicators of teaching excellence at the college level. These included knowledge of both subject matter and effective teaching methods, clarity of content presentation, ability to stimulate interest and thinking, preparation, organization, and enthusiasm both for subject matter and for teaching it to others. The last item is particularly powerful, because enthusiasm is frequently contagious. "The most influential teachers . . . were usually the ones who loved what they were doing, who showed by their dedication and their passion that there was nothing else on earth they would rather be doing" (Csikszentmihalyi 1997, 78).

Strategy: Allow opportunities to apply learning. Powerful strategies here are knowledge- or skill-building practice exercises or sessions such as labs and projects that allow students to use what they are learning as they are learning it, particularly if the activities can be completed in a real-world context. For example, in a course on technical training methods, one instructor arranged for students to work in teams to provide technology training for real clients in the community (nonprofit agencies). This win-win arrangement gave students an opportunity to apply their newly learned training skills to meet an actual learning need and for agencies to receive a valuable service that they could not have otherwise afforded.

Increase confidence

Strategy: Describe difficult concepts in concrete ways. When teaching unfamiliar, difficult, or abstract content, you will often need to give students more than one type of explanation. My daughter once related a story about a college chemistry course she had taken during which every time a student did not understand a particular concept and asked to have it explained again, the instructor repeated exactly the same words, only louder. What the instructor mistook for a hearing problem was actually a need for an alternative explanation. It is always a good idea for you to define and explain new terms, orally or in writing or both. In addition, providing a range of examples is useful when content is particularly difficult or abstract. A course website is a great centralized location for glossaries, examples, demonstrations, and alternative explanations of difficult concepts. It can be developed by the instructor, the students, or both.

Strategy: Progress from easier, more familiar, or basic content to more complex, abstract, or difficult content. When teaching a basic or introductory course, begin with what students already know and progress to increasingly more difficult concepts or skills, building in periodic reviews. When teaching an advanced course, begin with a review of the more basic, already learned information and build on that knowledge as the content becomes more difficult. Not only does this give students confidence in their ability to learn the new content, it also helps provide important associations to previously learned information. When there is a great deal of content to be learned or when the content is particularly difficult or abstract, some instructors hold periodic review sessions before the amount of new information to learn becomes overwhelming.

Strategy: Allow thinking and reflecting time. When asking students questions in class, it is important to allow them time for thinking before they respond. Research has shown that teachers often do not allow their students enough time after a question is asked to retrieve what they know from their long-term memory. Many students don't want to risk blurting out the wrong answer and appearing foolish to their peers. As instructors, however, we tend to be uncomfortable with silence; sometimes several seconds can seem like an eternity! We often respond to the silence reflexively, either by randomly calling on other students to answer or by jumping in with the answer ourselves. Rowe (1987) found that, on average, instructors wait less than one second for a response to their question. Further, she discovered that if instructors allowed just three to five seconds, they were able to elicit more responses and higher-quality responses from students. It is often a good idea to inform students during the first class session that you will be allowing them extra time to respond to your questions. This affirms to them that you really want them to respond and that you recognize that it often requires time to formulate a good response.

Strategy: Assess learning at various points during the instruction. Using evaluation techniques to assess student learning at various points throughout the instruction allows you to identify what informal and formal learning has occurred and where you need to revise or modify learning goals, instructional methods, or content. Assessment techniques might include quizzes, oral questions, application exercises, self-assessment instruments, and short-term projects. For example, an instructor in an undergraduate course on economics after each class session required students to complete an online questionnaire containing reflection questions about the class session and the readings. The questionnaire not only allowed the instructor to assess each student's progress but also provided continuous feedback on his teaching effectiveness.

Strategy: Provide timely, regular, informative feedback on learning progress. Students need to know what and how well they are doing and where and how they can improve. Follow up the learning assessment methods described above with prompt formal or informal feedback (e.g., written or verbal or both) on students' learning progress. Students also appreciate your being available for individual consultation at regularly scheduled office hours or before or after class. I recently began using an online midterm (multiple choice) in one of my undergraduate courses as a way to assess how well students learned various concepts presented in the textbook and class sessions. The exam is administered to the whole class in a computer lab, drawing randomly from a pool of items so that no two students receive the exact same set of exam questions. The students really liked this strategy because they received immediate feedback as soon as they completed the exam, including their grade, which items they answered incorrectly, and what the correct answers were. In this way, the exam served as both an assessment and a learning tool.

Strategy: Provide sincere praise for learning effort and success. Praise can be a highly effective motivational strategy throughout a learning episode—but only when it is sincere, used judiciously, and emphasizes the link between effort and learning success. When tied to competence and achievement of challenging tasks, it can boost a student's self-esteem (Dweck 1986). Wlodkowski uses a "3S-3P" mnemonic to guide the use of praise as a reward: "Praise (and other rewards) should be *S*incere, *S*pecific, *S*ufficient, and *P*roperly attributed for genuinely *P*raiseworthy behavior in a manner *P*referred by the learner" (1993, 232). An instructor of a doctoral seminar on statistics was known for his rigor and challenging exams. When he wrote "Good job" at the top of one student's midterm exam, that student told me that it was the highest praise he had ever received in his academic career. A little praise can go a long way toward boosting students' confidence in their learning abilities.

ENDING THE INSTRUCTION

Reinforce confidence

Strategy: Help students set new learning goals. When students are motivated and excel, they often want to continue their learning as a natural consequence of learning success. You can encourage and support their desire for more learning through enrichment opportunities. For example, you can recognize a student's learning competence and recommend advanced or honors courses in the same subject area or provide reading lists and other independent-learning options to be completed after your course has ended.

Promote satisfaction

Strategy: Use fair and consistent learning-assessment methods. All of your tests and other learning assessments should be consistent with the learning goals and the content presented. Remember, test results reflect not only your students' learning levels but also your teaching effectiveness. Providing students with examples of the types of questions that will be included on a test helps to alleviate some of the test anxiety they might experience. Some instructors use a game-like exercise (e.g., "Who Wants to Be a Millionaire?" or "Jeopardy") that is fun and provides an effective test preparation/review activity.

Strategy: Reward learning achievement. Reinforce connections between achievement and effort by giving praise, public recognition, and other tangible or symbolic rewards (e.g., grades, certificates) at the completion of a learning sequence. You also can acknowledge exemplary academic achievement by displaying student work, a strategy used often in subject areas such as the visual arts, music, and engineering. Some instructors choose the best examples of one or more assignments and ask those students to present their work to the class (or beyond). Doing so provides recognition to the stellar students, while it also helps their classmates to understand what makes an outstanding assignment.

Strategy: Allow students to use or apply their newly gained knowledge or skills. Opportunities for students to demonstrate their knowledge or skills can be provided through in-class simulations, internships, fieldwork, or project experiences. When students can see what and how much they have learned (particularly in a real-world setting), they experience a sense of learning satisfaction and accomplishment.

Planning Tool

This integrated framework for designing motivating instruction is illustrated in the table on page 35. The framework provides an organized, systematic instructional-planning tool to help create a learning environment, like the one described below, that inspires students' desire to learn:

> I can't quite remember the situation, at least not for the whole presentation. There were about thirty students present, one instructor, and one guest. Most of the class content was lecture. The instructor used the overhead projector extensively and threw out a lot of stimulating questions for student response and reaction. Whether or not it was used in this particular session I can't recall, but the instructor had a tremendous knack of drawing quiet students into the learning. I had a great feeling of being part of a learning environment.

4

Motivating Strategies

Enid Bogle

THE BEGINNING INSTRUCTOR soon learns that what works with one class doesn't always work with another. Even within the same class, dynamics in the classroom will vary from day to day, and the pedagogical strategy that excites one group of students might bore another. The experienced instructor knows that all students are capable of learning; but because students learn at different paces and favor different learning styles, the astute instructor builds a repertoire of strategies to generate interest and foster learning. Further, armed with that repertoire, the effective instructor quickly assesses a situation and makes on-the-spot decisions about which strategy to employ with each class or each student.

The problem for the inexperienced instructor is not just in recognizing that a problem exists but also in diagnosing its cause and having the wherewithal to choose the appropriate pedagogical response. Thus, while there are known strategies to motivate students (Keller 1983), the major concern is knowing when to apply the appropriate one.

The Role of the Learner

When students are not learning, it is our responsibility to assess the cause and engage them in activities that will motivate them. But what role do students themselves play in the learning environment? How can an instructor build on what each student brings to the learning table, especially if the student brings less than is desired?

Ideally, learners bring to the classroom certain skills and an *intrinsic* desire to learn. That is, learners pursue the act of learning for the inherent joy of obtaining new information and the rewards that acquisition of that new knowledge brings. With such students, our job as teacher is made easier because we do not have to encourage or cajole students to learn and do well but can offer them in an exciting way the new information, whether content or access to content. Lacking that intrinsic desire to learn, however, can be an impediment to students' success. Such students tend to give the minimum amount of effort required simply to pass the course; and they tend to be easily distracted by the slightest barrier to learning.

It is for these students that instructors should be ready with motivating strategies. The essential ingredient is to help students understand the importance of undertaking the learning task, maintaining interest in pursuing it, and eventually reaping the rewards for obtaining the information.

THE IMPACT OF CONTENT ON LEARNERS

Learning is thwarted when incongruence exists between the content and other factors of learning. Perhaps students lack the background necessary for understanding the material, or maybe they lack the foresight to grasp the relevance of the topic to their career goals. Your task is to match course content to the skill level of the learners and to present that content in a way that brings meaning and excitement to the learners so that they can make connections within the field or be able to transfer the information to other topics or fields. Get students to arrive at the "Aha!" of the information you present.

Your Role as Facilitator

In your role as facilitator of your students' learning, you must ensure that all obstacles to their learning are removed. Possible barriers might be a learner's lack of intrinsic motivation, unpreparedness, irrelevance of the content, or an uninspiring method of presentation. To ensure a meaningful classroom environment in the absence of intrinsic factors, you must focus on getting students motivated. You must know the content, be prepared, and exude confidence. Avoid seeming hesitant, tentative, or insecure. The instructor who exudes confidence, who is enthusiastic about the content, and who displays command of the significance of the topic is far more likely to capture the students' attention and propel them into being engaged with the lesson. It is then that the instructor must "move outside of the box" and develop creative strategies to present a body of information not merely to be remembered but that has immediate meaning and has the potential to be connected to future studies. Thus, despite what the learner brings to the classroom, the burden rests with the teacher in terms of the quality of the content and the presentation strategies. This presentation should vary; lecture with advance organizers, group work, demonstration, and site visits are all ways of capturing students' attention. Lack of these factors impedes successful learning. As a facilitator of your students' learning, you must provide *extrinsic* factors that will generate active learning by engaging the students in ways that will stimulate them to learn the content and, ultimately, develop their intrinsic desire to learn.

Your success in any class depends on *preparation*. Alert students will know when you are groping your way through the lesson; and weak students will not even bother to respond to a lackluster and, perhaps, inadequate presentation. It is better to be overprepared than to be underprepared. In fact, you lose nothing when you are overprepared. Not only will the additional information be useful for the next lesson, but also it can be used to set the stage for future inspiring discussions.

To whet the students' appetite for future discussion, you might offer comments such as "Let's see how this will fit into [an upcoming topic/activity] next time" . . . or "Will this apply to [the topic for the future lesson]?" You should also anticipate students' asking a few challenging questions and either be ready to respond or let the questions serve as a springboard to the next discussion. To maximize their motivating effect, be sure to thank the students for bringing those insights to the discussion, and indicate that together the class will investigate their significance. Doing so will make students more likely to seek the answers for the next time, or just be motivated to pose a question of their own that you can use to further the lesson. Thus, students become engaged in the teaching design and at the same time develop a new approach to learning the material.

Even more than preparation, the presentation strategy you use is of utmost significance. Try to begin each lesson by getting the students' attention and then maintain that attention. That might mean reviewing the previous topic; it might mean taking a stand that seems contrary to all that was said last time; it might just be a challenge to students to use ideas from the previous lesson. Your overall aim is to elicit and maintain interest, to energize the students to participate. Astute instructors will observe when a well-prepared lesson is off target and they will quickly shift focus, resurrect the lesson, and return to the main principles in another form. All of this means that you must have a contingency plan and be ready to put it in action.

With experience, you will develop a gut feeling that tells you when a lesson is going well. Do students ask pertinent questions? Do they make connections? Do they ask for clarification on difficult concepts? Do they answer review questions appropriately? These are important assessments. But these answers do not necessarily tell you whether the students are motivated to learn. Students who are motivated will achieve the objectives you outlined in your syllabus and will go a step further in pursuit of larger goals and pure enjoyment of the process of learning the material.

If students are not intrinsically motivated, what can you do to ensure not only that they are acquiring the information but also that they find their learning satisfying? You might begin by asking probing questions at the end of the lesson, or have students jot down three important points they learned and then share their knowledge with the class. Choose students at random to respond; if this becomes your routine, perhaps they will pay attention in order to have something to say if called upon. For this technique to be motivating, you need to find something in the response that merits commending. Never ridicule a simplistic or vague answer. By commending their effort, you help build their self-confidence, which might later motivate them to participate in the learning process.

SPECIAL CHALLENGES FOR TAS

Students who are not intrinsically motivated sometimes latch on to inexcusable reasons for not trying to do well. That a teaching assistant is not a "real" teacher is one such reason. If you are a TA responsible for a discussion section, laboratory, or your own class, knowing that some students hold this view means you must work doubly hard to assure students that you are qualified to be in charge.

What to Do When . . .

Knowing how to identify absence of motivation is important. Students who get good grades are not necessarily motivated; perhaps they simply perform on cue what is asked and expected. The student who is quiet might not be paying attention; neither is the one with the glazed stare. Be mindful of students who lack motivation, for then learning is not really taking place.

STUDENTS SEEM BORED

If students seem bored (not paying attention, doodling, reading instead of listening, yawning loudly and frequently, and so on), it is important that you identify the real cause: Is it related to the content? the learner? the instructor? There are many possible factors. Students might be bored because the content is too difficult or too simple, or the material might seem irrelevant. They might lack the background skills needed to process the material. Or your method of presentation could be dull or just merely a mismatch. Before you can remedy the situation, you need to know the real problem.

Begin by assessing the students' base knowledge by asking a few pertinent questions or having students do a self-assessment on the topic. Once you have identified their knowledge level, begin your presentation of the material at a point where students will grasp its meaning or, at least, develop some interest. You may have to step back and provide background material that your students should have—but have not—previously acquired.

But what happens when students are at different skill levels? Howard University instructor Richard Wright,[1] for example, asserts that a teacher should always "teach to excellence," then provide other means to allow students who are behind to improve their skills. By using this approach, the above-average students will not be bored and the others will be challenged to meet your learning goals. You should always attempt to present material that will neither bore some nor leave some behind. Sometimes it might be necessary to review or to ask students who think they have grasped the information to explain to the class what it is they understand; doing so reinforces for them what they have understood and, at the same time, it gives their classmates an opportunity to hear the information again through a different voice.

When students are bored, you also have to find a way to make the course material relevant to them. At times that can be difficult, especially when your course is required for general education and not for the major area of study.

---

1. Richard Wright made this assertion in a dialogue with TAs on January 5, 2001, at Howard University.

The former category of students might believe that taking the course is a waste of their time. How do you motivate these students? Consider offering a thorough introductory session focused on the benefits of liberal education and your course's place in the whole educational scheme, demonstrating its benefits for everyone regardless of the major being pursued.

You can also influence and ensure motivation by setting and reviewing goals with and for the learners. Know that establishing goals for the students to pursue is not enough: constantly review those goals with the students. Further, provide material in sequential form in manageable segments, so that students can develop mastery and satisfaction, then build upon their new skills by connecting them with the next set of tasks and new ideas. One example is the research paper. Break down such a project into small segments and provide students with appropriate guidelines and feedback for each phase of their work. This way, the task is no longer overwhelming, because students complete manageable segments for which they receive credit. Students will then be motivated to tackle complex assignments if they establish and manage these short-term goals; they will be less likely to be bored with the task, which otherwise might seem overwhelming and time-consuming. Encourage students to keep goals in mind and to evaluate them as those goals are completed.

As students gain satisfaction in completing their goals, they will gain confidence in their own ability and, eventually, develop an interest in learning, more likely an interest in tackling challenging assignments. Having confidence in one's ability does not by itself determine success, but it is a step toward pursuing and exploring other topics and becoming more involved in the learning process. When students develop ultimately a long-term involvement with the learning process, they become intrinsically motivated.

But do not assume that the length of time a student spends on an assignment translates into motivation. In other words, length of time is not equivalent to processing of information. It is, rather, the quality of the engagement that is significant. The astute instructor will engage each student in a discussion of what is taking place to ensure that quality and intensity are not substituted by duration and intensity. You might be rightly concerned about the time to be allotted for these discussions, given the number of students in your class; conference hours and small group tutorials are ideal times, in addition to e-mail chats, to continue discussions.

You might also counteract boredom by using different methods of presentation; students should not get accustomed to a routine of lecturing. Use group approaches, begin with a relevant video, send them to a museum, have them visit a laboratory, provide handouts with background or provocative material. Allow students to work independently and make presentations in groups or to the class. Your aim is to get them involved with the teaching and learning processes by providing them with an array of opportunities to foster their inclination to and facilitate their involvement in learning. You should know when students are bored, because they are unable to keep the pace of the class. When this occurs, emphasize mastery rather than speed, and evaluate individual progress rather than compare students' achievement with those of their classmates.

STUDENTS SHOW NO INTEREST

Students may have several reasons for showing a lack of interest in the class. And it might not be that they are bored. Finding the cause is essential. It might be that they did not want to take the class in the first place. Maybe it is required as a prerequisite, or it is the only three-hour course that fits their schedule. While it is easy to demonstrate the utility of your course for success in upper-level courses, it is extremely difficult to persuade a student to work hard in a course that is just a filler. However, your role is to motivate *all* students to do well. Begin by stating the virtues of the course and how it can be used not merely for practical reasons but for the education of the self. For instance, the student who says, "I'm a math major, why should I have to do a writing course?" needs assurance that a writing course is beneficial. Explain that mathematicians write proposals, make presentations, and prepare reports, while some write textbooks, all of which must be clear, precise, and organized. Another way of getting such students interested is to have your math major, for instance, write the procedure for solving a problem. An art major could visit a museum and prepare short abstracts or slide presentations for the class. In other words, you begin with what interests the students, and then apply it to the lesson.

Perhaps your best way to get students interested in the class is for you to demonstrate enthusiasm for what you are teaching. Being prepared is not enough; the excellent instructor brings life to the subject by using gestures, moving around, modulating the voice, adding some humorous comment. In short, capture your students' interest by *being lively*.

STUDENTS FEAR TAKING EXAMINATIONS

Your examinations should also be used as a teaching tool. As such, you should include different types of assessment with different goals. Get students involved with assessment. Discuss important concepts that everyone should know; get their opinions on why such concepts are important, and then use the process of examination as a review to see how much they understood. Invite students to suggest questions for a pool from which you might pull ideas for examination questions. (Of course, the students should understand that frivolous, simple questions that require no critical thinking will not receive serious consideration.) When students see ideas from their questions on an examination, they will feel that they are contributing and that their opinions are significant, and they will be more inclined to be active participants.

By varying the types of assessment, you achieve another goal: catering to students' different learning styles also requires different modes of assessing. In addition, students are kept more interested when variety and not sameness dominates.

STUDENTS ARE WITHDRAWN

It is not necessary that students be talkative to be learning. But when you are conducting a lesson by discussion, students should be encouraged to participate. Watch for students who outwardly are not paying attention by not participating and devise ways to bring them into the discussion or engage them in some comfortable way. One strategy is to ask reticent students to be leaders in small discussion groups; be sure to rotate the role, however, so as not to make anyone believe that you were trying to embarrass him or her. In large-group situations, another strategy is to ask the students for their opinion; if their contribution is not exactly what is expected, keep probing with leading questions until they give the desired answer. Through this approach, a withdrawn student gains confidence and, it is hoped, will be motivated to contribute again. Sometimes students are by nature withdrawn; or because of their cultural background, they might not feel comfortable engaging in discussions. For those students, find their comfort level and gently lead them into contributing. Perhaps you could make them responsible for preparing opening comments on a topic; thus, by your asking for clarification afterwards, you draw them into the ongoing class discussion. Try not to intimidate them, but allow these students to take small steps.

Once in a freshman seminar class, I brought in a newspaper article, offered a summary, then asked students to get in groups to defend or refute its issue. One student, who previously had hardly contributed to any topic, became so passionate in her group that her classmates could only listen in disbelief. As in this case, sometimes moving "out of the box" and doing something different can be very motivating. The nature of your course might not always allow such a total departure, but sometimes five minutes off topic to get a withdrawn student engaged is worth the time.

STUDENTS DO NOT PREPARE FOR CLASS

If students habitually arrive in class unprepared, ask yourself whether in the first class session you made clear that you were going to use class time to *explain, expand on,* and *extend* the material they should be working through on their own in their homework assignments. If you did make it clear, below are some possible strategies you might try to motivate students to develop interest in a lesson and to come prepared to engage in it, whatever your mode of delivery (discussion, lecture, group activity, or lab).

Student has too little time to prepare all assignments

Examine the student's course load and review his or her total assignments. If the load seems reasonable to you, refer the student to Student Services to be taught study and time-management skills. This approach is not specifically related to your class, but it teaches a student to balance homework assignments. On your end, too, review for yourself the specific significance of each aspect of your lesson to assure yourself that requiring that students be ready with each segment really adds to their total learning experience.

Student is a procrastinator

You might be able to resolve this problem by giving the class a mini test at the beginning of each session. Do not think of it as punishing the group for the sake of a few procrastinators. There is value for all students in your reinforcing the necessity of being prepared and your demonstrating how preparation facilitates their engagement with the lesson, and in your identifying (and then clarifying) misunderstandings and misconceptions. Also, at the end of each class session, remind the students of the importance of studying the assignment on which you will be building the next lesson.

Student has no interest in the topic

It is your responsibility to develop and enhance your students' appreciation for your topic. This can be done in a number of ways. One strategy is to explain at the end of one lesson how it connects to the next lesson. Point out the lesson's usefulness, tie the topic to out-of-class situations, or simply reiterate its significance to the field of study. Another way to spark their interest is to send them on a field trip to gather background or related material. Howard University TA Natalie Cole-Leonard,[2] for example, has used this approach in her literature class; she sends her students to a museum to view artwork of the period. She begins her lesson with discussion of the artwork, then moves into the literature related to it. She claims that this approach (pulling the art and literature together) stimulates class interaction with students. For a science class, you might assign a trip to the botanical gardens or zoo, then draw connections from the students' visit to the lesson. Every discipline can be connected in this way to some external activity that should elicit interest in the topic. But you need to know your students' interests to assess what will work.

Assignments seem difficult

If students do not prepare for the lesson because they have difficulty comprehending the assignment, provide them with study or reading guides for each lesson. Underscore significant concepts and explain difficult sections. Have the students write answers to simple questions to build their confidence, then gradually move on to more difficult material.

---

2. Natalie Cole-Leonard gave this suggestion during a conversation with graduate assistants, September 2000, at Howard University.

Motivated to Change

Each learner in your class brings a unique set of skills and traits to the learning tasks—students from different cultural backgrounds, students with different learning styles, students with very little enthusiasm for the subject, students who have special needs, students who are ready to be challenged to excel. Your role is to create and foster a classroom culture that encourages all of them to apply themselves. For the unmotivated among them, your job is to motivate them to change their behavior by your choosing and applying appropriate strategies. It is a formidable task to move students to achieve their potential for academic growth. In attempting to inspire and challenge them, you join a noble group of change agents.

5

Active Learning Inside and Outside the Classroom
Creating Multiple Learning Spaces with Technology

Dara H. Wexler and Patricia P. Tinto

ACTIVE LEARNING STRATEGIES can enrich education at the university level, both by stimulating students' engagement in the process and by encouraging them to recognize the practical applications of the material being learned. According to Meyers and Jones, "Active learning derives from two basic assumptions: (1) that learning is by nature an active endeavor and (2) that different people learn in different ways" (Meyers and Jones 1993, xi). By employing active learning strategies, a teacher "provides opportunities for students to *talk and listen, read, write,* and *reflect* as they approach course content through problem-solving exercises, informal small groups, simulations, case studies, role playing, and other activities—all of which require students to *apply* what they are learning" (1993, xi). Technological advances are now providing university teachers with new tools to broaden and diversify the learning spaces available for students using active learning strategies.

Meyers and Jones have argued that "changes in how we think about teaching, the growing diversity of our student body, and what researchers are discovering about the varieties of learning styles make a powerful case for active learning" (1993, 17). When planning for active learning inside and outside the classroom, it is important to ask the following questions. As an instructor, how do I (we):

 • encourage students to make connections between what they learn inside and outside the classroom?

57

- establish a safe and friendly climate?
- help students view an event through more than one perspective or lens?
- negotiate sharing the role of instructor with other instructors and/or with students?
- interact with diverse students?
- engage students in critical thinking about content and class pedagogy?
- enable students to be responsible for their own learning?

Just as people learn in diverse ways, so they may learn in diverse *spaces*. In this chapter, the term *spaces* refers not only to the physical locations where learning may occur (such as classrooms or schools) but also to virtual locations accessible through new technologies. Such virtual locations can encompass access (through computers or other media) to everything from movies and other popular cultural images, primary documents and other texts, and sounds to designed internet spaces such as online discussion forums and virtual museums. However, they always require the students to be active (often taking part in the construction or modification of the virtual learning space) and to be interactive—that is, to exchange information, views, and responses with other students and with teachers. The effective integration of technology into active learning strategies in a university setting—from the perspectives of both the student and the teacher—is a complex but rewarding endeavor.

Relying solely on physical learning spaces can severely limit interchanges among students and between students and teachers, as well as exposure to other perspectives from the wider culture. Access to newer technologies, however, grants instructors much greater flexibility, allowing the expansion of classroom boundaries (both physical and temporal), and the enhancement of student learning through the accommodation of individual learning styles and the exchange of knowledge, opinion, and feedback both among a broader spectrum of students and between students and teachers. When infusing technology into a course, questions to consider include:

- What kinds of conversation do you want to support and what are the most appropriate technological tools to achieve these (e.g., email, listservs, chat, video conferencing, synchronous versus asynchronous discussions, video streaming)?
- What type of accessibility and adaptations exist for diverse learners?
- What kinds of support are available for instructors and students?

- How often should you be available to students online?
- Is technological literacy a goal for your course?
- Can your goal be reached without the technology?

In the following sections we describe how technology can help build additional learning spaces inside and outside the classroom. We explain how these spaces facilitate the creation of active learning opportunities and discuss how popular cultural representations may be used to get students to think critically about the material being learned. Finally, we draw upon our experience of teaching a course blending active learning strategies with technology to show the application of these tools.[1]

Using Technology to Build Learning Spaces

In planning a course, one must consider the physical attributes of the classroom: the size of the room, availability of table space versus chairs and desks, accessibility of multimedia, flexibility of furniture, and the presence (or absence) of chalkboards. However, the limitations imposed by such attributes can be minimized by access to virtual learning spaces made available through technology.

The course we taught, "The Study of Teaching," was an introductory course designed to examine concepts of the role of a teacher. In preparing it, we were faced with multiple challenges, in particular, how to: (1) infuse technology into the course to help meet State Education technology requirements for future teachers; (2) involve students in active learning spaces inside and outside the classroom; and (3) bridge the gap between myth and reality about teachers and the work they do. To meet these challenges, we decided to take advantage of the Dialogue Project (Gates, Wexler,

---

1. The course "The Study of Teaching" serves as both a required course for those going into secondary teaching and an elective for students interested in education. It had an average of forty to fifty students (freshmen, sophomores, juniors) and met three times a week, fifty-five minutes each session. It included a field experience component that placed students in local elementary, middle, and high schools. This field experience required students to observe, take notes, and assist teachers and students for two hours each week, on ten different occasions. Given that this was an introductory course with a large number of students, we might have adopted a strict lecture format. Instead, we chose to give students the opportunity to create their own concepts of the role of a teacher by engaging them in a variety of activities in which they would work together in multiple ways.

Gao, Tinto, and Shedd 1998), an Internet-based communication vehicle developed by the Living SchoolBook, used to facilitate communication and learning among various K–12 and higher-education communities.[2] Membership in a Dialogue community included online opportunities for (1) conducting interactive dialogue among peers and instructors beyond the walls of the classroom; (2) submitting assignments, obtaining feedback from peers and instructors, and revising submissions; (3) posting and gaining access to relevant resources (web sites, primary documents, course materials); and (4) participating in one-to-one sections where individual students could be held accountable for their own work and where instructors could address students' individual assignments.

Providing Spaces and Opportunities for Active Learning

In promoting active-learning spaces, we are guided by the belief that students have a right and a responsibility to interact with other students; they should become resources for one another. As Billson explains, "A safe and friendly climate increases participation levels and class attendance" (1994, 26). To build such a safe, active learning culture, teachers should provide learning spaces that are protected yet varied, to allow for differences in the students' ages, cultures, and learning styles. These spaces, both online and within class, will then generate opportunities for:

• promoting interpersonal exchanges and communal learning, thereby stimulating students to get to know one another, learn one another's strengths, and help one another;

• broadening access to a wider pool of experiences and perspectives, thereby stimulating discussion and reflection, providing a safe venue to reveal one's own assumptions, and challenging those assumptions;

• outreach beyond the classroom or even the university to other learners;

2. The Living SchoolBook (LSB), in its eighth year of operation, is a research and development group within the School of Education at Syracuse University. Founded on the belief that new technology can facilitate and inspire the best work of teachers and students, the LSB encourages and enables the collaboration of educators, students, and professionals in the development and implementation of technology-based projects. The LSB collaborates with K–12 educators, university faculty, and community agencies to incorporate technology in teacher preparation, K–12, and other instructional programs. More information on both the LSB and the Dialogue Project can be found online at http://lsb.syr.edu.

- one-on-one student-teacher interaction; and
- speedy assessment tailored to individual students' needs.

CREATING SAFE SPACES TO EXPLORE
AND CHALLENGE ASSUMPTIONS

One active learning strategy we employed to create such a "safe space" for exploration and dialogue was to use technology to link the students' own school experiences with popular cultural images of teaching found, for example, in movies, cartoons, and television shows. By juxtaposing the students' own past and current school experiences with popular cultural knowledge (Wexler 2003), we challenged the students' beliefs and stimulated discussion and reflection on those beliefs. Since the students in the course each had multiple spaces in which they had crafted personal images of what it means to be a teacher (Adams and Hamm 1994; Daspit and Weaver 1999; Weber and Mitchell 1995), we presented them with popular cultural images of teachers as texts to be read, analyzed, and critiqued. Using these fictional texts provided the students with safe spaces to reveal their hidden assumptions and challenge commonly held stereotypes.

BROADENING PERSPECTIVES BY PROMOTING
STUDENT-TO-STUDENT INTERACTION

Beginning with the belief that students needed to know each other (Browne and Keeley 1997), we all took part in community builders, such as the Getting to Know You Scavenger Hunt, inside the classroom. For this activity we prepared a handout containing the following objective: "Get the signature of another classmate who . . ." followed by a list of statements with a space for signatures. This list included such statements as "Has designed a web page," "Likes hip hop," "Reads the New York Times online," and "Can speak another language." Embedded in this list were technology-related statements so everyone could become acquainted with who in the class had technological expertise. We also had students learn each other's names by making name plates that sat on their desks for the first few weeks of class, and created an online class directory that contained students' pictures and information, which was submitted and posted on the Dialogue Project.

In addition, we decided to explicitly value and promote student-to-student discussion both in class and online by using technology. For example, as a class we created an *Observation Question List* that was posted under Course Resources on the Dialogue Project. The list emerged from classroom and online discussions among students in which they voiced their observations about local schools. This activity helped to make the students more critical of assumptions and stereotypes that were unconsciously influencing their views. Student discussions also guided the selection of guest speakers we invited to class. These speakers addressed issues raised by students that pertained to teaching and the diversity of school cultures (e.g., racism, educational law, and students with special needs).

To allow students to interact with as many other students as possible, we promoted active-learning spaces and activities for both small groups of students and the whole class using a variety of group-based strategies. These included:

• *inexpert learning groups,* in which students were organized into different groups according to their various talents and abilities, with each expert group teaching something to the other expert groups;

• *cooperative groups,* in which the class divided into small groups, each of which was assigned a different task;

• *think-pair-share activities,* in which students were given a topic, first to think about individually, then to discuss and develop with a partner, and then, with their partners, to share with the rest of the class;

• *jigsaw,* in which a lesson was parceled out to individual students, each of whom was assigned to teach his or her part, in a predetermined order, so as to compose the whole;

• *centers,* in which different lessons and subjects were set up in different parts of the room to be learned separately from the others; and

• *small-group problem solving,* in which each group was required to work out a solution to a problem by themselves (Johnson, Johnson, and Smith 1991; 1998).

We also structured whole-class activities by using debates, role-plays, and various discussion methods. These discussion methods included:

• *fishbowl,* in which one part of the class formed a discussion circle while the other students formed a larger observation circle surrounding them, with rotation of the students in the two circles;

• *whips,* in which the instructor quickly canvassed all the students for brief and instantaneous responses to a given question;

• *panels,* in which small group of students each presented their views in front of the rest of the class; and

• *learning partners,* in which each student engaged with another student seated in the next chair or desk, to perform a small task or discuss an assigned question (Silberman 1996).[3]

As instructors we established two long-term small working groups for each student. These groups met face-to-face during class time and online outside of class. Students chose their own groups (using post-it notes on boards) based on criteria developed in class for membership in each type of group. One group was formed by content area (mathematics, social studies, art, science, physical education, and English), giving students the foundation for a working group that they could return to in later classes in their academic program. This group also supported the field component of the course. For instance, all mathematics students who were observing in math classrooms became members of a small online group formed to discuss issues arising from their school observations. The second group focused on the course readings; its members came from many different content areas, allowing each to draw on the knowledge and resources of people outside his or her own content area.

As the course progressed, we offered opportunities for additional mixed groups, both in the physical classroom and online. For example, one assignment asked students to create a group based on a common interest in an education-related topic, such as violence in schools, tracking, bilingual education, and charter schools. Each group then researched its topic to share with the class. However, instead of compiling all of the information into file folders to have available in the library for the entire class to view, each group constructed a virtual file folder. Finally, each group used the information in its file folder to generate a web page using interactive templates and consisting of an image, a description, connections with the students' content area, interviews with practicing teachers, links to relevant Internet and other resources, and a section of their choice. Educators in the field were then invited to critique these pages. These web pages became virtual multimedia projects that all class members could visit for information on relevant educational topics.

3. For details on how to implement these active-learning strategies in the university setting, see Johnson, Johnson, and Smith 1991; 1998.

CREATING INDIVIDUAL LEARNING SPACES AND
OPPORTUNITIES FOR STUDENT-TEACHER INTERACTION

Classroom opportunities for individual presentations were limited by the large class size and short meeting time, so individual accountability and student-teacher interactons were accomplished primarily online. For example, subject categories within the Dialogue Project consisted of reflective and analytical short journal entries and longer written assignments that were submitted to instructors through the one-to-one category. Using this category, students privately submitted assignments to the instructors.

Meeting the Challenges of a Course: Analyzing What Was Learned

By pairing technology, in particular the Dialogue Project, with active-learning theories, strategies, and opportunities, we were able to probe students' beliefs and assumptions about what it means to be a teacher. Using active-learning strategies and infusing technology into the course allowed us not only to meet the traditional challenges of teaching that we articulated at the beginning of this chapter but also enabled us to address the diverse needs of our students and involve them in active learning spaces inside and outside the classroom.

6

Assessment of Student Work

Michael Flusche and Patricia Featherstone

FOR GENERATIONS, we college teachers have been cloned by the same process. When we emerge from our graduate studies, newly minted degrees in hand, and take our first full-time teaching position—or when, as graduate students, we take on our first teaching assistantship—we all tend to do the same thing: We teach as we were taught. That is, we model our teaching style, techniques, and content on the one or two teachers who made the greatest impression on us as students. And this is good. Most of us have been blessed with an instructor or two who truly deserve to be imitated, and the art of good teaching deserves to be passed from generation to generation.

The limitation is that many of the models of good teaching that appeal to the academically inclined—those of us who go on to graduate school—are not the most effective models for the vast majority of students, especially for those who struggle in the classroom. Also, the models we remember most clearly might well be the most recent ones, from our advanced, graduate-level courses.

There are probably three types, or models, of great teachers that we remember—although, of course, none of these three exists in a pure state in reality. First, we all remember at least one great lecturer, the articulate scholar whose dazzling performance was a tour de force of intellectual pyrotechnics or whose vivid anecdotes made the material come alive. Some of these master teachers are legendary and occasionally are written up in the *New Yorker* or similar magazines. Another type, in a low-keyed and self-effacing manner, covered the course material in an efficient, clear, and logical fashion. We look back and marvel at how much organic chemistry, macroeconomics, or calculus we learned in each lecture as those teachers relentlessly pressed on. And then, we recall the third type of teacher, who put students first, who defined their task not as teaching physics, journalism, or marketing but rather as helping students learn physics, journalism, or marketing. These are the teachers who on occasion spent as much time writing us letters of recommendation as they did preparing for class.

Classroom Assessment

All of these great teachers probably shared a common practice. They read the faces of their students and noted their body language; they were genuinely concerned when their students did poorly on tests and exams; and from year to year they adapted their courses in light of what seemed to work. That is, they practiced an informal, intuitive, part-time version of what we now call "classroom assessment."

The good news is that we can, in this respect, be better even than our model teachers. For today's students, classroom assessment techniques give us extremely powerful and flexible tools that open up a new level and style of communication from instructor to student and from student to instructor. The techniques build upon all the lessons master teachers have been handing down for generations, and they take into account the things that students tell us about what makes effective teaching (Cross 1983, 1990; Feldman 1976; Pintrich 1988).

What, then, is this thing called *classroom assessment?* Simply put, it is a series of techniques that help instructors do systematically and thoroughly what good teachers have always tried to do: find out what students are actually learning in the classroom and how well they are learning it. It also subtly shifts the way we think about teaching by taking the spotlight off the instructor. Rather than stressing the improvement of teaching, classroom assessment looks to improve learning. It will frequently provide information that enables us to help students change the way they try to learn. It also helps students to assess their own strengths and weaknesses and to become more involved in learning the course content. Also, students see that we are genuinely interested in helping them learn and not just in covering the material and in giving them a grade. Because classroom assessment is always within our control, we can use it to become more effective by helping us clarify our goals and priorities for the course and even for individual class sessions. It can also help us diagnose how well a particular lesson is working and invent different approaches. Thus it is not surprising that students tend to see classroom assessments as supportive and helpful teaching devices, not as threats or goads. Classroom assessment addresses the uniqueness of each class, because its sole purpose is to help the class do better. And we all know that what works for the 10 A.M. section might not work for the 2 P.M. class.

Classroom assessment is powerful because it gives us an opportunity to give immediate feedback to students on how well they are doing, so they do not have to wait until the midterm or final exam to get the bad news. And it gives us instant feedback from our students that can lead to immediate changes in the course, so there is no need to wait until next year to introduce improvements. Best of all, effective classroom assessment techniques are available to every instructor. We do not need special training or a background in testing or statistics.

What It Takes

To get started using classroom assessment techniques, it helps if you build from success. It is best to experiment with classroom assessment for the first time in a course that is going well.

Second, it helps if you are willing to be flexible. Almost certainly, good classroom assessments will change the way a good teacher wants to teach the course. Old verities will suddenly not seem so certain, or at least not universally applicable. Lectures you knew were the model of clarity and focus will oftentimes not seem so brilliant when it becomes evident how many students misunderstood the intent of those lectures altogether.

Third, the whole process is pointless if you are not willing to act on the basis of what you learn. A cardinal rule of classroom assessment is, "Don't ask the question if you don't want to know the answer." That includes sharing what you learn with your students. Assessment that reveals something that you don't know how to deal with can leave you frustrated—knowing there is a problem you cannot fix. At such times, it is important to share your frustration with your students, and possibly with your colleagues, to see whether together you can devise a solution.

Instructors in institutions from community colleges to research universities across the country are daily inventing and adapting classroom assessment techniques to meet the needs of their classes. Two of the national leaders who have done the most to propagate the benefits of classroom assessment and to bring together what we know about it are Thomas A. Angelo and K. Patricia Cross. For years, their excellent annual summer institute at Berkeley provided hundreds of teachers with a systematic introduction to assessment and preparation to help their colleagues adopt its techniques. Their compendium, *Classroom Assessment Techniques: A Handbook for College Teachers* (1993), provides a thorough and practical guide to anyone interested in taking up classroom assessment. Besides presenting practical pedagogical advice, the book describes fifty assessment techniques and suggests how each can be adapted to fit the needs of different types of classes. (Much of the material in this chapter is drawn or adapted from that excellent handbook.)[1] A few examples suggest the range of the techniques (page numbers refer to the *Handbook*).

ONE MINUTE PAPER

An easy starter that is probably the most frequently used technique, and which is subject to countless variations, is the famous One Minute Paper (148–53). It provides quick and simple feedback to you and your students on what students have learned in a lecture or discussion. You simply finish the lesson three to five minutes before the end of the period, and in the time remaining ask the students to write on one-half sheets of paper or on index cards the answer to two questions: "What was the most important thing you learned in this lesson?" and "What important question remains unanswered?" As students leave the room, they turn in these sheets anonymously.

By looking over the sheets, you can get a very quick picture of what students derived from the lesson and then decide whether you want to spend any more class time on that topic or to clarify points that students felt were still unclear. Regardless, it is extremely important that you spend some time in the following class reporting back to the students and commenting on their responses in a general way to reinforce the lesson's main points and correct any misconceptions. Often, the students raise better questions in the One Minute Paper than they do in class; so in responding to the most frequently asked questions, you have the opportunity to expand or clarify the

---

1. Two videotapes that demonstrate various classroom assessment techniques and convey a feeling of how classroom assessment really works are "Classroom Research: Empowering Teachers," Catalog No. 38022, University of California Extension Media Center, and "Teaching-Directed Classroom Research," College of Marin.

most important points of the previous lecture. To prevent students from being disappointed that you did not respond to their particular question or comment, when you first solicit their feedback clarify that you will have time next class to address only the most commonly asked questions.

For students, completing the One Minute Paper has a number of benefits. First, it requires them to review quickly the whole lesson and organize and evaluate what they just heard; therefore, each student becomes actively involved in using the material, even though you might have a few hundred students in the class. At the same time, if they know that at the end of the lesson they must list a question that remains in their minds, they must be thinking about what they understand and do not understand—again, a form of active involvement. Interestingly, when students anticipate having to complete One Minute Papers, they begin to listen to the lectures in a more active manner and their responses tend to get better as the semester progresses. Even though the papers are not being graded and are turned in anonymously, students still tend to want to do a good job on them. By comparing the comments with those of other students in the class, they quickly see that there were other points of view on the same material. Finally, by hearing your synthesis of the feedback, they learn how an expert in the field assesses what is most important.

One of the beauties of the One Minute Paper is its flexibility. You can use it for lectures or discussions, as well as for laboratory sessions, films or videos, or field trips. One popular variation is the Muddiest Point (154–58), a technique in which you ask students to list what for them is still the least-clear point of the lecture they just heard (see also Mosteller 1989).

The task can be tailored to fit the situation; you might prompt students to address a more specific question or challenge them to integrate that lesson with a previous one, for instance. When properly set up and administered, the One Minute Paper is welcomed by students because they realize it helps them to learn—and, in a sense, to have a voice in the class, even if they have not spoken.

GOAL RANKING AND MATCHING

A second valuable classroom assessment technique is Goal Ranking and Matching (290–94). In the first week of class, you ask students to list in priority order their three to five learning goals for the course. Tell them you will analyze the goals, then report back and discuss the results. You will have compiled a list of your own goals previously. Also, as with all classroom assessments, think about what you will do with the answer; that is, decide how much you are willing or able to adjust the course to meet student expectations, should there be a wide discrepancy between what the students expect and what you intend to do. In many cases, you will want to use the occasion to articulate or clarify what the course is designed to accomplish, and help the students understand why it is that way. In other cases, you might be able to adapt its content or your teaching technique to more closely match the students' goals. It might be possible, for example, to let some students pursue their particular interests through a research project or term paper. If your course does not address the goals your students anticipated, they will appreciate knowing this early on so they can drop it and enroll in another.

Among the pedagogical advantages of the Goal Ranking technique is that it makes students aware of the degree to which they have or do not have identifiable learning goals. Use it as an occasion to discuss how the course fits into the college's or the department's curriculum and how it relates to other courses. Also, if you discover that the students have a very high or very low personal investment in the course, that could suggest some special adaptations of the material or its presentation. Unprompted or unprepared for, the students' responses are likely to be vague and very thin—but even so, in the hands of a skilled instructor, the feedback can present a learning moment if it can lead the students to become more active and involved in their own educations.

MEMORY MATRIX

A third very flexible technique can be thoroughly integrated into the teaching process, especially in introductory courses. The Memory Matrix (142–47) is a simple procedure that enables you to see how well your students recall basic information and are able to analyze and organize or categorize that information.[2] First, you develop a grid, its vertical columns headed by major concepts or areas that define the material, its horizontal rows listing different concepts or categories. In class, you distribute the grid

2. See also in Angelo and Cross 1993 the techniques "Categorizing Grid" (160–63) and "Defining Features Matrix" (164–67).

and ask students to write in the appropriate cells those items that fit. You can furnish the list of items to be categorized, or you can ask your students to supply them themselves.

Below is an example from Angelo and Cross (1993) of a Memory Matrix that might be used in an art history class. The students would fill the appropriate cells with the names of major artists the class has studied.

	France	**United States**	**Great Britain**
Neoclassicism			
Impressionism			
Postimpressionism			
Expressionism			

Source: Reprinted with permission from Angelo and Cross 1993, 143.

Having asked the students to complete the matrix individually, our art history instructor could then divide the class into small groups to pool their memory. She would be able to discover, for instance, whether or not her students could easily identify the country of each artist, distinguish Impressionists from Postimpressionists, and so on. As part of her feedback on the exercise, she could explain why art historians categorize artists in this fashion and why it is not always clear where a particular artist belongs. On a practical level, she could help her students prepare for their final exam. Alternately, the instructor could use the matrix as an in-class teaching exercise with an overhead projector, herself filling in the information as provided by the class.

Clearly, the Memory Matrix can be an effective teaching tool as well as an assessment technique, especially in courses introducing large amounts of material that students are seeing for the first time. Also, it is a device that students can adapt to use on their own to help them organize their studying of any material.

EVERYDAY ETHICAL DILEMMA

A variety of assessment tools focus on students' attitudes and values, which for some fields can be extremely important but problematic in the classroom. It is sometimes difficult or misleading to try to read personal attitudes from students' class discussions. The force of a strongly articulated view can skew discussion among students groping to clarify their own value systems. Some students are silent or extremely circumspect; others say what they believe to be socially or politically acceptable.

One classroom assessment technique that is both an excellent teaching device and a useful assessment of student values is Everyday Ethical Dilemma (271–74). In Everyday Ethical Dilemma, students are to write a brief and anonymous response to an ethical dilemma you pose relevant to the course. The challenge to the students is to clarify their own values by thinking through your hypothetical situation. As before, you analyze the responses and report back to the class the various views presented. By identifying the patterns that appear, you help students see the differences among themselves and the implications of each position. Discussion or argument could follow, ideally leading to the students becoming more aware of the various value systems found within the class, as well as the various perceptions of the facts as presented in the case. From the anonymous responses to your hypothetical situation, you get honest statements from *all* the students, not just the dominant personalities, and so you are better able to address the whole class in your responses and in teaching subsequent material.

Ethical dilemmas are most frequently useful in professional fields such as social work, nursing, and education or in liberal disciplines such as philosophy. But they also can prove useful in a first-year seminar orienting students to college life. One instructor, for example, presented her first-year students with the hypothetical case of Anne, whose roommate confided she was planning to help her boyfriend cheat on an exam. The assessment asked students to respond to the question, "What would you do if you were Anne?" and to explain their reasons. After the instructor analyzed the anonymous responses of her students (the majority of whom said they would do nothing), the exercise provided the occasion for vigorous discussion of academic integrity.

APPLICATIONS CARDS

A fifth example is the classroom assessment technique Applications Cards (236–39), in which students write on an index card at least one realistic application of the general principle or theory they have just learned. This technique forces students to think actively about the material and to connect it with what they already know. The pedagogical value of focusing on the practical value of the lesson is clear.

Instructors have used this device in a variety of ways. In an economics class studying Gresham's law, *good money drives out bad,* students were asked to give at least one example besides money of a situation in which Gresham's law applies. Physics students were introduced to Newton's Third Law, *to every action there is an equal and opposite reaction,* and then were asked to list three applications of the law to everyday life. In political science, one of the standard maxims of American political history is that *all politics is local;* students were challenged to imagine how to apply this principle in giving advice to a presidential candidate.

In commenting on the responses in the next class, you will be able to distinguish for the students which responses were excellent, which were just acceptable, and which were not acceptable. One of the pedagogical advantages of this technique is that students can learn from having the best examples pointed out to them. For this and other such techniques, author Thomas Angelo suggests that you disguise somewhat those responses you intend to criticize or reject (1993).

Helpful Lessons

From instructors' experiments with classroom assessment several lessons have emerged that help ensure success:

• Identify a question you would like to know the answer to, that is, whose answer will help you in conducting your class and improving student learning. A common question is, "How well do my students understand—?"

• At the start, be sure that your assessment technique will meet your needs. Not all techniques are appropriate for your class; use only those that are.

• Ease into classroom assessment slowly. Start with small, manageable techniques, such as the One Minute Paper, and develop the assessment style that works for you.

• Set limits on how much out-of-class and in-class time you are willing to invest.

• Always close the communication circle by giving feedback to students—not just about *what* they wrote but also about your reaction to it. In some instances, you will want to let the class know you will be departing from the original class schedule or syllabus to respond to what you learned from the assessment (Angelo and Cross 1993, 25–32, 53–59).

COSTS

As with every change in the way we do our business, there are costs and presumably there are benefits. Users of classroom assessment report three major costs:

• Just doing assessments takes time—in and out of class. That can mean more work for you and less time in class to cover the material.

• Following up on assessments also takes time. Revisiting material the class found confusing the first time forces you to cover less new information; you will have to curtail or drop some items, presumably of lesser importance.

• Learning something from assessments that you can do nothing about—whether it is students' prior academic deficiencies, their lifestyles, or the department's curricular surroundings—can leave you frustrated.

BENEFITS

On the other hand, practitioners of classroom assessment find three very powerful benefits follow systematic use of the techniques:

Students tend to respond very positively when the techniques are used constructively, when they see the techniques benefit them and they experience the excitement and interest assessments can generate in a course. Students see use of the techniques as evidence of your genuine concern and a type of cooperation between you and the class. In some instances, after they experience classroom assessments in one course, students will ask instructors who are not using assessments why they aren't. For many instructors, assessments can pump fresh excitement into a course that had grown tired and stale. When students become more actively involved in a course and begin to feel a sense of ownership, which assessments invite, instructor and students alike begin to see that course differently. Assessments can make the classroom a more engaging place to be on either side of the desk. When several colleagues take the classroom assessment plunge at one time, collegial interaction can be enriched. Swapping notes and suggestions can open new fields of conversation between you and your fellow instructors. Classroom assessment brown-bag lunches, for example, can be extremely enjoyable, because the techniques open up new styles of teaching that are interesting to discuss.

Conclusion

One of the most attractive aspects of classroom assessment techniques is that they can be used in large and small classes, occasionally, or integrated into the course structure. Ultimately, however, they all lead in the same direction: toward a redefinition of the student-instructor relationship and the role of the instructor in the classroom. Using classroom assessments can contribute to an atmosphere that supports active and collaborative learning and a more open and responsive teaching style.

In the end, assessments help answer the most important question that every instructor must ask—not "How well am I teaching?" but "How well are my students learning, and how can we together improve their performance?"

7

Ethical Issues in Teaching

Sandra Hurd and Hilton Hallock

ETHICAL DECISION-MAKING is part of the daily work of teaching. Each time we grade an exam, make accommodations for students with disabilities, or decide to share our personal opinion on a controversial issue during a lecture, we struggle with questions of fairness, honesty, competence, and equity. As these examples illustrate, ethical teaching is more complicated than "doing no harm." The concept of ethics requires us to consider how best to carry out our relationships and responsibilities related to teaching and faculty life.

As higher education has come under more public scrutiny, professional associations in higher education have developed standards of ethical conduct that address issues such as research methods, conflicts of interest in professional roles, and academic freedom and integrity. However, questions of what and how to teach are also infused with ethical considerations, and these norms are less likely to be codified (Markie 1994; McGrory 1996). Some expectations for ethical behavior in teaching are straightforward. For example, laws, institutional policies, and professional standards prohibit discrimination and harassment of students. We are expected to honor fundamental ethical principles such as treating others fairly and respectfully. We are obligated to model standards of academic integrity and quality scholarship. We are required to be competent in both the subjects we teach and the pedagogical strategies we use in our courses.

These basic responsibilities are certainly useful guidelines for our conduct as instructors, but when we begin to examine them in the context of our everyday work, we find that ethical decision-making often involves subtle distinctions, complex relationships, and conflicting interests. It is not always easy to know what to do; standards of conduct do not provide all the answers.

76

Societal expectations for faculty and for institutions of higher education change over time, and our individual roles and responsibilities evolve over the course of our careers. Other chapters of this book highlight how higher education itself could affect the ethical landscape of our work: What ethical concerns might arise from the discovery and use of new technologies? Are there particular ethical challenges that come with pedagogical strategies such as service-learning or interdisciplinary instruction? How does the diversity of student backgrounds and goals affect the ethical dynamic of the classroom? Do the growing numbers of adjunct and nontenured faculty face different ethical problems?

There is no way to prepare for every specific ethical challenge we might face as instructors, but that does not mean we should not prepare at all. Continuous reflection on ethics in teaching hones our skills in ethical decision-making, and conversations with colleagues enhance our understanding of the ethical issues we might face at different stages of our teaching careers and of evolving community standards. Ethical decision-making is shaped by community norms, so we encourage you to discuss general ethical issues with your colleagues, mentors, and students. Once embroiled in a difficult situation, you may feel professionally isolated, torn by conflicting loyalties, or even constrained by confidentiality from discussing the case.

This chapter focuses on several general areas of ethics related to teaching—relationships with students, responses to student needs and expectations, and academic integrity. It is not intended to be an exhaustive review; it should serve as a starting point for reflection on how we as teachers can use our knowledge and power to promote learning and development in our own academic environments.

Relationships with Students

Students' cognitive development, educational achievement, changes in occupational and other values, and career choices all are affected by their interactions with faculty, both in and out of the classroom (Pascarella and Terenzini 1991). Ethical decisions are embedded in those interactions. The quality of our decisions and actions influences how much and how well our students learn. Thus, ethical issues in teaching are central to the educational missions of our institutions and profession. We are expected to act ethically when we design syllabi, respond (selectively) to student contributions in class, evaluate students' academic work, write recommendations, and make admissions decisions because these are, fundamentally, expressions of fairness, honesty, and care in our relationships with students (Hansen and Stephens 2000).

As instructors, we are vested with power over our students, and we exercise that power and authority in formal and informal ways. Whether we are teaching assistants, novice professors, or senior faculty, our roles within the classroom and our positions in the larger academic community place us in relationships with students that are inherently unequal. Because we have that power, it is incumbent on us to explore the ethical implications of our relationships and decisions and to act in ways that support student learning and development.

DUAL RELATIONSHIPS

Dual relationships with students present ethical difficulties because our responsibility to be fair and objective with *all* our students can conflict with other allegiances. For example, a faculty member might know one of the graduate students in her seminar very well because she also serves as the student's dissertation adviser and their children go to school together. Even if we are confident that we can maintain our objectivity, the perception of bias can undermine our effectiveness as teachers and restrict student opportunities for learning. Extensive social interactions, close personal relationships, or other professional contacts (e.g., business partnerships, therapeutic relationships) outside of class with students can raise concerns about favoritism or conflicts of interest.

As instructors, we have ethical obligations to our students and to our colleagues and institutions. We must try to balance our roles as mentors or student advocates with our roles as impartial evaluators. Teaching assistants, in their role as liaison between students and supervising faculty members, often wrestle with even more complex issues of confidentiality, students' personal concerns, and quality teaching (their own and those of the course instructor). When we play multiple roles, the limits of our power and authority can be less clear, or our ethical obligations can appear to conflict.

None of us is *only* a teacher. And none of our students is *only* a student. Some dual relationships are probably unavoidable. However, when we assume the powerful role of instructor or supervisor, we take on the primary responsibility for avoiding the conflicts of interest inherent in dual relationships.

SEXUAL HARASSMENT

We address sexual harassment here, not because it is the most prevalent ethical violation in teaching, but because it is a classic illustration of exploitation of students and abuse of power in the teaching relationship. Faculty members are cautioned against, often prohibited from, having sexual or romantic relationships with students whom they teach, supervise, or evaluate. This was not always the case. As society has come to see such relationships as harassment, understand the harm to students' educational opportunities and achievement, and hold institutions liable when such harassment occurs, clearer restrictions have been articulated.

The ethical standards of the American Association of University Professors (AAUP) require faculty members to avoid "any exploitation of students for . . . private advantage" (AAUP 1990, 113). Sexual harassment that involves the expectation or exchange of sexual favors as a condition of academic benefits or professional advancement (*quid pro quo* harassment) is one such situation. Even when the parties perceive the relationship to be mutual and consensual, the risk of exploitation, intentional or not, is very real because one party has power or authority over the other. Further, the relationship can affect others around them; the student's classmates, for example, can feel their own work or education is impaired by the relationship as the result of unfair or unequal treatment.

The AAUP (1990) affirms that harassment of students is not only unethical but also inconsistent with the values of academic freedom. Discrimination against people on the basis of their gender or sexual identity is an example of unethical conduct. Such discrimination by an instructor could take the form of unwelcome behavior of a sexual nature that contributes to an environment that is intimidating for study, work, or social living (*hostile environment* harassment). Behavior that students find discriminatory or harassing can be overt or subtle, intentional or inadvertent. To prevent such ethical breaches, it is imperative that we acknowledge the unequal power we bring to educational and social relationships with students we teach or supervise, and understand the appropriate parameters for our relationships with them.

The Ethical Obligation to Respond to Legitimate
Needs and Expectations of Our Students

As classroom instructors, we have an ethical obligation to respond to the legitimate needs and expectations of our students. But not every student expectation is reasonable, and part of our instructional role is to understand the difference between those that are and those that are not. Expectations are situational, and what is reasonable will differ according to student characteristics, the mission and values of the institution, and the learning objectives of the curriculum or class.

Within a particular curriculum or class, students' expectations may remain stable over time, allowing faculty to develop long-term strategies for responding to those expectations. Instructors in the School of Management at Syracuse University have collected data about expectations from thousands of undergraduate students in a variety of courses over a ten-year time span. These data reveal remarkable consistency in students' expectations, falling into three overlapping categories: preparing for student learning, promoting student learning in the classroom, and supporting student learning outside the classroom.[1]

PREPARING FOR STUDENT LEARNING

In the first category, students include expectations about our knowledge of our disciplines, our preparation to teach particular courses, and our syllabi. Clearly, students have a right to expect that we will be knowledgeable and current in our disciplines. But when students use these words, they are not necessarily using them as we might. A faculty member doing cutting-edge research and submitting articles to the best journals could well con-

---

1. At the beginning of a course, the students are asked to identify their expectations about that course, its instructor, and themselves. Once compiled, the information is used to design specific course activities and to underscore for students their responsibility for their own learning. The expectations can be revisited periodically during the semester if students are not meeting them.

We are indebted to the following faculty colleagues, who have contributed to our efforts to understand the expectations of our students: Professors Paul Bobrowski, Fran Zollers, Elet Callahan, Paul Andreoli, Stephen Matyas, Ravi Shukla, Millie Doering, Mohan Tanniru, John Grabner, Leon Hanouille, and Gisela von Dran.

sider herself both knowledgeable and current in her discipline. What students are referring to, however, is an instructor's ability to communicate principles and concepts to them in understandable ways that include real-life, timely examples.

Students also expect faculty to be prepared to teach the particular courses to which they have been assigned. We are not all equally skilled at teaching core courses, electives, large classes, small classes, lectures, and discussion sections. Nor are we all equally skilled at teaching various levels of undergraduate and graduate students. Students, however, have the right to expect that we have prepared ourselves to teach the courses on our schedules.

The final expectation in this first category is that we have developed a carefully constructed syllabus. Students expect a syllabus to communicate clearly two kinds of information. The first concerns our course requirements, assignments, due dates, expectations for performance, and criteria for evaluation. The second encompasses other kinds of information important for their learning, for example, academic integrity policies, a statement about accommodating students with disabilities, location and time of office hours, rules about submitting assignments late, and an attendance policy.

PROMOTING STUDENT LEARNING IN THE CLASSROOM

In this second category, students identify expectations for how the class will be conducted, including expectations for the atmosphere in the classroom. They want us to control students who try to dominate discussions, to ensure that everyone behaves respectfully, and to listen to different points of view. Other expectations address the kinds of learning activities we use. Often students express this by saying they want the instructor or the class to be "interesting." Although some faculty suggest that students mean they want to be entertained, we understand "interesting" to stand for much more.

Students want instructors who promote active learning and collaborative learning, who account for different learning styles and ways of knowing and thinking, and who construct learning experiences with an understanding of how students learn and develop intellectually and socially. These concepts have not traditionally been an integral part of faculty training. Learning theory, however, becomes increasingly important as we shift the focus from teaching (the instructor's performance) to learning (what the students leave the classroom knowing). Viewed through the lenses of our ethical obligations, strategies such as active learning are more than hallmarks of good teaching; they are part of our responsibility to promote learning for all, not just some, students.

SUPPORTING STUDENT LEARNING OUTSIDE THE CLASSROOM

This third category of student expectations encompasses the myriad ways in which we can support student learning outside the classroom. Students expect us to be available and willing to provide help. Providing help is not just posting a few office hours and being there most of the time. It is being approachable and creating an environment in which students feel comfortable not only coming for academic help but also developing an appropriate relationship with us. Students expect us to see them as the unique individuals they are, with different values, perspectives, aspirations, and needs. This expectation is especially true for students with disabilities, whose special needs merit thoughtful accommodation.

Two extremely important student expectations that we have an ethical obligation to meet are to provide timely and constructive feedback on their work and to be fair in our grading. Most students intuitively understand that learning is a process and that their success in large part depends on our providing them explicit feedback about their performance so they can improve. The most powerful learning takes place when learners get immediate feedback. Most of us are not able to provide instantaneous feedback, but we need to be sensitive to issues of timeliness and to do our best to return student work as soon as possible. The quality of the feedback we give is also extremely important. Returning assignments marked only with a number or grade at the top does little to help students identify gaps in their knowledge or skills. Papers with no comments, or with singularly unhelpful comments such as "Lacks organization" or "Good job—B," leave students at a loss as to how to do better the next time. Students want to do better; it is up to us to construct assignments in such a way that we give them the timely and useful feedback that will allow them to improve. Fewer assignments that provide more feedback can be a powerful learning tool—less can definitely be more.

Fairness in grading is also extremely important. Faculty exhortations that learning is more important than grades fly in the face of students' experiences and goals. They understand early on that good grades are an important part of getting admitted to the college of their choice. They understand that grades make a difference for admission to graduate school or getting the job of their dreams. For better or worse, grades are important to students, and we have an ethical obligation to make sure our process of assigning grades is a fair one.

Grading is an unavoidably subjective process. Even with such ostensibly objective measures as multiple-choice exams, we must constantly deal with difficult issues: How do we account for effort versus performance? How do we evaluate the work of a student with a disability, or a student for whom English is a second language? How do we protect against the biases that we all experience as a part of our cultural conditioning? Being clear about our expectations and criteria and sharing those with our students are important first steps. But we must also be constantly vigilant and reflective about stereotypes and assumptions we make in order to avoid treating students differently based on criteria not linked to their learning.

The Ethical Obligation to Promote Academic Integrity as a Central Value of the Academy

Academic integrity is a core value of the academic community. Academic dishonesty limits opportunities for learning and harms students who act with integrity. As faculty, we have an obligation to protect and promote the academic honesty of our students. Sadly, many high school students cheat (*Who's Who* 2000), and such behavior continues into college (McCabe and Pavela 2000). In light of this reality, our obligations include educating our students about the importance of integrity, preventing acts of academic dishonesty, and taking actions that enforce standards of honesty.

EDUCATION

One of our important obligations is to communicate the importance of academic integrity. A conversation about what integrity is and why it is important is an excellent starting point (see Academic Integrity Exercise).[2]

2. We recommend the academic integrity exercise on pp. 86–87, developed by Professor Elletta Sangrey Callahan, as a starting point for discussion. In the classroom, an academic integrity discussion is most useful early in the semester as students are developing their

Once we have impressed on our students the importance of academic integrity, we must also communicate what standards we expect them to follow. If your institution has an academic-integrity policy, you must communicate those standards and procedures to your students. If you are in the unfortunate position of teaching in an environment without such an official policy, then communicate explicitly what standards you expect your students to follow and the consequences for not following them. We need to be aware of the special problems posed in learning environments where group work and collaborative learning are encouraged; we must be very clear about which work we intend to evaluate individually and which we intend to be collaborative. It is also important that we communicate clearly our commitment to enforcement; if students suspect we are not absolutely committed, they won't be either.

PREVENTION

There are several ways we can prevent acts of academic dishonesty. First, it is essential that we model the behavior we expect from our students. We must properly attribute any material we present to our students and cite our sources just as we expect students to cite theirs. Second, we can minimize opportunities for violations. Make sure tests are properly proctored, create new assignments and exams for each class rather than reusing old versions, and structure assignments such that dishonesty is difficult or not worth the students' trouble. For example, instead of assigning just a final paper, we can build in intermediate deliverables—a research plan, an annotated bibli-

---

understanding of the instructor's expectations. The exercise could be more meaningful to students if you adapt the examples to reflect particular courses they are likely to take or situations they are likely to face. If your school has a written academic integrity policy, students should be asked to read it, and the discussion should focus on specific provisions of it. If your school reports on the outcomes of policy violations, the discussion should also address the range of penalties imposed for various violations. There are a number of ways of engaging students in this discussion. One way that we have found successful is to ask each to write a brief response to one of the situations, and then have them share their responses in small groups before engaging the entire group in a discussion. This method allows students to think through their responses individually, understand through discussion with peers that there are multiple perspectives on ethical issues, then come to closure through a facilitated discussion.

We have also found this exercise useful as a faculty-development tool.

ography, research notes, an outline, a first draft—that allow you to monitor students' progress. Not only will we minimize the opportunities for academic dishonesty, but we also will create a valuable learning experience.

ACTION

When we do not enforce the rules we have set, students quickly pick up on our lack of real commitment. There may be situations in which we are tempted to forego taking action; the violation may seem trivial in the press of all our other obligations, providing proof could seem daunting, the time a disciplinary process involves might seem excessive, we might worry about long-term consequences for us and the students, or we might simply shy away from conflict. But enforcement is crucial, as difficult as it might be. Students will not value academic integrity unless we clearly demonstrate that we do.

Conclusion

Negotiating the demands of our ethical obligations as teachers at times can seem both impossible and overwhelming. It is both comforting and disconcerting to realize that much of the time there is no single right answer. So it is important to remember that we have many sources of support we can draw on in trying to find the best answers to ethical dilemmas. We can explore ethical issues and share experiences with colleagues. We can take advantage of the knowledge of mentors and advisers. We can seek the advice of professional staff, who have also faced ethical dilemmas in their academic lives and can share their thoughts and experiences with us. The conversations may be informal "hall talk." There also are more formal strategies for facilitating discussions about ethical issues and academic integrity:

- Institute brown-bag lunches on integrity issues.
- Ask members of the institution's academic integrity committee to do a presentation.
- Include sessions on academic integrity in TA training and new-faculty orientations.
- Ask staff from the center for teaching and learning to do a workshop on academic integrity.
- Start or join an online discussion about ethical issues in teaching with your professional associations.

It is most useful, of course, to prepare ourselves to face academic integrity issues by having these discussions early in our teaching experience. However, to do our best as educators attuned to changes in the learning environment, we need to engage in a continual, reflective process of educating ourselves and our students, to heighten our ethical awareness and theirs. Living a commitment to academic integrity is a never-ending process. As important as it is to try to do the right thing, it is important too to forgive ourselves when we make mistakes—they are inevitable—and then resolve to learn how to do better the next time.

ACADEMIC INTEGRITY EXERCISE

1. Rob Early, a sophomore, has been contacted by his statistics professor regarding a take-home exam he recently completed. The exam counts for 20 percent of his course grade.

Rob had worked closely with another student in the class, Melanie Shilling, throughout the semester and understood that teamwork was not only permissible but encouraged by the professor. When the exam was assigned, it seemed only logical to discuss their analyses and debate their conclusions with each other. The take-home exam was similar in format to the in-class examination. Melanie and Rob met several times to discuss their interpretation of this and other assignments they were preparing for their classes. While they never actually showed each other their solutions to the questions on the take-home test, they did discuss how they approached the problems and justified their answers. Rob used these discussions as the basis for revising his answers and reworking some of his conclusions on the take-home exam.

2. During an interview for an internship, Norm Ross was asked about leadership activities he participated in during college. Norm told the interviewer he chaired a committee to develop a mentoring program for incoming transfer students. This statement was false, although Norm had served as a member of the committee.

3. K. C. Leland, a citizen of Anozira, is a first-year graduate student. Anozira's culture and institutions differ greatly from those of the United States. Anoziran society is based on a very traditional family structure. The high levels of respect and obedience given to parents are also expected by teachers. At K. C.'s undergraduate college, classes are lecture style. When

students are called upon by the teacher, they are expected to repeat, word-for-word, material presented in the lecture or from the course textbook. Similarly, papers and examinations consist of reciting language from class or the text. No method of citation or discussion of sources is used or considered necessary. During K. C.'s first semester of graduate study, she turned in a three-page written assignment consisting of eight paragraphs taken almost word-for-word from the textbook plus introductory and concluding paragraphs.

4. Roberta Late, a freshman in her first semester, has been contacted by her information systems professor regarding a computer assignment she recently handed in. The assignment involved creating a document, the template for which was provided in the course handbook, demonstrating the ability to perform certain tasks in Microsoft Word, including formatting, importing and resizing a graphic, and creating a chart. The professor contacted Roberta because her assignment and several others he received were identical, except for the student's name.

a. Roberta acknowledges that she ran out of time to finish the assignment and copied the file from one of her teammates, substituting her own name.

b. Roberta acknowledges that she and two of her teammates worked together to complete the assignment. She explains that they created one computer file from which each printed out a copy with their own name on it to hand in. She notes that the information systems class emphasizes teamwork and promotes collaborative learning, that they all contributed equally to completing the assignment, and that she believes they all learned a great deal by working together.

c. Roberta acknowledges that she is a novice computer user and had great difficulty completing the assignment. She further explains that, although she sought help and advice from several of her teammates on various aspects of Microsoft Word, she completed the assignment sitting by herself at her own computer. Given the amount of help that she got, however, she is not surprised the assignments are identical.

Further Reading

Center for Academic Integrity, Duke University: academicintegrity.org
Fisch, Linc, ed. 1996. *Ethical Dimensions of College and University Teaching.* New Directions for Teaching and Learning, no. 66. San Francisco: Jossey-Bass.

McCabe, Donald L., and Linda K. Trevino. 1996. "What We Know About Cheating in College: Longitudinal Trends and Recent Developments." *Change* 28, no. 1: 28–33.

McCabe, Donald L., and Kenneth D. Butterfield. 1999. "Academic Integrity in Honor Code and Non-Honor Code Environments." *Journal of Higher Education* 70, no. 2: 211–34.

Murray, Harry, Eileen Gillese, Madeline Lennon, Paul Mercer, and Marilyn Robinson. 1996. "Ethical Principles for College and University Teaching." http://www .aahe.org/Bulletin/Ethical%20Principles.htm

Pavela, Gary. 1997. "Applying the Power of Association on Campus: A Model Code of Academic Integrity." *Journal of College and University Law* 24, no. 1: 97–118.

Sockett, Hugh. 1993. *The Moral Base for Teacher Professionalism.* New York: Teachers College Press.

8

The Multidisciplinary Possibilities of Feminist Pedagogy

Robin L. Riley and Diane Lyden Murphy

FEMINIST PEDAGOGY OFFERS practitioners and students possibilities for teaching and learning that can enrich traditional classrooms. While feminist pedagogy utilizes gender as a tool of analysis, it is not gender specific. Rather, it opens up opportunities for all students to engage ideas and course materials in innovative and transformative ways. Feminist pedagogy resists the assumption of a de-raced, de-gendered, de-classed student and instead acknowledges the influence that social locations have on histories and styles of learning.

In various disciplines, feminist pedagogy takes on different forms. In chemistry it might mean assigning students to do oral histories of people who work in science before they begin the actual doing of hard science. In history and political science it might mean repeatedly asking the question, "Where are the women?" In math classes it might mean taking care that test or practice questions are not directed only at men. In English it means reading literary and cultural texts through a lens focused on gender. In sociology it means prompting students to connect their lives through the traditional sociological method of joining history and biography while also asking questions about how gender is implicated with race and class.

Background

Feminist pedagogy comes about as a result of the critique that second-wave feminists[1] made about the exclusion and invisibility of women in educa-

1. The second wave feminist movement in the United States started in the late 1960s. It is important to differentiate between this and the later movement because the second wave was

tional settings. With the acknowledgment that education was one of the systems that helped keep a patriarchal ideology in place, traditional classroom practices, feminists argued, were directed toward reproducing a system of sexism in which male supremacy was kept intact. Accepted classroom practices in which mostly male instructors utilized materials and presented lectures that were male centered and directed at an assumed male audience were unacceptable to feminists intent on making women's presence in the classroom more welcome and on facilitating learning for women.

Feminist pedagogy, as a method of teaching and learning, evolved from the feminist critique of traditional classroom practices that situated both education and learning as neutral activities that occurred outside of ideology. Feminist pedagogy refused to situate education or learning outside of ideology. Feminist theorists, practitioners, and teachers recognized that, in fact, learning occurs within the same contexts of power and oppression that operate outside the classroom. They pointed out that in many ways the unequal relationship between student and teacher reproduced the oppressive gender, race, and class relationships that happened outside of the academy. Education, they argue, is therefore often aimed towards men and is alienating for women.

Currently, while feminist pedagogy aims to make education more self-reflective in terms of its male bias, it also works to influence curriculum and individual practitioners. The liberal feminists who were active at the onset of the second wave of feminism advocated simply for a larger presence of women in the public sphere, including educational institutions. They also assumed an essential commonality among all women. As feminism has evolved over the past thirty years, a more complex understanding of the category "woman" continues to be explored. Within contemporary feminism, women no longer are assumed to have an essential, shared nature. Instead, issues of difference between and among women are now acknowledged and engaged. As a result, issues of class, race, sexuality, and ability are taken up and attended to as aspects of identity that determine students' subjectivities in and out of the classroom. These subjectivities, it is hypothesized, influence how students learn. "A transformative feminist pedagogy should dis-

---

heavily critiqued for not dealing with racism and being actively homophobic. The current feminist movement is typically referred to as the "third wave" and, although many of the public voices of feminism still come from a second wave perspective, the third wave is concerned with unraveling not only gender oppression but also racism, classism, homophobia, and ableism.

close how subjectivities—particularly gendered—are being constructed and/or represented outside and inside the school setting, and enhance the development of 'compound identities' " (Hernandez 1997, 20).

Although the concerns about female representation and low numbers of women are still salient in certain disciplines, like science and mathematics, it is not enough, contemporary feminists argue, to simply admit more women to institutions of higher learning or to have larger numbers of female professors. Rather, the presence of women within these institutions must be acknowledged and welcomed by the creation of a curriculum and the utilization of pedagogical practices that are (1) more inclusive of the wide diversity of women's history, women's concerns, and women's lives; and (2) work toward undoing racism, classism, homophobia, and ableism and thus facilitating social change.

Practicing Feminist Pedagogy

A curriculum developed by feminist pedagogues works towards making all students feel welcome and valued. Angela Calabrese Barton (1998, 17), for example, a science educator and feminist pedagogue, argues against the pro forma teaching of science:

> Pre-defined knowledge sets and ways in which to introduce, practice, and monitor the development of them is based on assumptions that all students will assimilate into the culture of science equally and unproblematically; that all students will come to learning science with the same cultural capital, and that all students have the same use for science.

Feminist pedagogy resists the assumptions about a common student. Students are acknowledged to come in a variety of races, classes, and genders, with the accompanying social, learning, and educational histories. These differences require creativity on the part of teachers to develop a variety of approaches to introduce students to new ideas.

Because feminist pedagogy takes on various forms depending on the discipline in which it is utilized, it is helpful to think about it not simply as practice but also as a stance.[2] A feminist pedagogical stance refers to political and

2. Thanks to Margaret Himley for making this observation. Conversation with the authors, September 3, 2000.

epistemological positioning. It involves values and goals. This stance is enacted not only in larger numbers of women taking part in teaching and learning, but also through the use of more inclusive course materials, through open acknowledgment of power inequities between teacher and student, through encouraging teacher self-reflection, and through using the classroom as a space for interactive learning. There is no one set of practices for teachers to follow in terms of how these aspects of a feminist pedagogical stance are enacted in the classroom. The practice of feminist pedagogy relies on a number of factors including the flexibility of the discipline, the responsiveness of students, the availability of inclusive materials, and the creativity of the instructor. Still, there are certain commonalities among practitioners of feminist pedagogy.

Within feminist pedagogy, institutions of learning and indeed the classroom itself are denaturalized[3] and power differentials are named and acknowledged. The classroom is seen as a site where power is constantly being enacted. It is a site of conflict, difference, and power (Hernandez 1997). The classroom is recognized as a risky space where safety is always being negotiated, not assumed. In classrooms where feminist pedagogy is practiced, difference and conflict are not handled as a matter of classroom management as they might be in traditional classrooms, but rather are welcomed as discursive events that facilitate learning for everyone (Himley 1997).

Consequently, teachers are urged to examine their own practices as they relate to interacting with students. They might ask themselves whether they are unwittingly asking questions that are gender-specific, or whether they are consciously or unconsciously giving more opportunity or weight to male student responses (Rosser 1991). In addition, in the classroom students often reenact the very power differentials that feminist pedagogy seeks to eliminate. Students often interact with each other in sexist, racist, classist, or homophobic ways and teachers must quickly recognize, point out, and unpack these interactions in ways that allow learning for all students involved (Himley 1997).

In feminist pedagogy, learning is recognized as both a social and political

---

3. That is, the ways of thinking about teaching and learning as separate and unilateral and occurring outside of power relations are deconstructed. The teacher does not think of herself or himself as the holder of all knowledge but rather sees learning as a dialogic, reciprocal relationship.

process. That is, students are acknowledged to be both knowers and learners. Students are encouraged to simultaneously contribute relevant information from their lives to classroom discussion and to be engaged listeners. Because their presence in the classroom is not taken for granted, and they are seen, and see themselves, as valuable participants in the classroom, they become active rather than passive learners and become agents in taking responsibility for their own learning.

Feminist teachers, too, see themselves as both learners and knowers. Rather than serving as the all-knowing deliverer of truth, the teacher is a guide for student learning. Angela Calabrese Barton explains: "The knowledge base of teachers is both the foundation on which they are able to teach and also a vehicle through which they are able to learn; through teaching, teachers come to question their knowledge" (1998, 7). Because the power asymmetry between student and teacher is named and discussed in classrooms where feminist pedagogy is practiced, various aspects of the curriculum and courses are open to negotiation. While teachers are encouraged to enrich syllabi by choosing materials that will appeal to a wide range of students and that cover areas that include the students' subjectivities, students are encouraged to comment upon and negotiate syllabi, course materials, course requirements, and assignments, and to determine how classroom interaction will take place. Within these negotiations, the teacher is expected to advise students. She[4] is charged with mediating the students' wishes and her own goals for the class. The imperative is to suggest a plan for the course while simultaneously attempting to meet the students where they are conceptually. This delicate balancing act makes for an incredibly challenging teaching situation.

Thus, the feminist classroom is a space that is dialogic. With students as both receivers and givers of knowledge, learning is believed to take place best in the interaction among the students and between students and teacher. The life experiences and cultural perspectives of the students are viewed as valuable resources that each student brings into the classroom. Using personal narratives or, in the example set forth by Angela Calabrese Barton below, oral histories can productively disrupt not only the individual classroom but also the discipline itself.

---

4. Utilizing feminist pedagogy is not gender-restricted. Therefore, in referring to teachers in the third person, the authors have utilized both feminine and masculine pronouns.

Allowing lived experiences to bring to the forefront the positional nature of the knower and knowing in science denies the possibility in an objective reality. It opens up science and science learning to cacophony. It allows teachers and students to experience how knowledge about science and in science embodies the complex and contradictory locations of the lives of those who construct that knowledge. The creation of these spaces pushed against the boundaries of Western science and as a result, as a community, we were able to begin to de-center the traditional power arrangements in science. We were able to reposition ourselves in science. (Barton 1998, 55)

Shifting selves and disciplines is tricky and perilous work. It cannot occur without risk-taking and a little noise generated by both students and teachers.

The Feminist Classroom

In classrooms where feminist pedagogy is practiced, students are encouraged both to listen and to speak. Most often, students are seated in a circle so that they can see each other when speaking. The circle also helps to shift the focus from the teacher as the holder of all knowledge. It is often difficult to introduce students, accustomed to being passive receivers of knowledge, to speaking in classrooms. Frequently, students have difficulty in simply learning to look at each other when speaking rather than at the instructor even when they are directly responding to something another student has said.

Sometimes the students are giddy from the experience of being listened to as a knower for the first time. Unfamiliarity with this new process means that other students might be reluctant to speak at all. The teacher then is charged with managing both excessive talking and silence. Students may respond to a classroom situation in which they are encouraged to speak for the first time as if they are audience members of the Oprah Winfrey or Jerry Springer shows. The responsibility of the feminist instructor in this situation is to insist on thoughtful, informed interaction. That is, students may be encouraged to share personal stories only as a means of elaborating the course material for others and as a starting point from which to move the discussion forward. The teacher must model and emphasize the difference between opinion and what educator Paulo Freire calls "critical consciousness" (1970). Opinion is arrived at through unexamined exposure to media images and life experiences. A critical consciousness, conversely, is the result of thoughtful interaction that takes into account both a variety of materials on a particular topic, context, and politics.

More often, excessive gregariousness is not the problem; rather, silence is. Silence becomes a puzzle that the instructor has to solve. In order to do that, it is necessary to determine the meaning of silence. Sometimes students are silent out of shyness or fear. Sometimes silence comes out of privilege. White students, for example, not seeing themselves as raced, may think that they do not have to participate in a conversation about race, while students of color feel compelled to participate in these conversations, because often they bear the burden of representing all people of color in those discursive spaces. Other times, silence is a form of resistance. If it is resistance, the teacher might ask a series of questions about his own behavior and about what might be missing from the course materials that might make clear the puzzle of student resistance. Is there a gap or an omission from the course materials? Has the teacher positioned himself too clearly, not allowing the student to adequately struggle through the ideas being interrogated? Are the general ideas in the course too unfamiliar or too different from the status quo for students to grasp? The teacher then has to fill in the gap or make ideas more palatable in order to facilitate student learning.

Sometimes students too shy or reluctant to speak in large groups will open up in small group situations. The pedagogical goal in feminist classrooms, however, is not simply to have students find their own voices, but rather to facilitate the students' understanding that the situated knowledges that students bring to the learning context are merely the starting point for the students' learning journey.

In feminist classrooms, teachers take up aspects of identity that are made invisible or are ignored in traditional classrooms. As a result, students are able to connect aspects of their individual lives with course materials. Angela Calabrese Barton explains that she assigns students in her chemistry classes to do oral histories with members of the community as a first assignment: "The initial goals of introducing oral histories into chemistry class were to begin to make the practice of chemistry less abstract, to broaden the definition of science with which students came to class, to connect the theory of the classroom to practice" (1998, 38).

In this case, students begin their inquiry of science with an introduction to a scientist. In other disciplines, personal narratives articulated within the context of the course materials help students to connect experience with structure, which makes course material more relevant and allows them to make connections between the everyday and theory. Composition educator Adriana Hernandez suggests that feminist pedagogues allow students "To deconstruct and reconstruct the terrain of everyday life" (1997, 34).

While feminism as it is currently thought about and practiced no longer focuses exclusively on gender, it does always utilize a gender lens. It simultaneously works to end all oppressions, to uncover all "isms," to have all students feel as if education is for and about them, and has meaning and importance in their lives. The utilization of a feminist pedagogical stance in disciplines across the curriculum is essential not just for the learning of women but for all students. Hernandez writes, "A critical pedagogy that produces diversity of knowledge and subjectivities contesting domination and oppression is a fundamental practice for more egalitarian forms of life" (1997, 13).

Further Reading

The sources cited in this chapter will be helpful to instructors interested in exploring and adopting a feminist pedagogy in their classrooms, as will these:

Britzman, Deborah. 1998. *Lost Subjects, Contested Objects: Toward a Psychoanalytic Inquiry of Learning.* Albany: State Univ. of New York Press.

Ellsworth, Elizabeth. 1997. *Teaching Positions: Difference, Pedagogy, and the Power of Address.* New York: Teacher's College Press.

Gore, Jennifer. 1993. *The Struggle for Pedagogies: Critical and Feminist Discourses as Regimes of Truth.* New York: Routledge.

Luke, Carmen, and Jennifer Gore. 1992. *Feminisms and Critical Pedagogy.* New York: Routledge.

Pagano, Jo Anne. 1990. *Exiles and Communities: Teaching in the Patriarchal Wilderness.* Albany: State Univ. of New York Press.

Ropers-Hiulman, Becky. 1998. *Feminist Teaching in Theory and Practice: Situating Power and Knowledge in Poststructural Classrooms.* New York: Teacher's College Press.

Rosser, Sue V. 1995. *Teaching the Majority: Breaking the Gender Barrier in Science, Mathematics, and Engineering.* New York: Teacher's College Press.

9

Helping Students with Learning Disabilities to Learn

Bonnie McClellan and Emily Rocque

DISABILITY LAW—specifically Section 504 of the Rehabilitation Act of 1973 and the 1990 Americans With Disabilities Act (ADA)—requires that colleges and universities provide *access* to persons with disabilities, including learning disabilities such as dyslexia, written language disorders, and expressive language disorders. What do these and other learning disabilities imply for you as an instructor? That is, what specifically does the law require; and then generally, what can you do to ensure all students equal access to learning as you optimize the potential of the capable but "differently abled" students?

Teaching students who have basic differences in how they process and retain information can certainly be a challenge. But it can also be a journey to greater understanding and appreciation of intellectual differences and to more skillful teaching. The law, intentionally or unintentionally, provides us with a unique teaching *and* learning opportunity.

Learning Disabilities Go to College—An Overview

By its very nature, to have a learning disability (LD) in a college setting poses issues not easily dismissed. Deeply entrenched assumptions—such as that *articulate* means *smart,* that good spelling equates with *capable,* and that quick (to answer, finish tests, read a book) signals high intelligence—underlie our judgments regarding ability. The term "learning *dis*ability" by itself calls a student's ability into question. Unlike a physical disability, a learning disability is "hidden," is not easily identifiable, and even when identified will manifest very differently from person to person and situation to situation. A student with a learning disability might be very articulate and bright in class, write papers very well, and then do poorly on in-class essays or exams. It is easy to underestimate the capabilities of such students.

Effective teaching begins with understanding. Become knowledgeable about yourself—your own learning and teaching preferences, your responsibilities under Section 504 and ADA, and what it is to have a learning disability. You have a head start on this last and important task if you have ever struggled to find a word or express an idea, had difficulty starting or finishing a paper, felt overwhelmed, or wondered whether academia is where you belong. Start there, but now imagine how frustrated or discouraged you would feel if any or all of those conditions were not fleeting but constant.

The sections that follow offer a brief summary of disability law, a description of some ways learning disabilities can impact academic performance and behaviors, and then teaching suggestions for helping students with LD to learn.

Understanding Disability Law

Simply stated, the intent of the law is "inclusion." That the law is succeeding can be seen in the dramatic numbers of students with LD enrolled in undergraduate, graduate, and professional programs—an average of 95,870 students annually in two-year and four-year postsecondary institutions between 1996 and 1998 (Gephart 2000) and 57,999 freshmen alone in 1998–99 (Henderson 1999).

The requirements of Section 504 are simple and balanced: On the one side, the college or university must provide "equal access" to educational opportunity to students with disabilities; on the other side, the students must be "otherwise qualified" to participate in the institution's programs or activities. Accommodations and modifications—defined as changes in the status quo—must be "reasonable," appropriate, and established on a "case-by-case" basis. There is no prescribed, cookie-cutter set of accommodations or strategies for all LD students. Finally, all information related to a student's disability is "confidential" and can only be shared by the college or university with the permission of that student.

As an instructor, you have a legal responsibility to make sure that your course, viewed in its entirety, is *accessible*. Accessibility is the primary consideration of disability law. As a matter of standard practice, whether you are aware that a student in your class has a disability or not, you will want to re-examine how you teach students and how you evaluate them. Questions could arise, for example, regarding the time you allot for a test, the kind of test you give, or the number and length of your assignments. Ultimately, you could find yourself, together with the department chairperson or academic dean, rethinking the standards and essential skills of a course. Extending time for a test, allowing the taping of your lectures, or giving interim feedback on lengthy written assignments are common examples of the accommodations you might be asked to make for a student with a learning disability.

Investigating Campus Resources

Find out about the support services, programs, and other resources available on your campus. Most colleges and universities have an office of disability/learning services or a staff person designated to assist students with disabilities. These offices are an excellent source of information for teachers, as well as students. A student, prior to requesting any accommodations or modifications in a class, must contact an official source in the college. This source, usually an adviser in an office identified to assist students with disabilities, reviews the required documentation of disability presented by the student, determines appropriate accommodations, and serves as an adviser to students and a consultant to faculty. Counseling, tutoring, and other learning services available on campus *and* in the community are especially helpful for students getting established in demanding academic environments.

For your part, you can check with the campus computer center or learning labs to become knowledgeable about reading and editing software, voice-activated computers, and other assistive/adaptive technology available as tools for testing and online instruction. Take advantage of teacher-training disability workshops and courses available on your campus, as well as on nearby campuses and from disability organizations. Read, check the Internet, borrow videos from the disability services office, and see the other "Further Readings/Resources" at the end of this chapter. Above all, maintain communication with your students.

Understanding How LD Characteristics Affect Learning

By definition, persons with learning disabilities are of average or above-average intelligence who display a marked discrepancy between their cognitive potential and their achievement, or who exhibit unexpected and often dramatic differences between their abilities and their weaknesses. LD students often possess areas of exceptional talent or creativity, are generally hard working, and are capable of doing college work. But, not surprisingly, students with LD often lack confidence in their ability to learn. Emmy-winning television producer and author Stephen J. Cannell (1999), who is dyslexic, makes this point well in his essay "A Dyslexic Writer's Story."

Dyslexia, specific language disability, attention deficit disorder (ADD), and *perceptual impairment* are some of the diagnostic terms commonly used to diagnose the difficulties of students with learning disabilities. Frequent areas of difficulty for students identified with specific language disability are unexpected and sometimes severe spelling and editing difficulties, awkward or inappropriate word use, problems finding words, weak memory skills for learning tasks that are heavily language based, and slowness in processing information (e.g., in reading, listening, or making connections). Although not officially classified as a psychological disability, ADD is included here because much in this chapter's discussion applies and ADD is increasingly present in classrooms. ADD often bedevils students in the form of poor attention span and distractibility, difficulty breaking down tasks, and procrastination.

When working with students with learning disabilities, keep in mind that each student will have a unique combination of learning strengths and needs, and students will vary greatly in their ability to communicate their needs and advocate for themselves. Your awareness of the learning differences that influence what you see in student work and behaviors is a critical requisite in effective teaching.

Teaching Practices and Suggestions

"Different strokes for different folks" went the song lyric, which is exactly the prescription for the differently abled, the learning-disabled student. Your teaching challenge is to *enable* that student. Think of learning schematically, as a three-part process of getting information, keeping information, and showing information. That sequence parallels the major processes affected by learning disabilities: *input, processing,* and *output.* To address these three areas, you will need as many strategies and combinations thereof as you have LD students in your classes; there is no single solution. Teaching practices that are flexible and that evidence pedagogical insight benefit all students; but for LD students they are crucial. Ongoing communication with LD students regarding their needs and strengths is strongly recommended.

"Getting" Information: Input

How you present your course material has a tremendous impact on how well your students "get" it. A multisensory presentation approach that is broad and inclusive of all the ways ("styles") that students take in information—visual (seeing), auditory (hearing), and haptic (touch)—provides variety and reinforcement for all your students, but is essential for LD students ensuring that they can acquire information via their preferred reception style. (What is your own preferred style of reception? Be aware that most instructors teach to their own preferred style.) Following are some suggestions regarding presentation of your material.

ORGANIZATION

The more organized your presentation, the better; in fact, it would be hard for you to overdo good organization. Disorganization is an underlying condition of being learning disabled. Some LD students are victimized by their disorganization; others subdue it with compulsive, rigid organization schemes of their own on which they are totally dependent. With either type of student, your own disorganization will create confusion that directly interferes with your students' learning. Instead:

• Make your syllabus crystal clear. Spell out your objectives, grading policies, and expectations regarding attendance. Lecture topics and reading assignments, and their due dates, should be plainly delineated.

• Include a notice on your syllabus describing how to request services or accommodation or both for a disability. On most campuses, a student's request must be made to the disability services office or officer.

• Avoid last-minute changes in the syllabus. That is, say what you will do, and do what you say. Assignments with short turnaround times can prove impossible for some LD students.

• See the discussion "Lecture and Other Modes of Presentation" below for more organization tips.

READING ASSIGNMENTS

Much of what students must learn in college they typically are expected to learn through reading. For LD students that input mode can pose special challenges, which you can address:

• Identify textbooks early so students who read slowly have a chance to get a head start on the readings.

• Space reading and written assignments, disbursing the workload throughout the semester. Be sensitive to times of heavy scheduling in other courses (e.g., midterm exams).

• Think carefully about supplemental reading assignments: why you need them and what you want students to get out of them. Convey that rationale explicitly to your students.

• Integrate reading with your lecture series, identifying material you consider important.

• Emphasize the text's table of contents as an organizer, and keep its wording consistent with your syllabus.

• Make sure handouts and photocopied readings are legible and relevant.

• Allow time for students who require enlarged-print books or books on tape to acquire those materials.

• Request that your materials on reserve in the library be put on electronic reserve.

LECTURE AND OTHER MODES OF PRESENTATION

Lecture is generally an instructor's primary mode of information input. But lecture is also the mode in which LD students' various deficits can prevent them from "getting" the information. Students with poor *auditory* processing or attention will have trouble following all the talk, or they will be unable to write and listen at the same time, or perhaps both. Spelling and handwriting problems compound their difficulties. Poor *visual* learners might have trouble moving information into their notes from the board or overhead displays that change quickly. Many LD students do not pick up on facial expressions, gestures, and vocal inflection and will, therefore, miss the meaning in your conscious or unconscious emphasis and tone.

Appropriate accommodations for students who have difficulties listening and taking notes include shared student notes; having a note-taker from the disability services office accompany the student to class; taping your lectures; and receiving copies of your own notes, outlines, or overheads. For auditory difficulties, you might be asked to wear a lapel microphone for a student using an FM listening system. Here are some other suggestions:

• Insert a short, controlled break into your lecture, or make planned shifts in activities or presentation. These break up the prolonged periods of listening characteristic of the lecture mode.

• Be consistent and predictable. Begin lectures with a recap of the previous lecture and an overview of the current one, orienting both to the syllabus. End by coming to some kind of closure, then preview where the next class session will be going.

• Briefly outline the day's lecture on the board or an overhead, reading aloud for the auditory learners; or give all students a prepared outline of the lecture on which they will fill in the day's notes. This works *especially* well for courses in which there's a lot of material or new terminology to cover.

• Reading effectively is a three-part (before–during–after) process of previewing, reading, and reviewing. Model this process in the classroom using foreshadowing (before), probing questions and follow-up commentaries (during), and summaries (after).

• Emphasize both verbally and visually the key points of the lecture. Guide the progression of the information using words such as "first," "now," "therefore," "to conclude," and the like.

• Narrate what is visual, and make spoken information visual using charts and diagrams.

• Include interactive activities that use motor, tactile, and other senses. Involve students at an emotional level, as well.

• Make the abstract concrete when you can; use examples and models.

• Include time for discussion or a question-answer period to assess how well students have understood the material.

• Speak clearly, loudly, and at a pace slow enough that everyone can keep up or catch their breath. Face the class when you talk; do not talk when you must turn your back.

• Adjust your vocabulary to an appropriate level, or make sure you explain esoteric words and technical terms. Write key terms on the board. Students with LD don't always make the connection between how a word looks and how it sounds.

• Vary your presentation with films, demonstrations, props, and guest lecturers.

• Add active approaches to "getting," such as lab work and hands-on projects, field trips, peer presentations, debate, and role playing. Anytime students, LD or otherwise, can *do* as opposed to the overworked *see* or *hear*, they are more likely to remember.

"Keeping" Information: Processing

This is the part of a course when students are studying and reviewing, and it is mostly done without you. However, you can expedite this crucial "keeping" stage by providing students with an overview that includes the relative importance of each of the topics you have covered and your "take" on the material.

Here are some suggestions to help your LD students retain what they have learned:

• Reinforce content you believe students should retain.

• Your reinforcement should be immediate, frequent, and ongoing.

• Help students see relationships and make connections. Focus on the big picture as well as on the specifics.

• Be consistent, predictable, and reliable. Doing so will help students to anticipate test questions—perhaps the smartest strategy a student can devise.

• Provide study guides, ranging from a general outline of what you have covered to a slate of study questions, possible test questions, or both. Reviewing content and knowing in advance the kinds of questions that will be on a test can help students focus and organize.

• Hand out or have available practice test questions with model answers, letting students "rehearse" the test before they face the real thing. Mastery results from practice.

"Showing" Information: Output

Some LD students, despite being successful in the previous two stages (they "got" your material and they "kept" it), face in stage three the ultimate frustration of not being able to adequately "show" you what they know. Learning disabilities affect written language and test taking, both skills students traditionally must possess in order to show what they know during class, in their written papers, in presentations and projects, and on tests. But you can help them.

CLASS PARTICIPATION

In your grading, acknowledge whenever possible areas where the student is proficient. For example, some LD students shine in discussion but not on paper. Consider counting classroom contributions as a part of your evaluation of a student's understanding.

Recognize a student's consistent effort that might not always translate into good test or paper grades, such as their religiously attending class, keeping up with assignments, and the like.

For students who are nearly paralyzed talking or reading aloud in class or who have unusual difficulty expressing themselves, work out alternate ways they can participate. Informal discussions during office hours and substituting a project for class participation are two possible methods.

Seek ways to give value to qualities of emotional intelligence such as motivation, curiosity, perseverance, and effort.

PAPERS

Delimit topics, as an option for students who are overwhelmed by open-ended assignments.

Set up interim deadlines, preferably with feedback, for students who have trouble pushing a paper along all by themselves, or offer the option of several smaller papers rather than one long one.

Evaluate content, not writing mechanics and spelling, for exams and in-class writing. It is common for students with LDs to have difficulty spelling and seeing their writing errors. If written language competency is a course objective, provide LD students the opportunity to earn back lost points by submitting corrections.

Be flexible on paper deadlines. For students who require flexibility on due dates, set up an adjusted time line.

PRESENTATIONS AND PROJECTS

Think of alternate ways for alternative minds to show what they know. Certainly you must evaluate what a student has learned, but often there are novel ways to do that. Could students teach a portion of the material? Could a web or illustrated answer supplement or substitute for an essay question?

The portfolio method of grading lets students be evaluated on what they did with the information in a course. In courses such as music, art, and architecture, juries evaluate proficiencies as projects and performances.

Consider worthwhile extra-credit assignments for LD students, completed on their own time and in their own way, to supplement their grades.

TESTS

Extra time for tests is the accommodation most frequently provided for students with learning disabilities. The standard extension is time and one-half, but sometimes even more time is allotted and breaks are included.

Encourage students to take responsibility for making alternate test arrangements.

Test on content you believe should be reinforced; testing should not be a game of "gotcha!"

Make your test's layout and language crisp, clear, and uncluttered. Questions should be relevant and fair.

Frequent quizzes on smaller amounts of material help the LD student keep up and solidify material that will show up on the weightier tests, thereby reducing problems with memory. But do not "pop" a quiz.

Allow all students to drop a quiz grade or two, thus letting them learn from their mistakes without too much collateral damage.

Return tests quickly. It is essential that you give students reinforcement, correction, and feedback while the material is fresh in their memory and before they have to attempt another test with you.

In general, give an LD student the same test you give the other students, but modify your *procedures*. This could mean some combination of giving extra time, testing the student separately in a distraction-free environment, administering the test in smaller sections at separate times, allowing the student to select from among more questions, providing examples, being available to rephrase questions, and allowing follow-up discussion of the student's written answers.

Allow an alternative test *format* or combination of formats: essay questions versus objective, oral versus written answers, take-home versus in-class, a shorter version, a word bank for sentence completion, or fewer choices on multiple-choice questions.

Modify the *administration* of the test by allowing for a reader, tape-recorded exam, voice computer, or exam on disk.

Modify the *method of response*. For example, the student might be allowed to use a word processor, a scribe, or a tape recorder to record answers and to answer on the test itself rather than on an answer sheet.

Give partial credit when the student is headed in the right direction. Math and science instructors could grade the student's process more than the final solution.

Allow aids such as a spell checker, dictionary, or thesaurus; a calculator; or data cards (listing formulas, dates and names, technical terms) as memory aids. Allow the student to consult the textbook or lecture notes if memorization is not a learning objective being tested.

Specific Courses

Students with learning disabilities often have trouble with specific subjects, particularly foreign languages and math. These subjects' hierarchical and sequential presentation, the memorization load, their "foreign" terminology and vocabulary, the systematic rules and exceptions, and the performance requirements often play right into a student's areas of difficulty.

If yours is such a course that LD students cannot waive or substitute, there are still some things you can do to aid their learning:

- Slow the pace as much as possible.
- Increase the practice and reinforcement.
- Enlist all appropriate accommodations—perhaps extra time, alternate test and performance formats, and test aids such as calculators and vocabulary lists.
- Require tutoring or give individual help yourself or both.

Summary

We will conclude with a few words of caution to persons at either end of the teacher continuum—those who, without being aware or with kind intentions, lower expectations and standards and grant accommodations for which a student is not eligible and those who believe that students who receive extra time to complete a problem set or who have an oral component to an exam compromise the standards of the course or are receiving unfair advantage. You can enhance and accommodate your LD students' learning without fundamentally altering critical course content or lowering your standards. Doing either is as much an injustice to an LD student as is not providing educational access. Instead, standards and criteria need to be evaluated; methods need to be adjusted.

Students with learning disabilities can and *do* successfully navigate rigorous and challenging curriculums. Instruction and faculty attitudes play a key role in that success. Be open, be knowledgeable, be flexible, be creative. Enjoy these differently abled individuals. Stephen J. Cannell, dyslexic, award-winning television producer and author, makes clear how he got to where he is today: "I owe my career to my writing instructor at Oregon. Ralph Salisbury looked past my misspellings and gave me encouragement and hope" (1999, 78).

Further Readings/Resources

BOOKS AND ARTICLES

Kantrowitz, Barbara, and Anne Underwood. 1999. "Dyslexia and the New Science of Reading." *Newsweek,* November 22, 72–77.

Reetz, Linda, Mary Milleret Ring, and Geralyn M. Jacobs. 1999. "20 Ways to Examine Test Modifications." *Intervention in School and Clinic* 35, no. 2 (November): 117–18.

Vogel, Susan A. 1997. *College Students with Learning Disabilities: A Handbook.* 6th ed. DeKalb, Ill.: Northern Illinois Univ.

West, Thomas. 1991. *In the Mind's Eye: Visual Thinkers, Gifted People with Learning Difficulties, Computer Images, and the Ironies of Creativity.* Buffalo, N.Y.: Prometheus.

VIDEO

Understanding Learning Disabilities: How Difficult Can This Be? PBS Video, 1990. Produced by Eagle Hill (school), 1990, Peter Rosen, producer, and Dr. Richard D. Lavoie, director and facilitator of the videotaped workshop. Distributed by PBS Video.

ONLINE ARTICLES

http://www.ldonline.org/ld_indepth/teaching_techniques/exam_test_
  modifications.html
http://www.ldonline.org/ld_indepth/postsecondary/facultytips.html
http://www.inform.umd.edu/CampusInfo/Committees/PCDI/RA

ORGANIZATIONAL WEB SITES

International Dyslexia Association (IDA): http://www.interdys.org
Learning Disabilities Association (LDA): http://www.ldanatl.org/

10

Technology for Campus-Based Instruction

Anne Schaper Englot and Ken A. Smith

MATT WAKES UP to the sound of a digitized chime telling him he has an instant message. He sleepily rolls over and reaches toward the laptop perched precariously on top of a pizza box on his desk. He jiggles the computer's mouse, and his screen saver—an aquarium scene of fish lazily swimming back and forth—dissolves into an icon-encrusted window. The instant messenger has text scrolling across it: "Wake up! Wake up!" It's from his classmate Amanda.

"I'm up," he types back.

"Log into TopClass . . . we have to answer a question in our discussion section before class."

"OK. Later."

"Later," she messages back.

Matt minimizes instant messenger and points his Internet browser to the URL of TopClass. He logs in and finds his discussion group. Fellow group members Jennifer and Ryan have already started a threaded discussion on the assigned topic. Matt opens another window and accesses his class notes saved on the hard drive of his computer. Into yet a third new window he opens a folder located on the campus network and launches the PowerPoint presentation that his professor, Ms. Jones, delivered in class yesterday. Matt pages through the presentation, pausing on a slide that lists several web sites. Each web site on the list is hyperlinked to that web site's address on the World Wide Web. Matt clicks on the first web site and as the site opens, he pages through and jots down the information pertinent to the discussion question. He repeats the process with the next web site on the list and then closes the PowerPoint. He is ready to join the discussion. He maximizes the TopClass window and types in his commentary on Jennifer and Ryan's contributions. Amanda joins in next.

Before logging off, Matt checks his mailbox. Glancing at the clock on the computer's screen, he realizes he only has ten minutes before class. He pulls on his sweats and his baseball cap and takes his computer down the hall with him to the bathroom to brush his teeth while he waits for his e-mail to download. The computer is not plugged in anywhere. Instead he accesses the Internet with a wireless connection; a transceiver in his dorm sends a signal to a wireless card in the laptop.

As he brushes his teeth, he pages down through the loads of spam until he is sure there is no really interesting mail, shuts down, slips the computer into his backpack, and heads to class.

In class, Matt's professor shows the students how to link to the day's quiz using TopClass. When the quiz is over, the professor sends the class on a webquest. Each discussion group must use a few select web sites to answer a battery of questions concerning a specific topic, collect images related to that topic, and ultimately create a presentation summarizing their findings to deliver to everyone at the end of class. Afterwards, the presentations are posted to the course web site for other class sections to peruse.

During lunch in the campus laptop café, Matt and Ryan relax playing a computer game over the Internet. Amanda and Jennifer download MP3 files in the dining hall over the wireless connection.

The next class meeting finds the students out in the field recording notes and documenting their process by taking pictures with a digital camera. On the way back to campus in the van, their professor plays a DVD illustrating the correct lab procedure. Later, to analyze the data, they will access the required software program, which is housed on a local CD tower.

Meanwhile . . .

Ms. Jones wakes up, and over her morning coffee she logs in to TopClass to post the day's discussion question. She knows the students will need to access their class notes as well as the previous day's PowerPoint presentation in order to link to several web sites containing material on which she based the discussion question. Next, she sends an instant message to each group leader in order to get the discussions rolling. She wonders over the class time saved in the delivery of this assignment in this way. The process has become more efficient even as she has had to become a better manager in order to keep the course flowing effectively.

Ms. Jones loves the flexibility of being able to perform these tasks before she leaves her house in the morning. Formerly, she had to be on campus to physically post discussion questions at a library reserve desk, where students had to physically check for questions and record comments. This new ability to access the online discussion site from any Internet connection at home, in the office, or from the classroom has enabled the discussion to flow more freely and occasionally even to go into greater depth. Her students who commute or who work a lot of hours especially appreciate the increased flexibility, and they have demonstrated greater success with such assignments.

She yawns and stretches. She was up until 2 A.M. the previous night preparing a new PowerPoint presentation with updated references. Although this is the third year she has taught this course using PowerPoint as a teaching aid, she continually has to check the currency of web links and researched information on the Internet, to insert new digital images as digital media of greater resolution become available, and to check each presentation for compatibility with this year's version of the operating software. It is a trade-off: Even as time is saved in information retrieval, the time it takes to prepare multimedia presentations and design assignments increases.

After breakfast, she checks the assignment folder for another course she teaches, accessing the campus network from a secure modem connection. She reads through each student's assignment and sends grades and comments on them to each student through e-mail. By the time she arrives on campus, Ms. Jones has received several e-mails back from students with questions regarding their grades. Unperturbed, she refers them to the course grading policy posted online and linked to the course syllabus.

In class, while Matt, Amanda, and the other students are taking their quiz over the Internet, Ms. Jones is checking through her presentation for that day. She realizes that the web site she intended to show the students is downloading much too slowly to keep their interest. So she punts, quickly restructuring the lecture into the form of a webquest, in which each group answers a set of questions based on Internet research and puts a presentation together with images to illustrate the topic. At the end of class, the student groups deliver their presentations. Their grades on the quiz the next day are proof that once they were engaged in the learning process, the students retained a greater percentage of the material presented.

Although technology may fascinate her, Ms. Jones is no "techie." She became an early adopter because of the pedagogical flexibility the technology would afford her.

The scenario described above is not so far-fetched. Although not yet common, such technology-aided interactions are happening daily at institutions such as the State University of New York Morrisville, Wake Forest University, Seton Hall University, and Acadia University (Canada). Many other universities, colleges, schools, and departments are close behind them. Thus, the reality is that use of technology in classroom instruction will be a fact of life for many instructors very soon. What is important is that we use technology *effectively*—that is, to aid the achievement of learning objectives.

This chapter will introduce you to some of the key dimensions and issues in the effective use of technology in support of otherwise traditional, campus-based education. We approach our topic as early adopters who, having used such instructional technology to support a variety of courses over a number of semesters, have accumulated a reasonable amount of experience with regard to what works. We also have had many productive discussions with colleagues with similar interests, and we have read fairly broadly in this field. Although we are researchers by training, technology is not the focus of our respective research agendas. Nevertheless, our experience using technology in the instructional setting gives us a basis for sharing our insights, and our training as researchers has helped us articulate relevant questions that practitioners should consider (and that other researchers whose agendas do focus on instructional technology might investigate).

First we should set down a few definitions. *Instructional technology* can be broadly understood as any tool or method used to facilitate the delivery, understanding, and retention of course-related material, along with any tool or method used to support course administration. Such a broad definition would encompass the use of chalkboards and flipcharts in classroom delivery and the use of spiral-bound grade books for course administration. In this discussion, however, we focus on *computer*-based or *computer*-related technologies, while retaining the emphasis on course delivery and administration. We also confine our focus to *campus-based instruction,* as distinguished from "distance education." In the latter case, greater use is made of computer-based and computer-related instructional technologies because students do not set foot in a classroom or interact face-to-face with their instructor or classmates.

Finally, our reader should understand that our objective is a broad overview of the field as a *starting point* for those instructors interested in using technology in and around their classrooms. Our intent is to emphasize the promise of effective technology application—and also its costs and drawbacks—for the widest possible audience. Thus, we have avoided detailed discussions of discipline-specific requirements and tools. (We apologize in advance if we have omitted someone's favorite tool or technique, but we welcome correspondence that would help us continue to improve our own classrooms.)

Technological Foundations

Driving the accelerating use of technology for classroom teaching and learning is the convergence of a number of related technologies. The primary antecedent has been the widespread availability of personal-sized computers, or PCs. The power and speed of PCs, both desktop models and laptops, continue to rise while the cost of hardware and software continues to fall. The result is that virtually all faculty and students have access to a computer, even if they might not own one.

The potential of these small computers has been dramatically increased by the advent of local and wide-area networks that link multiple computers and allow them to share information. These networks can tie PCs to their larger mainframe counterparts in client-server configurations, or they can tie together many of the small computers in peer-to-peer networks. Many networks within institutions incorporate both client-server and peer-to-peer network infrastructures. The newest and largest network, of course, is the Internet: a "network of networks," if you will, that enables computers to share information around the globe. Computers can be connected to the Internet through permanent, hardwired connections or through temporary dial-up connections via modems that rely on standard telephone lines. Technology now exists for wireless connections to the Internet,[1] and current trends indicate that in the very near future data, graphics, voice, and full-motion video will be fully integrated and available at virtually any location.[2]

1. See "The Wireless Revolution," *The Chronicle of Higher Education,* Oct. 13, 2000: A59; and "SUNY's Morrisville Campus Sees Wireless Computing as Way to Create a Niche," *The Chronicle of Higher Education,* Oct. 13, 2000: A62.

2. See, for example, Covell 2000.

In this context, converging computer and network technologies create exciting new possibilities for teaching and learning. At the same time early adopters of technology report that the related costs in both money and time are significant. In the following discussion, we overview some of the promise and some of the pitfalls of using instructional technology: first the general implications of these trends, and then some immediate "pressure points" faculty must address when they consider using these technologies.

General Implications of Technology for the Classroom

STUDENT NEEDS

Students typically come to us with high expectations for our use of technology. Remember that IBM introduced the PC before most of our undergraduates were born. Having grown up surrounded by technology and being media-savvy and media-sensitive, many students *expect* it to be used effectively. Students today, for example, expect instructors to be available and responsive via e-mail. And because computer technology offers so many channels for communication (e-mail, voice mail, instant messaging), many students procrastinate on initiating contact, then become frantic if they do not receive an immediate response.

The computer-savvy student especially can be intolerant of the fact that different instructors are varyingly knowledgeable and capable in their use of technology. It can be somewhat disappointing for a student who comes to class expecting to be learning *from* the instructor to find that some of those instructors are less comfortable with the technology than the student is. Our students come from high school expecting the "sage on the stage," not the learner-centered "guide on the side" model of learning that seems to parallel the increased use of instructional technology. So, although they wish instructors were all-knowing, students often find themselves learning with, or even teaching, their instructors new modes of computing and technology use.

Students also can be intolerant of the limitations of campus technology equipment and support. Techies who purchased (or were given) a brand new computer as they headed off to college often discover that the hardware and software they encounter in the campus computer labs are a generation or two older than their own "newfangled" systems. At the same time, technophobe students who are totally reliant on campus equipment and support must contend with overworked staff who are busy troubleshooting one more problem with the network. Neither techie nor technophobe finds the experience very confidence-building.

Finally, although we find that students generally are wildly adept at certain tasks (downloading music and pirated software, for instance), they can be wildly *inept* at organizational tasks such as composing articulate, concise e-mail messages; effectively using electronic folders to organize their work; contributing productively to online discussions; or searching the Internet for high-quality course-related materials. Thus, despite their basic proficiency with the hardware and software, often students need to be taught how to use that technology *effectively* as part of their learning process.

FACULTY REQUIREMENTS

In general, technology-related requirements placed on the instructor are increasing. For example, many institutions require all instructors to have and use e-mail, and to provide at least a minimum amount of information (e.g., class syllabus, office hours) via the web. Some, such as Seton Hall University, include "effective technology use" among their criteria in awarding tenure, favoring such activities as participation in computing initiatives and the development of digital course materials.[3]

But it takes a major commitment of time and energy to become proficient with the various technologies available. Even on campuses where technology is given priority, training initiatives for those instructors who are less able often are slow to be started, understaffed, and underfunded. As a consequence, many instructors work long hours off the clock to learn how to use technology and apply it to its greatest potential.

3. The phrase "effective technology use" is from Dennis Garbini's talk at the Ubiquitous Computing Conference (see note 7). Seton Hall Faculty Guide, 1999 (rev. ed.): "Article 4: Appointment, Promotion, and Tenure Standards. 4.3: Scholarship, including Research or other Creative Work. a. Evidence shall include, but not be limited to: lectures and papers presented to professional organizations, articles in professional journals, books, personal research grants, commissions, awards, applied research, bibliographic research, manuscripts, scripts, manuals, works of art, public performances, audio or video tapes, films, computer software, multimedia presentation and emerging forms of information technology." Accessed at http://www.provost.shu.edu/senate/Policies/index. Upon arriving at this address, click on "Faculty Guide with Revisions as of August 24, 1999" to open document.

Creation of new course materials is very time-consuming and often requires a level of expertise beyond the basics. A dilemma for faculty, especially those at research institutions, is that time spent learning and developing effective applications of instructional technology is time unavailable for their research agendas. Even at predominantly teaching institutions, time spent learning new technologies takes time away from developing course content. Clearly, a critical issue for faculty is how to balance the different demands.

Finally, it is our observation that faculty who are early adopters of technology tend to enjoy a competitive advantage with respect to student expectations and student evaluations; that is, such an instructor scores points with students just for being technologically savvy. Likewise, it appears that different disciplines and different courses within disciplines benefit differentially from the use of various technologies. As a consequence, a "digital divide" or "caste system" can result, in which a very effective "traditional" or "low-tech" instructor is made to feel inadequate or unappreciated due to lack of (or resistance to) technology use. Or an instructor can feel coerced into adopting technologies because they are "hot," even if these technologies do not effectively contribute to students' learning.

INSTITUTIONAL SUPPORT

A third set of implications relates to institutional support. Effective use of technology is expensive. Technical and training support are required to maintain and upgrade the technology infrastructure and instructor skill in its effective use. Where support is inadequate, systems deteriorate and the cost of skill maintenance and development is transferred to the users—to instructors and students.

As an example, one of us (Englot) each year teaches a new release of AutoCAD to her architecture students. The new version of the software and its text often arrive only a week or two before classes begin, and it falls to her and the other instructors to make sure the new version is loaded on their personal machines. They receive no training, recalling the point made earlier that students often find they are learning with or even teaching their instructors. Consequently, the cost is significant, not only to the institution for the costly upgrade but also to the instructors in the steepness of the learning curve and time lost during the critical few weeks prior to the start of the semester.

A reason for these difficulties is the way in which technology expenditures are budgeted. With many past technology initiatives, institutions treated them as one-time, capital expenditures—equipping dorms with computer rooms, or wiring dorms and classrooms to a campus mainframe, for example. Such expenditures are put in the capital budget rather than the operating budget. Institutions have also viewed investments in technology maintenance and upgrades as alternatives to other capital improvements. Many times, technology projects are initially funded by grants or sponsored programs. But who will then pay for maintenance and upgrades after that initial grant has been exhausted?

One ameliorative approach worthy of consideration is the creation of a laptop environment, such as that implemented at SUNY Morrisville.[4] In such an environment, students are expected to purchase and use laptop computers as part of their educational program. The benefit is that a "laptop program" pushes the cost of computer purchases and upgrades onto the students themselves. A drawback is that the infrastructure to effectively support a laptop environment is somewhat more complex than that required for permanently installed computers, and the cost of maintaining a campus network and its servers is still significant. Thus, it becomes apparent that all institutions must begin to treat the cost of networks, hardware, software, and training as operating rather than capital expenditure.

COMPETITIVE ADVANTAGE

A final general implication returns us to the idea of "competitive advantage" mentioned earlier. That is, merely adopting and using instructional technology is unlikely to provide an instructor or institution with a competitive advantage that lasts. Rather, as technology spreads, the expectation of *effective use of technology* will set a threshold for competitive parity. What that threshold looks like might vary by discipline and by level of instruction (lower, upper, graduate), but it is likely that a significant level of effective technology use will be required to remain competitive. This dynamic is analogous to the spread of ATMs. First introduced by Citibank, the ATM gave those banks that implemented the technology early an immediate competitive advantage; in time, however, customers have come to *expect* their accounts to be accessible from any ATM, whether operated by their own bank or not.

4. See Brown 2000.

In the same way that ATMs have become a necessity for the banking industry, aspiring academics are discovering that their ability to use technology effectively is not optional. Technology is being used to facilitate active learning, collaborative learning, and independent learning. Conversations about teaching take place at computing conferences, and vice versa. And campuses known for leadership in teaching often are also the leaders in computing.

At Acadia University, in Wolfville, Nova Scotia, for example, the rhetoric employed to market the use of laptop computers is firmly tied to an educational outcome. Prospective students are promised that they "will use today's technology to develop the advanced analytical skills they need to adapt to ever-changing study and work environments." President Kelvin Oglivie declares, "We are moving the classroom into a new, dynamic, and exciting environment that brings students and faculty together in a fashion that has never before occurred. The dynamism of the classroom is unprecedented."[5] The word *dynamic* connotes an "active-learning environment," a buzzword in the field of education meaning roughly "learning by doing."

Far from being an anomaly, the relationship alluded to by Acadia among computing, teaching, and learning has been institutionalized at a number of the leading colleges in what is called the "ubiquitous computing" movement. At Wake Forest University—one of the progenitors of ubiquitous computing—belief in the transformative power of technology is impressively embodied in brick and mortar. The university's International Center for Computer-Enhanced Learning (ICCEL) is "founded on the belief that learning principles such as collaboration and interaction can be supported and enhanced by the appropriate use of technology."[6]

At Seton Hall University, its Teaching, Learning, and Technology Center (TLTC) is part of a more than $15 million initiative to enhance information technology. On the university's web site, technology is represented as being something that "not only enhances traditional models of teaching and learning, but also enables new kinds of teaching and learning and new methods of delivering the University's educational services."[7]

At SUNY Morrisville, a two-year agriculture and technology college, the

5. Accessed at http://www.acadiau.ca/advantage/.

6. Accessed at http://www.wfu.edu/technology/.

7. Attributed to Dennis J. Garbini (vice president for technology) and Stephen G. Landry (chief technology officer) in a publication circulated during the (January) 2000 Ubiquitous Computing Conference, Seton Hall University, New Jersey.

focus has long been on teaching. Therefore it is not surprising that its Teaching Excellence Center (TEC) was conceived by faculty involved in the institution's decision to "go laptop." The laptop initiative was spearheaded by President Ray Cross in his inaugural year, but faculty buy-in was the key to its successful implementation.[8] Instead of computer use being mandated across campus, a request for proposals to participate in a pilot project was sent out to Morrisville's faculty (this approach was repeated in a subsequent enlargement of the laptop initiative). By asking faculty to buy in to the program, the administration was able to reward early adopters without intimidating the apprehensive. Response to the laptop initiative has been overwhelmingly positive. The faculty members involved cite students' improved attention spans; improved communication between faculty and students, especially international students; and the exciting opportunity of connecting students to the global resources of the Internet. Christine Cring, director of the TEC, provides support to laptop faculty, as well as serving as a resource for faculty and staff who want to learn new skills. She created online tutorials and runs workshops on the effective use of technology. In 2001, SUNY Morrisville gained national attention by being named "#1 Most Wired College" in the two-year category in a Yahoo.com poll and being profiled in a *Chronicle of Higher Education* feature on wireless technology.[9]

The number of institutions developing ubiquitous computing initiatives is steadily growing, as is the number of faculty becoming adept at teaching using technology. Today, to teach with technology is innovative. But tomorrow? To us, these trends indicate it is unlikely that such initiatives or that adeptness will provide either institutions or instructors a sustained competitive advantage. At the same time, though, we believe that the rapidity with which technology changes continues to offer early adopters, be they institutional or individual, the opportunity to set themselves apart from their competitors.

8. Before coming to Morrisville, Cross had previously led Ferris State College in becoming one of the first "laptop" colleges in the nation. For more about SUNY Morrisville, visit http://www.morrisville.edu.

9. Morrisville held on to the title in 2002 despite the institution of more stringent criteria. Unfortunately *Yahoo! Internet Life* online magazine folded in August 2002, so the link to the site is defunct. "SUNY's Morrisville Campus Sees Wireless Computing as Way to Create a Niche," *The Chronicle of Higher Education,* Oct. 13, 2000: A62.

Immediate Pressure Points

Beyond these general implications, we have observed a number of immediate pressure points relating to the use of instructional technology. We call these "pressure points" because they have high visibility, high potential payback, and high risk if not implemented properly. They also are where faculty are most likely to get into trouble when they use the technology for the first time.

CLASSROOM DELIVERY

Probably the most common technology in the classroom is the use of computers with presentation software and digital projection systems to support the delivery of lecture and discussion material. Microsoft's PowerPoint software is the preeminent example of this tool. The use of presentation software requires the availability of a computer connected to a projector. These systems range from computers (laptop or desktop) and projectors mounted on carts that are wheeled into the classroom on an as-needed basis to permanently installed teaching consoles that can also include document cameras and video cassette and DVD players. Early projectors were somewhat limited in their brightness and resolution, requiring classrooms to be darkened and graphics to be simplified so as to be legible to all in the room. Recent advances in projector technology, however, provide users with resolution that rivals the best desktop monitors and enough brightness (lumens) to be visible in fully lit classrooms.

Presentation software is quite good for listing and/or summarizing the main points of a lecture or discussion. By visually reinforcing what students hear, presentation slides help transfer factual material such as names and dates. Presentation software is also effective in presenting material other than straight text. Tables, charts, formulae, graphics, photographs, and even video clips can be incorporated into presentations, all of which can help communicate concepts and ideas more effectively than can the spoken or written word alone. Good presentations can be informative and entertaining, which helps students stay focused. Finally, having presentation materials already assembled in the form of a digital presentation can contribute to in-class efficiency. Instructors need not spend a great deal of time writing on the blackboard; they need only jump to the appropriate presentation slide.

And if the slides are made available to students as handouts, they can spend more time interacting with the instructor rather than frantically trying to copy down all the notes.

However, the effective use of presentation software requires careful planning and a significant degree of skill. Given the power of the software itself, it is critical that faculty not allow themselves to become enamored by the bells and whistles, which can detract from rather than contribute to effective communication. Having been subjected to too many PowerPoint presentations (by faculty as well as students) that have used jarring color schemes, poorly composed slides, too much text in too small a point size, and distracting transitions and animations, we have come to the conclusion that clean and simple are better. An eye for graphic design is clearly an asset in this regard.

Today, many textbooks include PowerPoint slides with their ancillary teaching materials. Although these slides can help an instructor up the learning curve with the technology, the use of "canned" presentations involves its own risk. First, the fact that a set of slides was provided by a publisher does not mean that a presentation is immune to the composition and format problems discussed above. Indeed, we have even found typographical errors in the presentations provided with our textbooks. Second, covering the slides that accompanied a chapter does *not,* in our opinion, constitute effective teaching. Effective teaching requires that the instructor think through the learning objectives for each class session, thoughtfully determine how best to achieve these objectives, and *then* decide how to present the relevant material. Consequently, although the presentations provided by publishers can give us some good ideas, we develop our own presentations to ensure we know exactly what is included and why.

Importantly, digital projection systems are not limited to serving as the platform for formal presentation software. Anything that can be displayed on a computer monitor can also be projected on screen. Thus, when using a computer with a windowed operating system, it is quite possible to use PowerPoint to present the major points of a discussion, switch midstream to Excel to present a financial analysis in spreadsheet format, then switch to Word to show a related document, then pick up where one left off in PowerPoint. Course-specific software such as SPSS (statistics), AutoCAD (drafting), or PhotoShop (graphic art) can also be demonstrated and used effectively.

If the teaching station includes a document camera and video cassette or

DVD player, full multimedia presentations can be used. If the teaching station is connected to the Internet, the power of the World Wide Web also is instantly accessible. We have found that using the web in class to access information we have stored remotely (e.g., the details of an assignment we have placed on the course web page) or to provide an immediate example of a course topic (e.g., an article from *today's* issue of The Wall Street Journal Interactive) keeps the course current and heightens student interest.

We have found that using digital projection systems in our classrooms lets our delivery of course material be more creative, interactive, and efficient. However, the technology has its costs—the primary one being preparation time. Putting together PowerPoint presentations from scratch is a significant task, as is learning to transition smoothly between multiple software applications. Keeping presentations fresh requires ongoing research for new material and new examples. Our experience, however, has been that the benefits truly outweigh the costs, and we believe that the effective use of presentation technology should be considered a necessary skill for anyone entering the teaching profession.

INTERACTION OUTSIDE THE CLASSROOM

Technology also can provide the means for furthering interaction between the instructor and students, both individually and collectively. The simplest form of technology-based communication is e-mail.

Most instructors now list their e-mail address on their syllabus, along with their telephone number, office address, and office hours. E-mail significantly expands opportunity for students to send messages or queries to their instructors outside of normal office hours. Similarly, e-mail provides opportunity for instructors to contact individual students. Students routinely get an on-campus e-mail account when they enroll in classes, and the addresses are often included on class lists provided to faculty at the beginning of the semester. This new communication channel clearly has potential for good, but it also has potential for abuse.

Using e-mail effectively requires identifying when it is appropriate, versus telephone conversations or face-to-face meetings. E-mail is very good for sending quick announcements, short inquiries, and short answers. But if the content of the message is complex, other media would be more appropriate. A key limitation compared with face-to-face communication is that

e-mail lacks body language and tone of voice, which can help clarify, emphasize, or even ameliorate the content and impact of a message. Much research has been done on e-mail as a communication medium. Briefly, we
suggest the following suggestions to gain the benefits of e-mail while avoiding some of its worst pitfalls.

Set clear expectations. For example, let students know how quickly
you intend to respond to their inquiries. It is natural for students to want a
rapid response. Setting the expectation ("I will respond within twenty-four
hours . . . within forty-eight hours . . . by close of business on Tuesdays and
Thursdays") takes the pressure off and prevents students from feeling that
you have let them down. Likewise, set expectations for their responses to
your e-mails. If you will be relying on e-mail to send course announcements,
homework assignments, and the like, students must be held accountable for
checking their e-mail accounts frequently. Finally, set some expectations for
what kinds of messages you will entertain via e-mail versus by phone or face
to face. For instance, we expect students who must miss class to inform us in
advance, and communicating via e-mail is fine for this purpose. But we do
not discuss individual student performance on exams or assignments except
in person.

An extension of e-mail is the list server, or listserv. Listserv software allows
a single e-mail message to be sent (or "posted") to all members of a list by
addressing the message to a single e-mail address. It is not uncommon for an
instructor whose campus offers listserv capability to create a listserv of all the
students in his or her class or section, then post assignments or announcements to the entire class through the listserv. Listservs also can be config-
ured to allow a list *member* to post a message to the entire list, thus allowing
students to send a question or comment to all of their classmates.

The listserv's ability to broadcast messages to all list members creates the
potential for continuing class discussion outside the boundaries of the classroom. Students can post questions or comments to the list, to which the instructor responds. Because all members of the list see both the query and
the response, they all have opportunity to benefit from that individual interaction. Alternately, the instructor might choose to delay responding so that
other students can respond first. Some instructors award credit to students
who contribute constructively to the online discussion, thereby effectively
creating an extension of in-class discussion.

Like e-mail, using listservs effectively requires thought, expectation setting, and management. You must instruct students in what constitutes appropriate content for the listserv. Discussions can all too easily move off the course-related topic. This is particularly likely if the discussion is "unmoderated," meaning that you are not keeping up with the flow of the discussion yourself. Another potential problem is listserv "overload," when a listserv is so active or when your students (or you) are members of so many listservs that the resulting traffic fills their e-mail mailboxes. It can help to use message folders, mail filters, and "digest" options (i.e., all messages from a twenty-four–hour period are collected into just a single e-mail message). But unless effectively managed, listservs can seem more trouble than they are worth.

An alternative to the listserv is the web-based discussion server. A discussion server is a facility that, rather than sending posted messages to each member's mailbox, instead posts messages to a web site that members visit periodically. Two significant advantages are the absence of e-mail overload and the capability for "threaded discussions," in which messages are grouped by topic. We also consider it an advantage that a discussion server requires students to take the initiative to visit the discussion web-site on a regular basis to keep up with the discussion, rather than simply responding to e-mail messages that appear in their mailbox.

E-mail, listservs, and discussion servers all contribute to interaction outside of the classroom. A common element is that all three are active communication media that prompt students to engage in discussion of course materials. Another tool that supports the course outside the classroom is a course web page.

A course web page (or web site) is a repository of course information available to students anytime via the web. Simple course web pages include material that parallels information found in the course syllabus—indeed, some course web pages are no more than online versions of the syllabus itself. More sophisticated web pages might include course readings, assignments, examples, sample test questions, links to the course discussion server, or links to other relevant web sites. Like a good class presentation, a good web page requires a significant degree of skill and effort to construct. Design, content, and navigation must be carefully thought through and integrated. Effective web sites also evolve over the course of a semester, as material is added and updated as the course progresses. Our experience has been that, although costly to develop and maintain, an informative course web page reduces the number of administrative questions we receive from students and allows us to be more content-focused during class time.

Overall, we believe that technologies that support interaction with and between students outside the classroom have the potential to contribute significantly to student learning. Obviously, such technologies allow for more interaction with and around course material, but we believe they also provide additional opportunity for students with differing learning styles. Some students are verbally quick on their feet and engage easily in class discussion. Others are more reflective, hesitant to take a position until they have had time to think through a topic. Yet others are simply uncomfortable speaking in class, whether due to personality or cultural conditioning. E-mail, listservs, and discussion servers provide all these students the chance to share their thoughts, to their benefit and that of the other members of the class.

COMPUTER-BASED RESEARCH

A third pressure point in technology to support learning is the use of computer-based research. Online data sources and sophisticated research tools hold both promise and pitfalls. One promise is that, as more and more libraries and traditional sources of high-quality information become available online, instructors should be able to expect their students to readily access the best sources of relevant information. However, just as students were once taught to use traditional research tools such as library catalogs and journal indexes, they now also must be taught how to use online search tools. Without such training, students are apt to fall into the traps of using inappropriate information, misusing appropriate information, or even misappropriating others' information.

Access to libraries, statistical databases, government agencies, and other high-quality primary sources via the web yields many opportunities for creative assignments that require significant research. Unfortunately, the web also offers a great deal of information of questionable quality. Instructors must teach students to evaluate the quality of web-based material and to search for authoritative (rather than second-, third-, or fourth-hand) sources. Web materials are always placed there for a purpose, so students must be taught always to ask "Why is this here?" and to look for hidden biases. These classic research directives are even more critical now, given today's ease of access to vast amounts of online information. Librarians have traditionally functioned, in a sense, as gatekeepers—checking for scholarly, well-regarded material. When students get their information directly off the web, bypassing the gatekeepers, they now must ask the critical questions. (We do not mean to imply, of course, that on-campus libraries make available only information of high quality and without bias! However, the openness of the web exacerbates the research problem.)

In a related vein, information available from the web is often inconsistent or contradictory or both. Many times, research assignments actually benefit from this ambiguity, because students are required to think critically. But they need to be taught how to triangulate, to cite multiple sources, to piece together an argument that reduces (rather than eliminates) the uncertainty. Thus, if anything, the online environment emphasizes the importance of students' developing strong research skills early in their academic careers.

A real threat in the online environment is in facilitating violations of academic integrity. The extreme example is online term paper clearinghouses, from which students can download a complete paper on any subject for a fee. More common, though, are instances in which students use large portions of online documents without proper attribution or when students are able via the web to locate solutions to standard homework assignments (case write-ups, for example) posted on course web pages at other institutions.

You can take several steps to capitalize on the positive potential offered by computer-based research while avoiding its most egregious pitfalls. First, you should avoid research assignments that lend themselves to standard solutions. Instead, give your assignments a twist, in the form of a unique question that students can research on the web but for which a "canned" solution cannot be found. One of us (Smith) has taken to assigning business case questions based on current events in the news. Second, you must change your written assignments from semester to semester, even if you use the same topic or examples. Fraternities and sororities, for instance, have long kept files of previous homework assignments, exams, and the like. But the advent of the web makes it possible for students to look for solutions at other institutions. (One of us, Smith, found a complete set of case notes to an assigned case on the course web site at another institution.) Simply asking a different question about the same topic forces students to think through their answers, even if they are able to access answers to previously asked questions. Third, for the sake of your colleagues, take steps to protect solutions you post for the benefit of your classes. You probably will be able to create password-protected directories, where you can post case solutions with access restricted to members of that particular class. Finally, you must teach students, and then require them, to cite electronic sources correctly.[10]

THE DIGITAL DIVIDE

We have based most of this discussion on the premise that students typically are comfortable with technology. Our own experience has been that most are quite adept. If anything, their skills and expectations are likely only to increase as technology use makes greater inroads into elementary and secondary classrooms (see *Business Week,* Mar. 19, 2001). However, it is wrong to assume that *all* our students are equally facile and comfortable with technology. As colleges and universities continue to reach out to meet the needs of students from disadvantaged backgrounds, instructors are likely to encounter at least some students who have had limited exposure to technology—that is, who are, and who feel that they are, behind. And as more and more students enter college already tech-savvy, institutions will provide fewer and fewer resources for basic or remedial computer courses, with the result that the weaker students become doubly disadvantaged.

As is typical when students have any weakness, the disadvantaged students likely will attempt to hide the deficiency until it begins to adversely affect their performance. Even then, our experience has been that such students are somewhat evasive and resistant to help. This leaves us with two basic questions: To what extent is it appropriate to *require* the use of technology in courses where technology is not part of the fundamental course content? What can be done to bring the disadvantaged student up to speed?

With regard to the first question, we believe that technology has become a necessary component to mastering the sciences, architecture, business, engineering, to name a few, and that the use of technology can reasonably be required in such disciplines. However, for other disciplines (such as philosophy, foreign languages, dance, or drama) technology use is not a *requirement* for mastery, even if it can facilitate learning. Nor is the fact that

---

10. The APA style guide, for instance, addresses the proper citing of online sources.

technology use makes the course easier to administer for the instructor sufficient justification to require students to use technology in that context. As in all instructional design, *learning objectives* should drive decision-making.

With regard to the second question, we are afraid that here, again, the answer is to add to faculty workload, without the certainty of any reward other than the satisfaction of helping a student through a difficult transition. We ourselves have tutored students in some fairly basic technology skills to help get them up to speed; we also have written up step-by-step instructions for specific tasks and have compiled answers to frequently asked questions (or FAQs). Computer labs, help desks, and support staff can carry some of this load; but even so, we do not see these extra requirements on instructors going away anytime soon.

Concluding Thoughts

This discussion only scratches the surface. In addition to the general implications and immediate pressure points we outlined above, there are many other questions of interest to instructors who are exploring the use of technology to support learning. Formal research is well under way on many of those questions. But, we believe, for the purpose of this discussion, simply asking is sufficient to generate valuable reflection.

• Do the differences between undergraduate and graduate students (level of maturity, experience, etc.) have significance with regard to the effective use of technology in the classroom? For example, do these students have different needs and expectations?

• Likewise, do the differences between part-time and full-time students have significance with regard to the effective use of technology in support of learning?

• What impacts, positive and negative, does technology use have on students with disabilities? How can technology be used to overcome disability-related limitations?

• How are different learning styles affected by technology? Do different technologies support different learning styles? How?

• Is technology changing the definition of "on-campus" instruction? Given the many ways students can interact with faculty and course content outside of the classroom, should we be considering alternatives to the "contact hour" as the appropriate measure of academic credits?

• Should competency in a subject matter be measured in terms of academic credits? Or is there another model to explore regarding the measure of educational achievement?

Our own experiences using technology to support on-campus classes suggest that the positive potential is great. Although we have focused here on common technologies that can be used in a wide variety of contexts, we are also impressed by the potential of particular technologies and software applications that are available to support the unique needs of specific disciplines (e.g., computer-aided design in architecture, virtual prototyping in engineering, textual content analysis in the social sciences, translation tools in linguistics and language studies, to name but a few).

In summary, we are convinced that technology can be used effectively to enrich the learning experience of students. Although realizing the benefits of technology requires significant investment by both institutions and individual faculty members, we believe that they are investments higher education cannot afford not to make.

Further Reading

Brown, David. 1999. *Always in Touch: A Practical Guide to Ubiquitous Computing.* Winston-Salem, N.C.: Wake Forest Univ.

———. 1999. *Electronically Enhanced Education: A Case Study of Wake Forest University.* Winston-Salem, N.C.: Wake Forest Univ.

Brown, David. 2003. *Ubiquitous Computing: The Universal Use of Computers on College Campuses.* Bolton, Mass.: Anker.

———, ed. 2000. *Interactive Learning: Vignettes from America's Most Wired Campuses.* Bolton, Mass.: Anker.

Brown, David, Gordon McCray, Craige Runde, and Heidi Schweitzer, eds. 2002. *Using Technology in Learner-Centered Education: Proven Strategies for Teaching and Learning.* Boston: Allyn and Bacon/Longman.

Covell, Andy. 2000. *Digital Convergence.* Newport, R.I.: Aegis Publishing Group.

11

Discussion Sections

Buffy Quinn and Mark Monmonier

EXPERIENCE HAS TAUGHT US a lot about discussion sections. Both of us have run lecture courses in which teaching assistants handled the discussion sections, and one of us (Quinn) served as a TA for a variety of introductory courses, including a lecture course taught by the other (Monmonier). In this chapter we explore the function of discussion sections in undergraduate instruction and the roles of both TA section instructors and the professor in charge of the course. We also offer a variety of suggestions about how to make discussion sections work.

Discussion sections typically are weekly small-group meetings associated with large-enrollment courses usually intended for first- and second-year students. A three-credit introductory course in the humanities or social sciences might meet twice a week for a one-hour lecture given by the professor plus once a week for a one-hour discussion section taught by a teaching assistant. Lower-division courses of more than fifty students typically have multiple discussion sections, each of whose enrollment rarely exceeds thirty students and is commonly fewer than twenty-five. (We have seen some much smaller sections . . . when scheduled at 8:30 in the morning!) The smaller enrollment in the discussion section allows for greater interaction between students and the TA instructor than the student is likely to have with the professor in the large lecture.

The discussion section is amenable to discussing assigned readings or material already presented in the lecture. But a discussion section can further enrich a course if it fosters a wider variety of activities or formats. These might include lectures by the TA—in a setting less formal than the large class and which encourages questions; roundtable discussions, in which the TA encourages participation by all students (perhaps by calling on them by name); and exercises, on which students work independently or in small groups. Discussion sections also afford an opportunity for the TA to review or clarify lecture material, test student understanding of lectures or assigned readings, hand back and go over examinations, and explore timely instances of issues or problems related to the course. Making use of two or more relevant formats or activities during a single week's discussion section keeps students engaged and motivated. A discussion section also is an excellent time for TAs to encourage students who need help to stop by during office hours or make an appointment.

Productive Partnerships

Discussion sections involve partnerships: the teaching assistant with students in the section, and one or more TAs with the professor in charge of the course. The organizing tool for the partnerships is the syllabus, usually planned by the professor before the TAs are assigned to the course. The typical syllabus identifies a topic for each week's discussion section. Some professors encourage teaching assistants to develop the week's activities themselves; other professors expect TAs to use lesson plans or worksheets the professor has prepared.

Teaching assistants and the professor should meet at least once a week to plan the discussion sections and address any problems students might be having with the course. These "staff" meetings are especially important if more than one teaching assistant has been assigned to the course; students might appreciate a TA who is especially innovative, but they expect all the course's discussion sections to cover essentially the same material. The weekly staff meetings benefit both TAs and professor. They are an opportunity for the professor to review each TA's lesson plan, worksheets, quizzes, and other materials, as well as offer advice about presentation or points requiring careful clarification. They may also serve as a vehicle for TAs to give the professor feedback about the course, because students are usually more willing to discuss problems of clarity or workload with a TA. Such feedback will be especially useful to professors who are restructuring a course, introducing new material, or exploring different approaches. They might use what they learn from the TAs to compile a review sheet or contribute to a list of relevant test questions. And if the TA knows of students who are not completing the assigned readings, in the next lecture the professor could remind the class of the relevance of the readings—perhaps with a pointed illustration of how the textbook complements the lectures and prepares students for examinations.

TAs who plan to devote part of their sections to open discussion can use the staff meeting to review a list of discussion points, which might usefully reinforce or build upon concepts presented in the professor's lecture. Conversely, direct references by the professor during lecture to material already or soon to be covered in the discussion sections promote engagement and a sense of cohesion. Students need these reminders that the lecture and the discussion sections are closely integrated components of the same course. Synergy of TA and professor arising from carefully coordinated teamwork is essential to success and mutual satisfaction.

Weekly staff meetings also allow TAs to plan ahead two or three weeks. Mutual understanding of the week's agenda is especially important when the professor asks TAs to design or organize discussion activities themselves. TAs need time not only to plan their lessons but also to refresh their own understanding of the concepts involved—and perhaps to ask the professor for help or clarification. Advance planning also gives TAs an opportunity to review and reserve an appropriate video or to design worksheets or in-class projects.

In preparing each week's lesson plan, TAs should note the learning goals for that week and make a list of tasks to be accomplished, for example, taking attendance, handing back a quiz or reminding students about a coming test, fielding general questions about recent lectures, introducing a video, splitting up the students for small-group discussions, and having the groups report out. Assigning an estimated time to each task can reduce the likelihood of the TA running out of time. Allowing sufficient time for a satisfactory wrap-up is essential too, even if it means reducing the complexity of a worksheet or viewing a shorter, more carefully selected portion of a video. Estimating time accurately is a skill that takes practice, and the professor and veteran TAs can be especially useful until it is learned.

Another typical TA duty is helping to prepare and then grade examinations and projects. When an examination includes essay questions, the TAs and the professor must develop a mutually workable strategy to ensure that test questions are scored consistently and students receive timely feedback. If two or more TAs are to score the same question, the answer key should include essential parts of a correct answer, the number of points to be awarded for each part, and a rationale for adjusting a student's score upward or downward. Conscientious grading can be extraordinarily time-consuming, so TAs need to plan their personal work schedules to accommodate it. Then after the tests are returned, they should allow time for meetings with individual students to explain why points were lost for particular answers. Although grading is one of the more onerous parts of teaching, it can be highly effective in correcting students' misunderstandings and promoting their effective study habits.

Your First Day

Now that we have addressed the purpose of the discussion section and the role of professor and TA, we would like to offer some practical suggestions—particularly to TAs—for making a discussion section work. Some ideas will work better for certain disciplines than for others, but most can be adapted to an individual situation.

As with any class, it is important that as an instructor you establish the structure and style of your discussion section from the very first day. A syllabus is a good tool for getting lots of information across. Even if the professor in charge of the course doesn't require it, preparing a syllabus of your own for your discussion section is a good idea. At minimum, give students your name, phone number, e-mail address, and office hours. Include a statement regarding the rights and responsibilities of students. Students who are wary about talking to a professor will benefit from feeling that you are accessible and willing to help them throughout the semester.

Include a statement of your policies on tardiness, absences, participation in discussions, make-up assignments, and the like. Your syllabus is an important tool for establishing your expectations for students and your classroom ground rules. Will you allow eating? Do students always have to read assignments *beforehand,* or will reading afterward be okay? Can they come in late? Should they call you if they will miss a discussion section? Make decisions about which issues are important in your management of your classroom.

Students will also have expectations of you. Let them know how you will help them throughout the semester; for example, will you hold review sessions before exams? read drafts of papers? provide your lecture notes for students to review? Emphasize your availability during office hours; then make yourself available. Keeping office hours is a major service and responsibility to your students. Throughout the semester, invite students to seek help from you. Do not wait until the week of the exam to remind them.

When students come to your office, make it worth their time. Have your lecture notes and the textbook handy for students having trouble with the professor's lecture style or those who have missed class. If you choose to provide your lecture notes, we have found that allowing students to manually copy them is more effective than simply letting students photocopy them, because it allows students to ask questions if something is unclear. If several students come to copy your notes at the same time, simply photocopy them so each student has a set to copy from.

A discussion section's small enrollment is an opportunity for students to get to know one another and for you to know them and learn their names. You might never remember all their names, but try to learn as many as possible. We have even discovered that students don't mind your making a mistake if they see you are making the effort. An easy way to begin learning names is to have each student make a name card and tape it to his or her desk such that you (and the rest of the students, if possible) can read it. Ask the students to bring their name cards the first few times the discussion section meets. If you have the resources, take a picture of each student holding the name card. Taking pictures can also be a good "getting-to-know-you" exercise for the entire section. You might let the students take pictures of one another. A seating chart is another good idea; during the next section meeting, give each student a copy of the chart so everyone can begin learning names.

Another good first-day activity is to devote part of the time to introductions. Tell your students who you are (where you are from, what you are studying), then let them say who they are. As an icebreaker, you might ask them to reveal an unusual fact about themselves. We have had students who were struck by lightning (twice!), share Elvis Presley's birthday, and like to skydive. Or you might have students introduce themselves with an alliterative adjective; Mike, for instance, could introduce himself as "Meticulous Mike, because I keep my dorm room so neat," or Sarah as "Sailing Sarah, because I have a boat."

Making Your Discussion Section Worthwhile for Students

Students sometimes view discussion sections as simply that: a time to discuss. While talking about issues and ideas raised in the professor's lecture is an important part of your time with students, you should also work to make sure they feel the time is a valuable part of their coursework. By varying the activities throughout the semester and within each section meeting, you will keep the students engaged and even create an occasion they look forward to.

DISCUSSION

Getting students to participate in a discussion of course issues can be difficult. In a perfect world, they would have completed all the assigned readings, made thoughtful notes, and come to the discussion section with clear insight and sound logical arguments at the ready. But this is no perfect world. They probably will read the assignments, but it is your job to get them talking. Occasionally, students will be so eager to discuss a particular topic that your job will be simply to let everyone have a turn. With topics that are politically sensitive or difficult to grasp, however, students will not always be so eager. One way to encourage participation in discussion is to call on students by name. Ask broad questions to help get them thinking about the material: What is the author's main argument? What is the author's affiliation? What scientific principle is stated here? Very basic questions encourage students to speak up, and thus help get the discussion started.

Sometimes students are reluctant to join a discussion because they are shy about expressing their opinions. If the discussion is moving slowly and you think that might be the cause, suggest that each student write out one idea she or he took from the readings. Then collect the ideas, and redistribute them randomly. Call on one student to read aloud whatever idea he or she was given. Students usually have no problem offering the idea in this scenario, because they are not themselves responsible for it—or how "stupid" it might sound. And you now have an idea up for discussion.

CURRENT EVENTS

Introducing current events into the section helps students relate their academic exercises to the "real world" and is also good for generating class discussion. By looking through the newspaper every day, you will probably be able to collect articles that relate to the discussion or lecture. Photocopy the articles (include the paper's name, page number, and date) to distribute to everyone. Give students a few minutes to read the clipping and then ask,

"Why did I have you read this article?" Students should be able to make the connection between the article and the course and to see the relevance of the course to their lives. If you have several long articles, you can divide the students into several groups and give one to each group. Ask the groups to summarize their article for the rest of the class and highlight points that have been touched on in the course.

WORKSHEETS

Completing worksheets often can be a useful learning activity. For instance, if the professor has introduced a number of difficult terms in lecture, you might design an exercise in which students match terms with their definitions, writers with their works, quotes with their sources, or formulas with their applications. You might also have students work in pairs, so they can help each other. If you walk around the room as they work, offering suggestions and assisting them with difficult questions, you can get a feel for the students' knowledge of the material. Don't think of a worksheet as an exam, and don't present it to the students that way. Instead, remind students that the point of the exercises is to reinforce lecture material. Exercises can be especially helpful as review, when students are studying for the exam.

VISUAL AIDS

Visual aids are valuable tools in stimulating discussion, including overhead transparencies, slides, maps, and videos. Locating appropriate resources takes time, so begin planning for them early. Publishers sometimes provide overhead transparencies with their textbooks; ask the professor whether she or he might have some filed away. You can also make your own transparencies. If you want to use slides, check with the campus library about what might be available, or, again, use your own slides or borrow some from your colleagues. If you do decide to use slides, make sure to arrange *beforehand* for a slide projector with an extra bulb. The library will also be a source of maps, as will the local auto club.

You should also consider using videos. Most commercial videos run about sixty minutes—just a little too long to use in the typical fifty-five–minute discussion section. Movies, which can contain highly relevant and engaging scenes, obviously run too long to play in their entirety. We suggest instead that you select two or three short segments. Note exactly where on the tape the various segments occur, then fast-forward to the first one you will use so it is ready to go. Use your notes to help you find the subsequent sections quickly. During discussion, allow the students to comment on one segment before going on to the next. You will also want to have questions ready in case students have trouble getting started.

GUEST SPEAKERS

Consider having a guest speaker visit your discussion section. You could invite another student or TA, a faculty member in a related department, or someone from the community. In your invitation, explain your rationale for having a guest speaker and what you have in mind for that class meeting. Together, decide on the goal of the speaker's talk, the students' role, and the length of the presentation. Discuss such matters as whether you will need to make photocopies of materials, provide audiovisual aids, or arrange for a larger room. Having a guest speaker does take planning, but students seem to enjoy getting a different perspective. If you teach several sections of the same course, the speaker might not be able to visit each section. But don't let that keep you from the opportunity to enrich even one of your sections with a great guest.

EXAM REVIEW

If the professor in charge of the course does not hold exam reviews, you might want to review lecture material in your discussion sections. Suggest that the students study their notes beforehand and come with their questions ready. This gets students reviewing their notes and helps direct the review session away from the easiest material. Encourage students to answer one another's questions. Remind and reassure them: They are not being tested in the review session, and if they can answer a question there, they should do well on the exam.

An alternative to holding a formal review session before the exam is to review periodically throughout the semester. At the beginning of each section meeting, ask students to look over their lecture notes for that week to see whether they have any questions. This opportunity for the students to ask questions about material while it is fresh in their minds can also alert them to information missing in their notes. You could use this time to invite students to your office hours, too.

Developing Your Skills as a Teacher

Just as a review session is your students' opportunity to get feedback on their learning, asking students for feedback is important in assessing your own development as an instructor. A feedback questionnaire can help you find out how students are responding to your teaching methods and to the discussion section in general. Many departments provide a standard form for evaluating TAs at the end of the semester, but you should consider collecting information throughout the term. One way of getting this feedback is simply to ask your students how you are doing. One TA did this when two of her discussion sections were going well but one was not. She told us that during one meeting of the problem section, she asked the students what could be done to make it go more smoothly. The students suggested that she call on them by name and arrange their desks in a circle. After she made those changes, the students were more engaged and discussions more fruitful. On their end-of-semester surveys, the students commented that they appreciated her listening to them and taking their advice.

Or you can have students comment anonymously. A few weeks into the semester, you could have them all write comments or suggestions on slips of paper, which you then collect for later review. Some students will feel more comfortable doing this rather than commenting directly to you.

Teaching assistants also can learn a lot from one another. Sharing experiences with your office mates will likely happen naturally; but it is also helpful to arrange to meet off campus to discuss what each of you has tried, what has worked, and what still needs work. TAs in our department met in a private dining room at a local restaurant (at no additional cost, since it was an off-night) for discussion, even compiling a list of helpful hints. (That list is a principal source of ideas for this chapter.) Such a joint list gives a meeting focus. Each TA could be encouraged to bring along a favorite teaching idea to share, much like bringing food to a potluck supper. In addition, last semester's list makes a good starting point for reinforcement and refinement next semester. If the meeting's focus is professional development, the department will probably help defray the cost.

Classroom observations by peers or others are another useful learning tool. You might ask the professor in charge of the course to visit one of your sections. It is wise to schedule the observation for after midterms, but not too late in the semester. The observer typically sits in a corner, watches, listens, and takes notes. The observer can see things you might easily overlook, such as your not erasing the board thoroughly, talking too rapidly, writing too small, or using overheads not readily legible at the rear of the room. Observational reports often contain helpful suggestions for presenting concepts and examples, fielding questions, and engaging students in discussion.

Written reports can be especially useful if your mentor visits your class several semesters in a row. Cumulative reporting affords an opportunity to document your specific response to earlier suggestions as well as overall improvements in your teaching that reflect increased experience, knowledge, and self-confidence. Written reports by your mentor can be an important part of your teaching portfolio, as well as helpful in landing a job, a summer session appointment, or an outstanding TA award.

Making a Good Match

Teaching assistants can be justifiably anxious about their assignments to courses and to professors, and professors can have concerns as well. But the matching process need not be overly stressful or arbitrary. Our department, for example, asks TAs and professors to submit their preferences, then the chair and the graduate director sit down to work out the list. Although it is seldom possible to accommodate everyone's first choice, most people are happy with the result. Such polling also helps avoid aggravating the personality conflicts that occasionally arise between faculty and graduate students within a department.

Be wary, though, of letting unnecessary anxieties make for missed opportunities, especially for TAs preparing as future teaching faculty. If your department's curriculum allows, work with different instructors in a variety of introductory courses; doing so can offer especially useful insights into diverse pedagogical challenges and teaching styles. Think of your discussion section as an adventure—to be taken seriously, but also an opportunity to be playful with your teaching at the same time.

12

The Studio Course

Barbara Walter and Jane Hendler

IN A STUDIO COURSE, the processes of learning and creating are as important as the product. Often students work on their assignments during class time, during which both these processes and the product are discussed. Learning evolves over time in successive cycles of action and reflection. Students might rework an assignment several times, so they learn and practice techniques and skills during class and on their own. Through discussions and critiques, students learn how to talk about and evaluate their work.

The Learning Environment

The studio classroom is not a static space. The space must have the potential for interaction and the flexibility to maximize participation and communication. Once you have received your room assignment, visit the space so that you can become familiar with its environment. Feeling comfortable in the classroom can help build your confidence. Talk to someone who has taught in that room; ask about its idiosyncrasies. Does the marching band practice in the room above?

Think about whether the space can accommodate your special needs—for audiovisual equipment, for moveable furniture, for window shades. Will its size accommodate the number of students enrolled? Are there enough seats? Try the acoustics. Will you have to speak loudly to be heard in the back? Try to check the room early enough so that you can change to another room if necessary; if the room cannot be changed, at least you will have time to request shades or more seats. If the assigned room will not always meet the needs of the class, for special occasions perhaps you can reserve a room elsewhere that will, such as a slide projection room, computer cluster, or

seminar room. Also, decide what your multimedia needs are, so you can reserve projectors, videotape monitors, and the like. Is there enough chalk-
board space, or will you need an overhead projector?

Make a list of contact people and their phone numbers. Start with the departmental secretary; in addition, list your faculty adviser, faculty mentor,
and peers. Find out whom to contact if there is a problem with the room or
if you need to leave a note for your class. Do not forget the physical plant,
audiovisual services, and security.

Course Preparation

Review any teaching material given to you. Make sure you understand the
goals of the curriculum, so you can translate those goals into course objectives and requirements. Express these clearly in your syllabus. Once you
have organized the semester in the syllabus, decide what supplies, materials,
and texts will be required in order to accomplish those objectives. First, find
out what is on-hand within the department without having to be ordered.
Which supplies and materials are you responsible for providing, and which
will the students supply? Find out whom you need to contact, how to do the
ordering, and by when. If students pay materials fees, in your syllabus list
what those fees cover.

The curriculum will dictate the more concrete objectives presented in
your syllabus, but also give some thought to other worthy goals. Some of
them might deal with the students' behavior and attitude. For example,
your teaching philosophy might include helping students to become independent thinkers with mutual respect for one another. Begin to form a
strategy for moving toward such goals and any others that students themselves might have. Consider what might bring them to a university. What
might they want from the course and from you? Some students will want job
training, others a good grade or to make their parents happy. You might
want them to learn specific information, values, or social presentation. What
objectives you and your students set for your course will have an impact on
how you teach and what.

Making Assignments

Be sure to make clear the objectives of each of your assignments. State their
requirements, limitations, and variables. Give them time frames and due

dates. Will the assignments stress process, closure, or both? Explain how each will be evaluated. After presenting an assignment, allow time for the students to ask questions. This process of clarification can itself be a valuable part of the students' learning experience. At times, they will ask questions about routine matters, such as due dates or course requirements, which have straightforward answers. But some questions are more appropriately answered with another question, in cases when you want students to make connections through self-discovery. An example of this could be a student asks if something is finished. The question in response could be, "Do you think so? The fact that you asked tells me that you suspect that it is not. Where does the suspicion come from? Can you describe what gives you that impression?" Coming to an answer on their own also can help build students' confidence. Ask a question that will lead students where you want them to go or that helps students to clarify what they are really asking. Finally, pay attention to the questions students are asking; doing so will help you gauge what students are learning and where they are still confused.

A studio course typically includes some work days, during which students work on their assignments during class time. In preparation for a work day, establish guidelines for how you intend to use the time. Emphasize that the students need to attend class on work days. What process they use in completing the assignment is as important as their product. For you to evaluate and guide that process you must witness it. It is advantageous for both you and the students to be able to talk about their creative process during the experience, rather than after the fact. Also, tell the students how to prepare themselves. Do they need special supplies? Do they need to bring research to class? Finally, follow through; do not treat a work day as an occasion not to teach; all that changes is your teaching method.

Critiquing Assignments

There are many ways of assessing an assignment, but critiquing is a particularly useful method. Critiquing gives students immediate verbal feedback and allows for discussion, response, reaction, and further response. Before you bring your students together for a critiquing session, share with them the general goals of the critique and the specific requirements and guidelines that they should focus on for that project.

A distinguishing feature of studio classrooms is the practice of *peer* reviewing or critiquing. Collaborating with their peers to critique assignments maximizes students' learning in a studio environment in several ways. First, students begin to develop a self-reflective response to their own work. Second, they receive constructive feedback that will help them redirect or revise their approach to their project, so they can continue with the next steps toward its completion. Further, through peer critiquing students can strengthen their skills of critical judgment, in that they will learn to make informed responses to a variety of aesthetic approaches. Finally, the emphasis on learning as a *process*, and not merely as a product, is enhanced as students begin to recognize learning as successive cycles of action and reflection.

In addition, peer critiquing contributes to the affective aspects of learning. As students begin to understand their roles and responsibilities in critiquing, they likely will become more self-confident, more independent, and more open-minded in their responses and attitudes toward inquiry. A benefit can be better group dynamics and mutual respect and support among students in the class.

To make peer critiquing effective requires planning and modeling on your part. First-year students, in particular, could find the idea of publicly sharing their projects intimidating or confusing. With a little forethought on your part, you can avoid sessions that become unproductive or frustrating. To help direct the critique you may want to plan a strategy. For example, providing students with a list of questions that may be addressed during the critique may take some of the stress out of speaking for students. This helps to pattern the critique and focuses comments on the object of the critique rather than on the person. Are there particular points that you want the critiques to address? You may also ask the students what points they think should be included in the discussion.

TYPE

You can structure critiques in a variety of ways: instructor versus peer, large-group sessions, small groups, one-on-one formats, and either oral or written feedback. Each type has both advantages and disadvantages, depending on the type of project to be critiqued, how familiar students are with critiquing, classroom dynamics, and time available.

Large-group peer critiques (involving the entire class) can be especially useful if you want to model the process itself. The particular advantages of large-group sessions are that many viewpoints can be expressed and you can more readily facilitate discussion. However, because large-group sessions take longer, time considerations might require you to use small groups instead. Rather than the whole class critiquing twenty students' projects one at a time, it will take less time if students critique in small groups of maybe three or four. Another disadvantage of large groups is that some students will be less assertive and less at ease speaking out.

Small-group critiques have several advantages in addition to encouraging the quieter students to participate and managing classroom time more efficiently. They are more intimate, in that students often respond more candidly to one another's work. But be aware that small groups function less effectively if the group members are friends or if they all tend to be quiet. To avoid such problems, you can appoint a group leader to facilitate or constitute the groups with good mixes of quiet and assertive students. Another peer-critique method is to pair students for one-on-one sessions. This method is effective for the student who would benefit from having just one classmate act as a sounding board, observer, and listener in helping to solve a troublesome problem or approach. Working in pairs can avoid the anxiety caused by large-group sessions, and it allows students to concentrate on just one other project. Its disadvantage is that students receive only one point of view. When you are doing the critique yourself, meeting one-on-one with each student offers the advantage of giving both of you a better sense of how the student is understanding the project.

You also will want to think about whether to use oral or written critique or a combination of both. Consider the time constraints, whether the critiques are intended to be formal or informal, and whether students would benefit from having a record of the discussion. Asking students to write a critique of other students' work could help them to articulate the cognitive processes and their personal reactions to other students' projects. The written critique is shared with the creator of the project.

TIMING

A good time to critique is at the end of the students' first major project. At this stage, with their product completed, they would reflect on the project as a whole and consider alternatives and future directions. Sometimes, however, you will want to critique at an intermediary stage; peer critiquing can be useful here, in that you and the students' classmates can give the student some direction for revision and reshaping to be completed before the completed product is submitted for evaluation. Other times to consider critiquing students' work include at midterm and finals; these are good points at which to use an instructor-student conference, so you can give individual attention to each student's project.

Students always should know ahead of time whether an assignment will be critiqued and what the topic of the critique will be.

An atmosphere of mutual support, trust, and respect is key to a productive critique, but fostering such an atmosphere requires that you establish some ground rules and guidelines for students' participation. Make students aware of your rules prior to the critique session. Here are some guidelines to consider: Everyone should be expected to participate. Both strengths and weaknesses of each project should be discussed. Comments should never be personal, but instead should be directed at the work. Disagreements will develop and some comments will be subjective, but critiques are discussions, not evaluations.

When you are modeling critique for students who are unfamiliar with the process, or when you are facilitating a large-group session, try to keep your own critique focused and relatively short. Avoid letting your critique continue for so long that students become bored and restless. If the class becomes too divided over an issue, or if a situation of class-versus-instructor develops, try to refocus the discussion by asking questions. Or end the discussion temporarily, stating that you will return to the issue later but that the critique needs to move on.

As your students and you become more proficient at critiquing, you should find that questions become the primary mode of interaction. Ask more questions than you make statements. Begin the critique with comments or questions from someone other than the student whose project is under consideration—this strategy helps avoid the situation where the student merely defends or excuses everything before anyone else contributes. The strategy is especially useful if your students are inexperienced or insecure. The following questions can help launch discussion among the group:

• Does this project solve the assigned problem or give convincing alternatives?

- What do you think its creator was trying to do? Your impressions?
- Is there anything you would change? Weaknesses?
- What would you keep? Strengths?

And to the student whose project is being critiqued:

- What questions do you have?
- What did you intend with this project? How clearly has that come across to your audience?

The intent is to have the student realize how the work is understood by others. How close to their goal did they come? What did they want to communicate and was it received as they intended? Be as specific as you can about changes that need to be made before the final evaluation.

SUMMARIZING THE OBJECTIVES

Summary and self-evaluation are important components of critiques. You can prompt a brief summary at the end of each project's critique by asking the student who created it what she or he thinks are its particular strengths or weaknesses and how the project might be revised. Solicit responses from the student; where did he or she have difficulties, and what worked successfully?

In addition, you might find it beneficial to solicit from the class a critique of the assignment itself. Ask students to try to relate the current assignment to future assignments and goals. This exercise will help them to recognize that the particular processes, skills, and knowledge they applied on the current project are a foundation upon which to base their next level of learning.

The Student Portfolio

You might find it helpful to require that each student keep an individual portfolio that will serve as a collection site for past as well as current projects. Portfolios can be used to organize everything a student has worked on to date—including unfinished drafts and notes on future projects, as well as formal presentations. Another way to compile a portfolio is to have students select their most representative works—works to date, best effort, or works in progress. A portfolio also can be used for course evaluation purposes.

A particular advantage of having students compile studio portfolios is that they are a portable record of work that students can carry outside the university setting to job interviews or to prospective graduate schools.

Grading

In a studio course, grading is less objective than in courses where grades are based on written tests. But that is not to say that evaluation in a studio course is purely subjective. Your grades typically will be based on a variety of criteria. Because the creative process itself is also important, the product is not the only variable to consider. In a studio course, what progress the student makes from the beginning to the end of the semester might be important; work ethic, attitude, effort, and risk taking also might be factors you could consider.

Whatever balance of factors you decide to include in your evaluation, outline your criteria for grading in your syllabus, then stick to them. Clearly state your objective and subjective standards. And always apply the same criteria to everyone in the class; you cannot change the standards from individual to individual. On the due day of the assignment, review the assignment's objectives and other criteria with the class. What were the immediate goals? Follow the guidelines that you set when you gave the assignment.

Resolving Conflicts in the Studio

In the intimacy of a studio course, teaching to the individual student as well as the group takes on new meaning. In contrast to the large lecture course, in the studio course you come to know each student by name and face, and that familiarity often makes student more willing to speak out. Because of this greater opportunity for personal interaction, for both students and instructor, compliments, conflicts, and complaints are more apparent. The compliments are easy to deal with; the conflicts and complaints are more difficult to resolve.

If a conflict arises between you and a student, or between classmates, try to establish the history of the conflict. Is it a simple misunderstanding or miscommunication? Is it a difference of opinion? Has it been building over time, or has it just started? A conflict or complaint is much easier to resolve while it is still small. What is your point of view as the instructor? What is the point of view of the student? If you feel that you cannot easily resolve the situation, get some help. If you need help, go to your adviser or mentor first. Explain the situation and ask for advice. If the situation is still unresolved you may need to ask for a mediator who will meet with the parties who are involved. A faculty member or department chairperson may agree to mediate.

Because of the subjective nature of the studio course, conflicts over grades may occur. If you have been as specific as possible in the syllabus listing the requirement and basis for evaluation and you have stuck to the requirements when assessing grades, you may be able to use the syllabus to point out areas of deficiency. Disputes on the subjective side of the evaluation are more difficult to contend with. It will help if you have listened carefully during the critiques to the responses from the whole class. Writing notes to yourself after the critiques to keep track of each student's progress on projects and participation in critiques will help immensely. Include notes on the general responses from the other students. Also write down your response. When a student questions a grade, you can refer to your notes to address areas of dispute. If the conflict is unresolved, ask your mentor to review the student's work. Give the mentor your guidelines and requirement so he or she has a clear idea of what the student was expected to do. You may need to have a meeting with the three of you, the mentor, your student and yourself to resolve the problem. Work toward the best outcome for all involved.

13

Optimizing Laboratory Learning

Joanne D. Burke, Christine L. Bean, and Ruth A. Reilly

There are two knowledge explosions in science education, and teachers must be able to deal with both of them. They must be able to convey a framework of facts and theory (theoretical knowledge), as well as show students how to obtain the knowledge practically. With the advent of new technology (including the use of computers and the Internet), the "how" may become as important as the theoretical knowledge.

—*Boulton and Panizzon*

THE SCIENCE LABORATORY offers a unique opportunity to delve into scientific concepts and to advance higher-order thinking skills for students as well as instructors. It should be the place where students discover and learn the process of doing science. The National Commission on Mathematics and Science Teaching for the 21st Century report, "Before It's Too Late: A Report to the Nation" (2000), has emphasized the need for America's students to raise their performance in mathematics and science in order to succeed and remain competitive in an integrated global economy (National Commission on Mathematics and Science College Teaching for the 21st Century 2000). The purpose of this chapter is to review the theoretical role of the laboratory experience, to consider the role of instructors and students, and to identify specific guidelines for the planning and execution of a successful science laboratory experience.

Learning Theories, Technology, and the Laboratory Experience

LEARNING THEORIES

Laboratory participation is a distinguishing component of science classes, offering a number of unique learning opportunities. The laboratory is a place where students can test theoretical concepts in a hands-on environment. A laboratory environment that encourages active student participation can develop and reinforce important interdisciplinary skills such as critical thinking, problem solving, use of group dynamics, and writing across the curriculum. Laboratory work is also an opportunity for reflection and discussion, which enhances learning (Lazarowitz and Tamir 1994).

Students who might otherwise feel lost in a large science lecture benefit from interaction with fellow students and instructors in the lab's more intimate format. To the extent that the laboratory and its small-group work can offset the impersonal nature of a large lecture, the laboratory experience provides a powerful resource through which students can be reached in a more personal manner.

But just because a student spends time in a laboratory does not necessarily mean that true learning occurs. Unfortunately, many labs follow a "cookbook" approach, in which students are told what to do, follow set procedures in verification-type experiments, and enter their all-too-predictable results in preprinted laboratory worksheets. Little effort is made to creatively involve them in the scientific problem or in the design of the experiment, or to engage them in group work to analyze and discuss the observed experimental outcomes (Hilosky, Sutman, and Schumuckler 1998; Tobin, Tippins, and Gallard 1994). Even if there is some merit in having students learn to follow instructions, cookbook labs are a missed opportunity to develop students' higher-order thinking skills.

Pedagogical strategies that can enhance student learning in the laboratory include the incorporation of *cooperative learning*, in which students work together to analyze the problem, develop strategies for assessment, and consider rationales for the results. The students often realize they are in the process of learning and discovery together (Huff 1997; Towns and Grant 1997). In a cooperative learning environment, content is imparted primarily through learning activities, not through formal lectures. For students accustomed to passively sitting back and taking notes, the challenge to accept responsibility for their own learning and that of their lab mates can be a novel one.

For example, Glendon and Ulrich reported that nurse educators were successful in implementing cooperative learning strategies in the teaching of their courses (1992). The researchers noted that the change in role from lecturer to facilitator for the teachers, as well as from passive learner to active participant for the students, could feel uncomfortable initially. But, if the instructors explained their rationale for the new course design and helped to facilitate progression to a more cooperative format, the results could be quite impressive and the skills that students developed enduring. "Cooperative learning should be considered whenever the desired learning outcomes include higher-order thinking, concept formation, problem solving, inference making, conflict resolution, or values development" (Kleffner and Dadian 1997, 66).

Some concerns about cooperative learning have been voiced. Doesn't the process slow down above-average achievers? No—as long as group goals and individual accountability are components of the model (Huff 1997). What about grade inflation, and poor students coasting on the efforts of their more-capable classmates? Again no; with good planning, teaching experience, and individual as well as group evaluations, grade inflation need not occur (Glendon and Ulrich 1992; Huff 1997).

Another useful teaching model for laboratories is the use of *case studies,* as advocated by Herreid (1994). In the process of analyzing case studies and arriving at solutions, students are engaging in higher-order thinking processes. Cases can be particularly well suited to illustrating topical societal issues. Used in conjunction with current science reports and press releases, case studies can enhance the relevancy of scientific principles to everyday life. To be effective, case studies should be relevant, interesting, issue-oriented, short, conflict-provoking, decision-forcing, and have teaching value (Herreid 1997/1998).

Still other researchers look favorably on *problem-based learning.* Des Marchais, for example, has discussed a problem-based curriculum used at the Sherbrooke School of Medicine in Quebec, Canada (1993). Students there described it as an approach to learning that was more participative and dynamic than traditional instruction. They felt that it motivated self-learning; forced integration of basic science information; and ultimately made studying more concrete, enjoyable, and rewarding.

Technology and the Science Laboratory

An emerging trend in the science laboratory is the use of computer programs that allow students to "conduct" simulated experiments. For instance, with such a program students can manipulate Mendelian traits in genetic experiments to elicit different outcomes without actually having to wait for crossbreeding or offspring. Unlike the real thing, computer specimens behave predictably during experiments, and no critters unexpectedly escape from unlocked cages (Jensen 1998). Often the simulation programs are less costly than animals are, and they bypass the need for institutional permission to conduct live animal experiments. Human and animal rights activists in particular tend to view such simulations as positive alternatives.

But do the simulations really provide an equivalent laboratory experience, or are they merely an alternative? In a real biology laboratory, not all the experimental animals live, some escape their confines, and others behave in unexpected ways. Unlike an actual laboratory setting, these streamlined, programmed experiments largely bypass the need for students to develop unique solutions to real problems. Students are not required to make detailed observations of unexpected results, because a simulation program offers only a limited number of outcomes.

Jensen identifies two major concerns about the increase in the use of computer simulation programs in the biology laboratory (1998). First, as the quality of simulation programs improves and their use becomes more widespread, the cost of such software will decrease, making it harder to convince administrators that hands-on experiments are still needed. When comparing the costs of laboratory supplies with the one-time purchase of a computer simulation, administrators could well favor the latter. Second, computer simulation programs are becoming more available at the same time that distance learning is growing exponentially. Although many experiments can in fact be done at home, in a student's kitchen, can that experience of science really be equated to a well-designed, interactive laboratory course? As educators, we need to think about whether we want to teach our students "that science is a computerized simulation with predictable results, or that science represents life filled with unpredictable surprises" (Jensen 1998, 249).

Clearly, computer simulation programs are not the same as an actual hands-on laboratory course, but they do represent one aspect of a far-reaching explosion in technological advances available to the science educator. Whether we choose simulation or hands-on experiments will depend largely on our goals and objectives for the laboratory session. If your objective is to demonstrate the polymerase chain reaction to general microbiology students, a simulation or demonstration could be sufficient because the cost and time of an entire class performing the activity could be prohibitive. On the other hand, if your objective is to teach hematology students to perform white blood cell counts, each student must have the opportunity to actually perform the cell count procedure repeatedly. Judicial use of simulation programs can help to expand the limits of our science laboratories as well as stretch science education budgets.

Computer access and programming provide powerful tools for teaching science concepts and applications, too. Because computer programs run most sophisticated laboratory equipment, it is essential that students gain familiarity with the computer. Statistical programs allow for the storage, manipulation, and analysis of data. Computer linkages give students easy access to a host of reference libraries; and because such links typically are anonymous, students who feel intimidated asking for help might see reputable web sources as places to get information in a non-threatening environment (Nickerson 1995).

Planning and Implementing Enriching Laboratory Experiences

LAB INSTRUCTOR RESPONSIBILITIES

To make a science course and its coordinating lab coherent and successful, the course instructor(s) needs to ensure that instructional efforts are coordinated among everyone: faculty members, laboratory instructors, and all those involved in the course (whether the latter are laboratory coordinators, graduate teaching assistants, or undergraduate TAs). It is the faculty member's responsibility to clearly identify the goals for the lab; and the lab instructors must have a clear understanding of those expectations. Everyone should have reviewed the department and university professional codes of conduct and standards. Everyone should have a copy of the course text, lab books, supplemental materials, rosters, and syllabus. In addition, the course faculty member should commit to giving the lab instructors (especially TAs) feedback on their own progress in a timely fashion throughout the term.

Teaching a college science laboratory course can be very challenging. However, experienced faculty, former laboratory assistants, and published articles are available to provide insight and guidance. Many constructive, practical suggestions for teaching assistants were discussed by Mannara and associates (1966). Because laboratory assistants act as liaisons between the faculty in charge of the course and the students in the laboratory, the assistants' abilities to guide students in the application and discovery of scientific principles are critically important. Cooperation and communication among assistants is essential when a course has multiple lab sections. Ideally, everyone should meet together weekly to review materials, go over successes and problems that arose during the previous laboratory, and plan strategies for the upcoming one. By meeting together, all the lab assistants hear the lead faculty member's message simultaneously, and that enhances the continuity and consistency of the course. Working together to establish standards for student learning and evaluation is critical. Policies regarding switching labs, assignment expectations, grading, plagiarism, and attendance should be the same for all lab sections. If possible, all students in the course should receive information about the laboratory during the lecture session, so that when they disperse into their individual lab sections they are all "on the same page."

Students need to know that the lab instructors they are working with are competent and committed to helping them understand and master the material. *Understanding* goes beyond just reciting back information given out in a class; it cannot be transmitted from instructor to student. Instead, it is students who have to grasp the concepts, process them, and ultimately develop some type of mental model for their own understanding (Newton 1996). Just as instructors have the responsibility to teach and guide, students must take responsibility for learning in the laboratory. When all parties are committed to the learning process, the science laboratory provides a unique framework and opportunity to advance students' understanding of and excitement for science.

PLANNING THE COURSE

Goals and objectives

Usually the science department or lead faculty member is charged with initially designing the laboratory course, although input from all parties involved can provide additional theoretical and practical guidance. Good planning is the first step in a successful teaching experience. The goals and objectives of the course typically will not only reflect the specifics of that course but also embrace the fundamental principles of scientific inquiry.

A review article in 1994 by Lazarowitz and Tamir presented four guidelines for designing science laboratory experiences. Science laboratories should provide (1) concrete experiences and help students confront their misconceptions about scientific processes; (2) opportunities for data manipulation through the use of microcomputers; (3) opportunities for developing skills in logical thinking and organization, especially with respect to science–technology–society issues; and (4) opportunities for building values, especially as they relate to the nature of science. If you are responsible for a lab section, establishing clear goals and objectives for each laboratory experience strengthens your students' entire course experience, because lab sections are an essential component of any science class.

Your goals and objectives for the lab should consider the needs and interests of your students as well as the level of the course. You can enhance the match between the laboratory experiences and the students' own experiences by assessing the students' backgrounds and competencies during the first laboratory session. Either a written test or lab practical can be used to assess their abilities and knowledge from previous courses. A short competency quiz on the basic skills necessary for success in the lab can help identify those students who might need extra help. Such an evaluation also could include laboratory techniques such as pipetting or making a simple solution or students' ease in using the computer. It is important to articulate what skills are required for successful completion of the course so that student competencies and deficiencies can be identified early in the term. Then you can choose strategies to address deficiencies and ensure students' progress toward mastery of those laboratory skills.

Your assessment should also serve to alert students if the course is not appropriate for them—whether too basic or too advanced for their current level of expertise. Each student should have taken any required prerequisites; department policy might even require students to have earned a minimum grade in those prerequisites or to have taken the courses recently. But meeting course prerequisites does not necessarily translate into students' possessing the cognitive and technical skills necessary for success (Modell and Michael 1993). So it is imperative that students understand at the beginning of a course what abilities and knowledge they need.

When planning a lab session, it is essential to develop goals that are reasonable given the time, economic constraints, intellectual capacity, and environmental impact of the laboratory experiments. You need to consider the length of the laboratory period and what students reasonably can accomplish in that time frame. Keep in mind, too, that it typically takes longer to conduct a laboratory with novice students than with more experienced students. If possible, it is wise to conduct any new experiment the first time with a relatively small number of students so you can fine-tune it before you present it to a large group.

Remember that a science laboratory is an opportunity to offer students practical learning strategies. To accommodate their many learning styles, it can be beneficial to offer several types of experiments. Varying your instructional style within the lab curriculum to include survey work, observation, bench experiments, simulations, computer work, etc. will keep students from becoming too comfortable or bored, as well as give students with different learning styles a chance to succeed.

Developing course material and evaluation strategies

Course materials help communicate to students the specific goals and objectives of the course. The course syllabus, course assignments, and evaluation parameters serve as a contract between the faculty, including the lab assistants, and the students. The tools to be used to evaluate students should be established prior to the first laboratory, and the evaluation criteria should be clearly defined.

In a laboratory course, experiments and their subsequent documentation can be key components of the laboratory experience and evaluation. Providing model laboratory reports can help students understand the basic elements of scientific documentation and reporting. To ensure that each student develops individual technical skills, students should keep individual lab journals to document their work, results, and discussions of results. You should collect the journals periodically throughout the semester and provide each student with concrete feedback. A student's lab journal should document how the various lab tasks are being divided among group members. Your timely review of lab journals can make clear when development of the group process requires tasks to be rotated.

By using the data from class experiments, students make concrete examples of the scientific method come to life. In the discussion portion of their reports, students should consider why the experiment did or did not work. Remember that it takes time and experience to write a good lab report. Making students' first assignments simpler and later assignments increasingly complex allows them to develop their reporting skills and demonstrate their mastery of those skills as they improve. To guide their development, it is important that you provide timely and concrete verbal or written feedback.

Students are not the only ones who benefit from feedback. At minimum, ask students to complete a short, midpoint evaluation to appraise the course; you should report back the results to the class. An evaluation midway gives you time to make changes in your teaching before the conclusion of the term (Modell and Michael 1993). Also, from such an evaluation students find out how their classmates feel about the course, and some might realize their individual concerns are not shared by the majority of class members. Changes can yield big rewards for both students and instructors. By administering such a survey, you demonstrate that you take student feedback seriously and are responsive to it; students feel empowered by voicing their concerns and playing a role in shaping future course outcomes.

Lecture and laboratory familiarity

It is critically important to fully understand the theory behind the laboratory being conducted. One of the best ways to prepare is to attend class lectures with your students. This allows you to hear exactly what the students are hearing so that you will be better equipped to answer their questions and expand on the concepts presented in the lecture and laboratory meetings.

It is also highly advisable to practice each laboratory experiment prior to the students performing it, preferably in the room where the lab will be held. It is important for you to know in advance whether all the necessary materials and equipment are available and in working order. Determine where the extension cords and electrical outlets are. Can your overheads be seen and your voice heard in the back of the room? Where is that extra bulb for the projector, and how do you change it? All these things require planning, and such planning can make the difference between a smooth lab and a chaotic one. A smooth-running laboratory means that everyone can spend their time in the laboratory on the experiment at hand, not on mechanical problems. Being prepared will build your self-confidence and credibility, and it minimizes students' frustration.

CONDUCTING THE LABORATORY

Getting to know students is essential to good teaching

One of your first goals should be to get to know your students by name as early as possible. Introducing yourself, announcing and posting office hours, providing your telephone number and e-mail address, and encouraging questions all promote open communication. It is also important to provide very clear expectations of the students during the initial laboratory, as this sets the tone for the term. TAs especially—while they should be open to students' questions and concerns—need to establish that they are in charge from the very first day.

Beginning each lab by briefly reviewing what was covered in the last one provides continuity and helps students to see the big picture. By eliciting questions or concerns about what has been covered to date, you give students an opportunity to review and clarify their course experiences. When you introduce the current lab experiment, state its goals and objectives; at the end of the laboratory, review how these goals and objectives were addressed.

A lab instructor must plan for constructive ways to help students develop the skills they need. Move around the laboratory; be an active observer of the students' skill levels so you can assist them in developing their technique. Encourage questions and group problem solving. Prompt students to consider possible answers based on scientific principles and logic as a way of approaching problems, which will benefit them in writing their lab report discussions. Do not ask questions that can be answered by yes or no; ask open-ended questions to develop students' critical-thinking skills (Lamb 1997). Instead of a simple question such as "What quality control measures were used in this experiment?" ask "What additional quality control measures could be added to this experiment to ensure reliable and accurate results?"

Incorporating safety information

You must give students concrete safety information and emergency guidelines (Lamb 1997). During the first laboratory session, present the safety protocols in both oral and written formats. Information in the safety manuals should be reviewed and updated annually to remain accurate and comprehensive. Requiring students to review the safety manual and to sign and date their name on a log sheet also reinforces the importance of being familiar with safety protocols.

The following information should be discussed and written in a student safety manual:

• *Safety and emergency equipment.* Review all safety equipment (safety shower, eye wash station, fire extinguisher, chemical spill kit, fire alarm, telephone, first aid kit) so students are comfortable with where to find the equipment and how to use it.

• *Chemical safety.* Material Safety Data Sheets should be kept for each chemical used in lab and accessible to students. Proper handling and storage of chemicals should be reviewed.

• *Blood-borne pathogens/infectious agents.* If human blood or body fluids are used in the laboratory, students should be encouraged to get a hepatitis B vaccination. Universal Precautions must be described for each procedure the students will perform (see Bean 1990). Discuss the equipment available (gloves, eye shields, lab coats, safety hoods) and explain the procedure for reporting an accident (include a sample accident reporting form in the student safety manual). Explain the policies for bench top cleaning and hand washing.

• *Waste management.* Describe disposal policies for chemical and biohazardous materials (including contaminated gloves and paper towels) and for sharp objects (glass slides, pipettes, needles) in puncture-proof containers.

• *Instrument safety.* Before each lab, check that instruments have been properly maintained; check electrical outlets and cords. (Bean 1998)

Encourage additional exploration

Encourage students to explore topics on their own, on the Internet, and in disciplinary journals; but do not assume that all students already have experience in seeking out these resources. As an early laboratory exercise, plan a visit to the campus library for a demonstration of how to locate such information. This activity is particularly useful for courses at the freshman and sophomore levels. Reinforce the lesson by requiring students to find a current journal article pertaining to the laboratory experiment and turn it in. You could also require that students' laboratory reports cite Internet and journal articles in their abstracts and/or discussion sections. Exploration of this kind helps develop students' problem-solving skills and ensures that they are able to find and use these resources for future coursework.

Conclusion

The college science laboratory offers students the opportunity to integrate theory gained in lecture with practical hands-on experiences in lab. Well-planned and executed labs will expand the students' knowledge base as well as enhance the learning experience for both students and lab instructors. A well-prepared, knowledgeable lab instructor is an effective liaison between students and the course instructor. The information presented in this chapter can help prepare you for this important and challenging role.

14

Teaching Writing-Intensive Courses

Steve Braye

EVERY TEACHER TEACHES WRITING.

This seemingly simple premise ushered in a wave of educational re-
forms, from writing-intensive courses to writing centers to writing-across-
the-curriculum movements. But while the premise might seem simple, the
implications arising from the premise were not. Realizing that premise required changes at all levels of teaching, in every discipline, in every classroom. It changed the way we look at thinking, disciplinary knowledge,
assessment, and pedagogy. And it meant encouraging every teacher to see
the relationship between what they were teaching and their students' abilities to communicate complex thoughts through writing. No small task.

Even more, pedagogical and curricular innovations such as writing-
intensive courses and writing-across-the-curriculum movements are only initial steps in realizing the implications of using writing to reflect complex
thinking processes. In the thirty years that colleges and universities have developed programs to raise faculty awareness and knowledge about the teaching of writing, our collective knowledge about writing and its relationship to
thinking has steadily increased, helping us to improve what we do and how
we do it.

Understanding the basis for each of these movements will influence how
you conceive of your own teaching and courses, what assignments you develop to encourage learning, and how you interact with your students.
Whether you teach classes of three hundred or thirteen, you *will* be expected to use writing-intensive strategies to improve the writing and thinking of your students.

This chapter will help you learn about and apply these strategies to your own teaching, so you can understand why they are important pedagogical innovations and how they can improve your teaching. We will explore why these innovations have come about, what they offer you, and how you can use them to generate the best learning environments possible for your students—no matter what level, discipline, or subject. Finally, we will explore the many possibilities of writing-intensive courses, why colleges and universities have embraced them in various forms, and what practical educational means you might explore in order to teach more effectively.

What Are Writing-Intensive Courses?

Defining writing-intensive (WI) courses is not a simple task. There is no one definition that is accepted from school to school, no one description that can satisfy the myriad of purposes and goals each institution sets for writing-intensive courses. Even worse, any one description, from the quantitative—"A writing-intensive course should assign at least five pages of writing per week"—to the qualitative—"Writing is used as a tool for learning as well as for communication"—can set off heated discussion among faculty members, who often disagree on the best ways to use writing across the disciplines.

But there are general principles that describe writing-intensive courses, principles that we will explore here in order to become familiar with the "writing-intensive" label and gain some sense of what WI programs attempt to do. These principles can help you incorporate writing-intensive concepts into your classes, improving the learning of your students in every course.

Writing-intensive definitions generally include the following elements, in one form or another:

- Emphasize the writing process.
- Require significant amounts of writing.
- Assign a variety of writing types.
- Offer discipline-specific writing instruction.
- Write to develop critical thinking.

In the discussion that follows, we will attempt to define these elements and explore assignments that will help you develop writing assignments in your own classes.

Emphasize the Writing Process

Taking class time to emphasize the writing process often turns courses that assign plentiful writing into writing-intensive courses. Every course uses writing in some degree to achieve course objectives. But writing-intensive courses assist students through that process, helping students to reinforce what they learned and practiced in first-year writing courses while helping them develop a more mature writing process.

Learning to write is a developmental process, which needs reinforcing at each level of a student's educational development. Often, faculty fail to recognize this fact and become frustrated when their students' writing does not match the thinking an upper-level course requires. First-year writing requirements often attempt to introduce students to the stages in a mature writing process, offering time for them to practice these stages so they can *begin* to develop a mature writing process of their own. Writing-intensive courses are based upon the idea that with further emphasis on these stages, along with time to develop these stages as one's complex-thinking ability develops, students will continue to develop a more mature writing process— one that matches more closely with the critical-thinking abilities that a carefully structured college curriculum will inspire.

Emphasizing the writing process means discussing the stages that writing takes as we move from assignment to idea to draft to completed project. Often, it means helping students practice each stage of writing: prewriting, writing, revising. Too often, instructors assign papers and expect wonderfully written products to magically appear three weeks later. They might even assume that students used the entire three weeks provided to produce the thinking and writing that is submitted. More often, though, students are motivated by deadlines, meaning we receive rough drafts as final products, often the first rough draft the student produces. So instead of evaluating writing produced by a mature writing process, we evaluate what was produced in a forty-eight–hour blitz.

By breaking down assignments and requiring students to practice each stage of the writing process, faculty encourage students to develop more sophisticated writing skills and end up evaluating more complex projects. This is easily done. Rather than basing assignments on a final deadline ("I'm giving you the assignment today, and I expect to see it in three weeks"), faculty can ask for the assignment in stages, helping students to recognize how a strong written product should be developed. You might ask for a proposal or outline or memo the first week, demonstrating not only where students are in their thinking about the project but also that they have used the first week to work through the prewriting stage. During the second week, you might ask to see introductions, bibliographies, or pieces of the project, pushing students to the second stage of the writing and thinking project. This allows you to require students to participate in revising workshops, visit the writing center, or undertake other activities that help them develop their revising skills. You end up with better overall projects, more reflective of the thinking and writing the student can achieve; and students submit work they recognize as stronger, helping them to learn more from completing the project and often earning them higher evaluations.

This plan does not mean catering or pandering to students in any way. It means demanding the thinking appropriate to the assignment and enabling students to see how to reach this level. In fact, it means precisely defining the thinking you want them to achieve in the assignment and designing the assignment accordingly. Therefore, how you break down the assignment varies with the complexity of the assignment itself. The process instructors might use to break the assignment into stages depends upon the level of the course (200, 300, 400); the type of student enrolled (major, minor, non-major); and the writing experiences students have had prior to the course. A 200-level introductory course for majors and non-majors, often taken by first- and second-year students, would use a far different writing process than would a senior seminar in the major, where the level of critical thinking required might be raised significantly, causing certain writing problems, but where the disciplinary form might be considered old hat. So the maturity of the writing expected matches the thinking expected.

Finally, foregrounding the writing process helps instructors encourage students to connect writing and knowing. In this way, students recognize the importance of the writing process to every discipline and put aside questions of the evaluation process ("Why grade my writing? This isn't an English course"), which can take time away from the teaching we hope to do. You help students to recognize that a poor writing process influences their ability to think about a subject (more on this below), and a poor paper might reflect a poor process and lack of thought, rather than an inability to understand the material.

Require Significant Amounts of Writing

Any course that focuses on the writing process will demand some writing. But past research has demonstrated that students do not write as often as they need to in order to develop their mature writing process. They might write one paper for every class. But spending two or three weeks (at most, in many cases) out of fifteen weeks practicing writing does not provide the practice necessary for students to develop their writing process. They need to "write every day," experiencing the process over and over again. So most WI programs ask for "significant" writing, or some variation on that phrase.

Yet this seemingly simple requirement still proves to be highly contentious. How does the campus define "significant"? For most instructors, who do not understand the writing process well themselves, "significant" can simply imply a greater number of pages, with no thought given to the complexity of the writing required. But it needs to mean both.

Significant writing offers students plenty of opportunities to experience each stage of the writing process and demands that they produce writing that challenges their writing and thinking abilities. Therefore, just assigning one longer paper will not do. Instructors need to structure their courses to offer students multiple opportunities that vary enough (see the discussion of variety below) to demand that they practice many different parts of the process. In the end, then, students finish a course feeling they have completed lots of writing that has challenged and developed their writing process.

Assign a Variety of Writing Types

Writing-intensive courses assign "lots of writing" that challenges the writing and thinking abilities of students on many different levels. The writing might ask students to explore a concept just introduced. Define a concept introduced in earlier courses. Summarize a discussion or series of articles. Create poster sessions, lab reports, speeches, or newspaper articles. This variety of assignments requires students to use a number of different writing modes to develop and present different kinds of thinking and knowing.

Teaching that uses different modes of writing recognizes that writing forms reflect and value certain kinds of thinking. Resumes, a strict formal presentation of oneself, serve a specific purpose to a clearly identified public audience. Note-taking proves to be much more individualistic and abstract. Writing-intensive courses want to offer students experience with all types of writing, because one type, note-taking, for example, might shape the ideas that emerge in another, perhaps a formal report. At the same time, WI courses recognize that a student's inability to handle the former writing task will impact the performance on the latter. Writers cannot ignore one stage in idea development and expect to overcome it, and writing helps to develop ideas at every stage.

Thus, WI courses encourage a variety of writing assignments. Two pairs of terms have come to define the major distinction here: *formal* or *informal* writing, and *writing-to-learn* and *writing-to-communicate*. The former pair focuses more on audience; the latter focuses more on purpose.

Formal writing follows specific structures that are accepted and understood by the intended audience. It nearly always reflects some completed act of thinking. You prompt formal writing when you require a lab report, a book review, an essay, or some other completed structure that you can model for students. Formal writing has a clearly intended audience and stresses revision and accepted language conventions (usually by emphasizing grammar in the evaluation).

Informal writing reflects the formative thinking process of the student. It is messy, yet coherent. It is going someplace, but the odds are that students need to reflect upon this mess in developing complex thinking. You prompt informal writing when you assign in-class writing assignments, reading-response questions, or reaction papers. Informal writing usually serves the writer, offering the chance to put forth ideas in a more disorganized manner, then reflect and revise these ideas for later use.

Both types of writing can be evaluated, but the criteria for evaluation are quite different. Informal writing evaluation focuses much more on the thinking process, while formal writing evaluation will be based upon effectiveness of argument, use of form, and language conventions. And both lead to important development of complex thought.

Writing-to-learn tends to be the same as informal writing. Here, students are writing for themselves, to learn the material of the course. You might ask students to summarize some key concepts, offer questions to assigned readings, or reflect upon an idea in a few sentences.

Writing-to-communicate, like formal writing, has a different audience and purpose. This writing is public writing, using the accepted conventions and styles of a discipline to communicate within that discipline. Students might demonstrate their ability to write using technical language, a lab report format, or accepted disciplinary documentation styles. Certainly, students learn a great deal by practicing this type of writing. But the label comes from the goal of the writing; here, the goal is to take ideas and present them in accepted formats so they can be communicated to an outside audience.

Whatever terms might be used on your campus, accomplishing writing in a variety of ways helps students to develop their ideas better and often more quickly while practicing all aspects of their writing process.

Offer Discipline-Specific Writing Instruction

First-year writing courses generally focus upon one of two outcomes: preparing students to write for college (i.e., giving them the basic tools to adapt to writing in the disciplines) or introducing students to the stages in the basic writing process while offering them the opportunity to develop their own process. Given the limited time such courses have available, both outcomes are not possible. In many cases, campuses with WI programs ask first-year writing courses to introduce the writing/thinking process while helping departments design WI courses to teach discipline-specific writing.

There are a number of advantages to this approach. Faculty within the discipline are practitioners of writing from that discipline. They are experts in that style of writing, which an instructor who teaches first-year writing courses could never be. They understand how to create knowledge in the discipline, how to make claims, what burdens of proof exist, and how the writing structures can be manipulated to specific ends. With this departmental approach, then, students learn from experts, rather than from novices who might understand the general approach of writing in the discipline but who have not practiced and experienced the form themselves.

Second, the writing assignments that rely upon these discipline-specific structures are integral to making knowledge in the discipline. In many first-year writing courses that teach "writing in the disciplines," a knowledge base and assignment must be manufactured in order for assignments to require writing "in science" or "in social science." But when these writing forms are taught within the discipline, serving the objectives of a course in that discipline, the writing is not merely a constructed activity designed to give experience in the form. Instead, the form is the appropriate means of expressing the knowledge being created in the form, one integral to the other. Therefore, students can see what the form enables them to express and why.

Finally, using writing in this way enables instructors to teach variety in the writing process, helping students to understand that different kinds of papers require different writing processes. A biology lab report, for example, might be written in a linear fashion, from beginning to end, because the parts of the report reflect the actual process of hypothesis and planning and experiment. Some students find that this linear structure reflects their own ways of organizing knowledge and might find writing this type of paper easier. An argument in philosophy, though, requires a more holistic approach, where students can start anywhere in the process they choose, engaging in lots of revision and rethinking of the entire piece. Students who tend to like playing with abstract concepts might find this approach easier and enjoy attempting to pull together the whole project. Such writing instruction helps students to see that there is not a single writing process. We vary our approach based upon the kinds of thinking and arguing we are generating.

Write to Develop Critical Thinking

There is one major reason that colleges have embraced writing-intensive courses when they might be less than supportive of first-year writing courses themselves: the connection between writing and critical thinking. If one accepted conclusion has come out of research about writing, it is that writing promotes critical thinking in ways that no other intellectual activity can match. This is not to suggest that writing is some sort of potion, enabling students to magically master all kinds of thinking. Instead, it suggests that the activity of writing (active, dialogic, and recursive) requires many of the thinking processes (assimilation, evaluation, analysis) that we associate with higher levels of thinking, levels of thinking it can be difficult to access in other ways.

Like most discussion of critical thinking, William Perry's work with developmental thinking and college-age students serves as the starting point. If students do enter college seeing black-and-white perspectives, omitting grays and areas of dispute, writing activities demand that they translate their thinking into coherent arguments to delineate the supporting arguments and ramifications for their ways of thinking/acting. But writing also often exposes weaknesses in their thinking, pushing them to think in more complex ways about their ideas and arguments. Thus, writing enables them to reach higher levels of critical thinking.

Writing, especially writing assignments that demand complex thinking, asks students to see thinking as a messy, complex task rather than as a step-by-step process. Many students believe if you do the right kind of thinking, you will come to the right conclusion. Instead, we must help them to see the chaos of thinking, to unsettle their thinking and push them to explore alternatives, to encourage them to see in ways that help them reach beyond themselves. Class recitations and discussions can offer this opportunity. But writing assignments, which should demand problem posing and dissonance, offer the time to research new perspectives and question old assumptions and conclusions—while offering new interpretations and ideas. They all help students to think in more mature ways.

Designing Writing-Intensive Assignments

Even though our definitions for writing-intensive courses vary, using writing-intensive principles in our classes clearly offers new ways to inspire learning. So how do we translate these principles into our classrooms? How do we design effective writing assignments?

One of the first changes instructors need to make in the way we think of writing is to think of our course goals in relation to the writing and thinking our students are doing. Too often, we use writing indiscriminately in our classes. We develop assignments without considering the specific kinds of thinking our students need to do to complete the assignment, and without using assignments to lead students to discover new insights and reach new levels of critical thinking. Instead, we think in terms of a "project" or "essay," usually some paper modeled after writing in a specific discipline, and we treat what the students generate more in summative than in formative terms. But high-level thinking does not just occur through student effort or modeling. Students must think their way through higher and higher stages in order to arrive at sophisticated levels of critical thinking.

By determining the kinds of thinking you want your students to do at various stages of your class, you can design assignments to demand higher-level thinking and offer students the means to get there. When we do not conceive of writing assignments as demanding certain types of thinking, we tend to be vague in what we ask students to do, even though we may have, in our own minds, a clear idea of what their writing should achieve. An assignment that asks students to "define and discuss" might seem to ask for high levels of critical thinking. But most developmental-thinking schemes would place such an assignment on the lower end of the critical-thinking spectrum. Only by recognizing the distinct thinking tasks required by the verbs we use in creating our assignments, words such as *apply, analyze, formulate, persuade,* and *argue,* can we ensure that our students are certain of the thinking tasks we would like them to perform. (In the same way, we can improve our assessments of writing, basing them upon specific thinking tasks rather than on vague affective reactions.)

So you should begin the design task by determining your educational objectives for the writing you will assign. By setting these objectives first, you can decide what types of writing (formal, informal; writing-to-learn, writing-to-communicate) you will use in order to help your students reach your objectives. Once established, your objectives can be shared with your students, discussing them from the first moment you give the assignment. Sharing the objectives with your students will help them clarify why they are completing the assignment and can help them adapt their writing to the purpose, audience, and style the assignment requires.

Next, determine what types of writing you will use to achieve your purposes. Again, resist thinking of writing assignments to mean essays or papers. A wide range of writing tasks are available, and by using them in sequence, asking for definitions at the formative stages and for analysis at later stages, you can help students recognize how to arrive at higher levels of thinking.

Too often, in thinking about the range of tasks available, instructors forget the shorter tasks all of us use to develop our thinking. Good writing often starts with personal writing, anything from class notes to personal reactions to specific ideas. Spend time thinking about the range of informal writing you might use as (perhaps ungraded) assignments; these will shape student thinking, while offering you the means to see them work through your assignment.

Many teachers use "microthemes," or short write-to-learn assignments, to help students get started on larger thinking and writing projects. Generally, microthemes are short essays (themes), often written in class or from one class to another, that focus on specific concepts that will be used in larger class assignments. They ask students to articulate their thinking processes, which helps both students and you see where the students are in their understanding of new ideas. Microthemes might ask students to define a new concept, explore debates between ideas, or offer reactions to specific situations. These microthemes can be ungraded or simple to grade—used to expose areas where students need to do more thinking and reading rather than as summative judgments of larger assignments.

For example, you might want the students in your introductory class to produce a statistical report in a social science writing style. It would be easy to assume that they understand the style and the kinds of thinking that must occur before they are able to produce a satisfactory report. But you demand a great deal of your introductory students. You want them not only to demonstrate comprehension of basic theories and statistical styles; you also want them to interpret the findings and apply them in a meaningful manner. So you might begin with microthemes, where you ask students to summarize the basic theories and theorists, cite necessary information in the appropriate styles, and apply data presented in class to a new situation. Each of these is a lower-level thinking activity, which pushes the students in the direction you want them to go. In our social science example, you might ask students to write two pages applying given data to a new situation. You do not have to grade such a paper, in which students will likely make lots of thinking and writing mistakes, not able to complete such a complex assignment the first time. But they are practicing for a later, formal writing assignment, where they can take what they learn here and reapply it in a more sophisticated manner. (Students who choose not to complete the microtheme assignment, or put no effort into it, will not perform as well later on. They must practice thinking in order to be good at it.)

Finally, you can bring these various informal writing tasks together in the students' larger, formal assignment. This time, you hold them accountable for complex thinking, arguing in your evaluation criteria that they should not only be able to apply data but also be able to interpret it and speculate about future studies. You also hold them accountable for the lower-level thinking skills you have had them practicing in the informal assignments. Students need to define important terms, cite correctly, and summarize major ideas in order to do the higher-level thinking required by the formal project. Students see how daily class assignments connect to develop thinking, and they understand how skipping any part of the process limits their ability to think in complex ways.

Conclusion

Good teaching asks students to perform at the highest levels of thinking possible. Writing-intensive strategies, using lots of carefully designed writing assignments to meet specific course goals, inspire students to think critically and enable them to express their thinking in the many ways colleges demand. See writing-intensive strategies as ways to become a better teacher. Use the ideas discussed to reconceive your course objectives and realize them in innovative ways. You and your students will find the time well invested.

Further Reading

Bazerman, Charles. 1981. "What Written Knowledge Does: Three Examples of Academic Discourse." *Philosophy of the Social Sciences* 11: 361–87.

Bean, John C. 1996. *Engaging Ideas: The Professor's Guide to Integrating Writing, Critical Thinking, and Active Learning in the Classroom.* San Francisco: Jossey-Bass.

Belenky, Mary Field, Blythe McVicker Clinchy, Nancy Rule Goldberger, and Jill Mattuck Tarule. 1986. *Women's Ways of Knowing: The Development of Self, Voice, and Mind.* New York: Basic Books.

Bruffee, Kenneth A. 1993. *Collaborative Learning: Higher Education, Interdependence, and the Authority of Knowledge.* Baltimore, Md.: Johns Hopkins Univ. Press.

Elbow, Peter. 1981. *Writing with Power: Techniques for Mastering the Writing Process.* New York: Oxford Univ. Press.

Fulwiler, Toby, and Art Young, eds. 1982. *Language Connections: Writing and Reading Across the Curriculum.* Urbana, Ill.: NCTE.

Kurfiss, Joanne G. 1988. *Critical Thinking: Theory, Research, Practice, and Possibilities.* ASHE-ERIC Higher Education Reports, no. 2. Washington, D.C.: Association for the Study of Higher Education/ERIC Clearinghouse on Higher Education.

Perry, Willliam G., Jr. 1970. *Forms of Intellectual and Ethical Development in the College Years.* Troy, Mo.: Holt, Rinehart, and Winston.

White, Edward M. 1994. *Teaching and Assessing Writing.* 2nd ed. San Francisco: Jossey-Bass.

15

What! . . . Writing in a Science Class?

Anne W. Stork and Chad Sisson

AS SCIENTISTS, WE ARE WRITERS. Any given day can find us in the midst of writing a grant proposal, research paper, review article, or book chapter. Knowing how to write is essential to our survival: job offers and promotions often depend upon our research articles getting published and our grant proposals funded. But we not only write to communicate. We also use writing to think through our ideas; often it is during the process of writing up our data for publication, for example, that we realize the significance of our results.

New scientists can be surprised by the amount of writing they have to do. This is because as undergraduates most of us wrote very little; we might even have chosen the sciences as a career to avoid writing. When we were students we might only have written exam questions and lab reports; instruction on how to write was usually limited and any feedback on our writing tended to focus on the "science" and ignored the "writing." Writing was usually used as a means to be evaluated. We seldom were shown that writing was a tool we could use to think about science.

The consequence of not being taught how to write as students is that later, when we have to write as scientists, we usually do not know how. Tackling our dissertations and first grant proposals fills us with dread. The quality of the writing we produce as new writers frustrates our faculty advisers and editors. On our own we must stumble through learning how to write and how to use writing as a tool for thinking.

So why don't science faculty focus on writing with their students? The answer boils down to this: Science faculty teach within the context of their culture. Traditionally, that culture has viewed writing as something discussed in English classes by English professors. How often have we heard our peers and mentors say, "This is a science course, not an English class" or "I grade for content, not writing"? Yet clearly, writing is an essential skill for a scientist.

But we think graduate teaching assistants can play a key role in fostering change in such attitudes in the sciences. TAs are restricted in what they can teach their students, because they are typically handed a predetermined curriculum. At the same time, TAs have a certain freedom—from concerns with tenure or promotion or issues of curricular change. Consequently, TAs have the opportunity to experiment and develop their own teaching style. That is, they can emphasize the importance of writing through small changes in class format and ungraded additional assignments.

A first step is to devote class time to writing. While it now might seem unconventional to include writing in a science course, if we begin to treat writing as a tool, like we do statistics or experimental design, with each class we graduate attitudes among scientists will begin to change. More immediately, we will also start to see improvements in the quality of our students' writing—and our own!

Certain teaching situations allow TAs more freedom than do others. You might think you lack the latitude to modify your course; but chances are you could include a writing activity that takes just five to fifteen minutes of class time each week with little disruption to the curriculum. For more significant changes (such as modeling the writing process in class or incorporating peer review), you might require permission from the professor in charge of the course. Regardless, give some thought to how you might focus in your class on some aspect of writing, such as writing-to-learn (students write as a way to clarify concepts and synthesize ideas), writing style (what makes scientific writing clear and easy to understand), and writing process (how to create a piece of writing).

Writing-to-Learn

INFORMAL WRITING

Many students dread writing, in part because writing is usually used in the classroom as a way to judge performance. However, if you use ungraded writing assignments (i.e., "informal" writing) in your courses to help students clarify concepts and synthesize material, they will discover the rewards of writing as a learning tool (Fulwiler 1987). Because informal writing is un-graded and not held to the standards of "formal" assignments, students could consider it a waste of time . . . so why use informal writing in your class?

Writing is active

Making a lab interesting for students is a problem most TAs can relate to. How often do you find yourself halfway through a lab session and looking out into a sea of blank stares and nodding heads? Add an informal writing task. Writing is an active process that engages students with the subject and can help get them involved with what you are trying to teach. Students expect active learning in the laboratory, so let them explore the subject through writing.

Informal writing gives students freedom

What better way is there to stifle students than to force their ideas into an uncomfortable (formal) format with a set of new rules and expectations? But including informal writing can help students express their ideas on a subject without the threat of a bad grade.

With freedom comes voice

With this freedom of expression, students will begin to explore ideas more thoroughly and creatively. Especially in science, many students think that if they follow the prescribed format closely and run the grammar checker, they have succeeded in writing a paper. But does their paper have a clear point or say anything of substance? Having a clear purpose and style in your writing often is called having a "voice." Informal writing can help students (re)discover this voice, then help them translate that voice to other writing assignments.

Writing allows you to connect with students

Reading students' informal writing can reveal that many cannot concep-tualize a principle past its mathematical equations or definitions that they use in the lab. Finding out this type of information can give you a heads-up on what subjects are confusing your students.

The process of writing is a powerful learning tool

In many informal writing exercises, the more successful solutions come near the end of the exercise. The students will use the writing process to work through possible solutions to the problem, finally coming to a more acceptable conclusion because they have actively written their ideas down. Make this learning technique a topic for class discussion, and point out how writing can be a problem-solving tool. Here is an example from our experience at the University of New Hampshire:

> Sandra was frustrated by her students' inability to think through the lab's problem sets. At first, she was dubious that she could "modify" the lab as it was written in the lab manual. But after talking with fellow TAs, she decided to restructure her lab sections to include some informal writing. Her labs generally involved collecting and analyzing data, resulting in a formal report due the next week. In order to help students think about the concepts investigated during the lab session, she made up discussion questions that students responded to at intermittent points of the lab. When students produced a graph or set of statistics, for example, they would write initial responses to the corresponding questions. They would then discuss possible alternative explanations with their lab partners, and then write a more complete answer. Students turned in the written responses along with their formal lab reports the next week. Sandra used the informal writing to help her evaluate their understanding of the lab.

USING INFORMAL WRITING

Informal does not mean ignored

To make sure students get the message that informal writing is time well spent, respond to everything students write. Underline a few important points, relate what they wrote to a topic in the class, or pose a question for them to think about. However you choose to respond, always personalize your response, and find something positive to say.

Make informal writing an expected part of the lab

If you frequently ask students to write in class, they will realize that informal writing is a part of the lab and not a surprise addition or afterthought.

Share examples of informal writing

Show the rest of the class some of the important points made by their classmates. Discuss the ways writing can be used to develop ideas, create hypotheses, and discover conclusions. You can also use these pieces of informal writing to initiate change in a curriculum or approach to a class. Use them as "proof" of the need for change or to relate student needs with the design of the curriculum.

Experiment with informal writing exercises

You might want to begin with simple exercises to get students used to writing in a science class. Here's another example:

> Chad decided to add informal writing to his lab sections. On the first day of class, he asked students to write five-minute responses concerning the "most important" or "most confusing" point of the class. Later in the semester, as students became accustomed to regularly writing during lab, he challenged them with more involved informal writing exercises. For example, his students had a formal lab report due on biometric variance. Before turning the paper in, he had the students write a letter to an imaginary ten-year-old sibling explaining the concept of biometric variance using commonplace examples. Later, he shared with the entire class one of the more creative examples involving pancakes of varying diameters. This assignment spurred a valuable discussion on the importance of communicating science to a general audience and gave Chad some insight on the students' overall understanding of the concept.

Be creative in how you use informal writing, and observe how students respond to each type of exercise. For instance, informal writing can be used to prepare for group discussions. Or, try beginning class with informal writing by having students relate ideas from lecture to what they are doing that day in lab. Writing can also be used to summarize ideas presented in class or discussed in small groups. Bean's *Engaging Ideas* (1996) is a wonderful reference for informal writing assignments if you would like additional suggestions.

Don't be afraid to fail

When an assignment bombs, talk about it with your students. Explain that you are trying to make this a more enjoyable lab section for them while expanding your abilities as a future professor. Make them realize that they are helping you in the process of improving the college classroom.

Writing Style

Most students will appreciate some help on improving their writing style, and you can meet that need with as little as fifteen to thirty minutes per class.

> Lara was frustrated: Her students were consistently turning in writing that was wordy, vague, or confusing. She decided to give them some guidance as to how to improve their writing style. She decided to start small by spending fifteen minutes at the end of lab to work on writing clear sentences. To do this, she wrote a poorly written sentence on the board. Her students then broke into groups to rewrite the sentence so that it was more readable. Each group presented their "new and improved" sentence to the class. At the next TA meeting, Lara reported, "The writing exercise was magical! The students were so excited to get some instruction on how to write clearly."

If you would like to try revising sentences with your students but don't know where to begin, read chapter 10, "Revising," in Pechenik's *A Short Guide to Writing About Biology* (1997). Pechenik provides a wealth of examples on how to revise for content, clarity, completeness, and conciseness.

Show exemplars . . . both well written and not

Often students produce poorly written papers because they have no idea what a well-written paper contains. To change this situation, give students two papers, one well written and one poorly written, to read before class. Then, in groups, have students discuss the quality of writing in each. To identify the components of a well-written paper, have them consider the writing at the level of the sentence, paragraph, and entire paper. What do they find makes a paper easy to read versus a struggle? As a class, discuss the findings of the small groups, and formulate a game plan for producing well-written papers.

Students can learn a lot from the successes of their peers. To capitalize on this, make available well-written student papers that you have collected over time. (Be sure to get permission from the authors to circulate their papers. Another caveat: change your writing assignments regularly to discourage plagiarism.)

The Writing Process

MODELING

Inexperienced writers tend to sit down, write one draft, and think they are done. But students who take this approach shortchange themselves from developing their ideas; writing produced in a single draft risks being thin, unfocused, and disorganized. Techniques such as freewriting, ("write non-stop for a set period of time" [Bean 1996]), discussing ideas with colleagues, and writing multiple drafts allow writers the chance to figure out what they really have to say (Elbow 1998, 102). Here is another example from our own experiences:

> Anne wanted her students to break out of the habit of writing just one draft for a science paper. The next day, she started class by presenting her students with a controversial statement open to acceptance or rejection. She gave them ten minutes to write down any and all responses to the statement, urging them to write freely and to turn off their editing impulses. After all the students had written down their initial thoughts, they took another ten minutes to discuss their ideas in small groups. Each student then reassessed his or her ideas and formulated a point of view. Did they agree or disagree with the statement? What reasons did they have to back up their opinions? They then had twenty minutes to compose their ideas in the form of an essay. Once all the students had completed an essay, they exchanged papers with another student for review. Anne encouraged her students to have the reviews focus on the clarity of the author's argument and allowed ten minutes for the reviewers to mark their comments. At the end of class, reviewers re-

turned the first drafts to their authors. The students each then incorporated the reviewer's comments outside of class, and turned in a revised draft the next class period.

What was the result of spending a whole class period on writing? Before the class writing exercise, the students' papers were thin, unfocused, and did not have much to say. But afterward, the ideas in Anne's students' papers were well developed and had a point of view.

Would you like your students to learn to use new writing techniques, but you can't devote an entire class period to writing? Consider spending just fifteen minutes of class time on freewriting for an upcoming writing assignment. Students probably learned this technique in their English classes, but they might not realize that it will help them in their science writing as well. If you would like to teach your students about the writing process but don't know much about it yourself, read Elbow's *Writing with Power* (1998).

REVISIONS AND REVIEWS

Even after modeling writing an essay in class, many students will continue to hand in first drafts as final pieces of writing. To help them learn that "rewriting is the essence of writing well" (Zinsser 1998, 84), try building multiple drafts into your curriculum. The simplest way to do this is to ask students to turn in both a rough draft and a revised draft of their papers. The drawback of this approach is that students get little feedback on how to revise their writing, and what feedback they do get is too late to incorporate into their paper. A more involved approach is to require that students swap rough drafts outside of class and review each other's writing. But you might need to provide guidance on how to review another's paper. Also, the students might not take reviewing each other's papers very seriously.

A third approach, which will take some planning on your part and could require permission from the course professor, is to set up mandatory peer review in class. Realize that the more carefully you set up the peer review process, the more successful it will be. To make this work, you must take some class time to teach the students how to review a classmate's paper. State explicitly what they should be looking for and how they should respond to the author. To signal to the students that the review process is important, announce that you will be collecting and grading not only final drafts but rough drafts and reviews. The website "Resources for Scientists Teaching Science" (http://instruct1.cit.cornell.edu/courses/taresources/) offers several examples of peer review guidelines that TAs have handed out to their students.

FEEDBACK ON STUDENT WRITING

Finally, do not overlook the influence that your comments on their papers can have on improving your students' writing. But think carefully about how you respond.

> John used to think that the way to be of most help to his students was to litter their papers with lots and lots of comments. He thought that the way to teach students how to write clearly was to fix their mistakes. But spending hours and hours grading papers didn't seem to be paying off: The quality of his students' writing did not seem to improve as the semester progressed. John began to think about the types of comments he was receiving on his own writing. Comments such as "vague" or "awkward" in the margins or a barrage of microediting did not help him. On the other hand, big-picture comments, such as "the message in your last paragraph was very powerful—try starting with it on your next draft," were very instructive and helped him make major revisions. Comments that revealed patterns to his writing, such as "you often present five main ideas in one paragraph—try focusing on one idea per paragraph," helped him learn how to revise. John realized that he needed to change the nature of his comments on his students papers to help them see the patterns in their writing if he was going to help them progress as writers.

Here's some more good advice, from Keith Hjortshoj at Cornell University: "As you comment on your students' papers, don't consider yourself their grader or editor; consider yourself their reader. Remember, your goal is to help them communicate their science more clearly."

Conclusion

As scientists, we are writers. However, most of us do not receive training on how to write effectively. Be a part of reversing this trend. Take the plunge, and start incorporating writing into the science courses or labs you teach. If you are a bit nervous about your ability to teach writing as a scientist, start small by incorporating just five minutes of writing tasks into your classes. Even small doses of writing in a science curriculum will begin to help produce scientists who view writing as one of their essential tools.

Beware of feelings of self-doubt ("I'm in no position to teach writing— I'm a struggling writer myself!") If you would like to become a more accomplished writer, then you are the perfect candidate for adding writing to your courses. You will find that, as you help your students develop their writing skills, you will also see positive changes in your own writing.

16

Service-Learning
When the Goal and Process
of Education Are One and the Same

Yoram Lubling

The whole secret of the teacher's force lies in the conviction that men are convertible. And they are. They want awakening. Get the soul out of bed, out of deep habitual sleep, out into God's universe, to a perception of its beauty, and hearing of its call . . . [a] force to shake the world.

—*Ralph Waldo Emerson*

MY AIM HERE is to commend to you the pedagogy of service-learning—a form of active learning in which the educational environment is consistent with the press of ordinary experience, and where students develop physical and intellectual skills and habits and do not merely engage in the memorization of text. My pedagogical goal here, then, is to abandon traditional emphasis on the "education of the mind" through the transmission of classical texts, and instead adopt an emphasis on the "education of character." The reason for adopting the latter came from my recognition that, while the best of world wisdom is passing through my students' minds, it fails to bring about a change or transformation in their actual lives. In my view, if students leave my class and the space around their activities doesn't positively change, then I failed educationally. The central question of education— "What precisely did the student learn?"—then, continues to fly in the face of all my teachings. Why shouldn't education be evaluated by real results and gifts?

Consider, for example, the Holocaust as an historical event and as a teaching opportunity. It is clear that mere *knowledge* about the Holocaust, and other significant historical events, does not prevent the continuation of racism and bigotry. What is missing from the traditional teaching process is the actual *understanding* of the event. The state of understanding is different from knowing in a very essential way. Understanding is an existential event that challenges the whole person's intellectual and motor habits. To understand the Holocaust, then, means the possibility was eliminated that the student can still remain a bigot, or participate in future holocausts. In this case, education leads to a transformation in the life of students and their environments.

Knowing, on the other hand, involves no existential challenge to the whole person. If the Holocaust presents a challenge at all, it is merely a formalistic and cognitive recognition of information. As such, because there is no existential challenge there is also no transformation of character. The student can walk away from the class, join the Institute for Historical Review, vote for David Duke, and burn black churches. In this case, education does not lead to any positive change in the life of the students and their environments.

It seems to me, however, that the traditional assumption in education—that recognition of information alone can bring about change of conduct—was clearly handed a death-blow by the events of the Holocaust. To continue and hold such an assumption will lead the teacher into the web of a contemporary paradox. On the one hand, as a cultivated person the teacher must acknowledge that the Holocaust is of utmost significance in understanding human history. On the other hand, that teacher will also have to admit that such a significant event has failed to transform the state of knowledge or morality. How can something that is so central and significant bring no transformation at all? The question is, then: Is the Holocaust really not that significant as to change basic assumptions about reality, or is it our educational framework that fails us by not allowing historical events to challenge cognitive structures?

Clearly, the answer is the latter insofar as we live in the world through a particular set of assumptions. For traditional education is based on a dualistic worldview, in which education is seen as a mere cognitive process. If any transformation of character is to take place by mere cognitive knowledge, although it is not required, it will be through magic. This view makes the false assumption that learning and acting upon that learning is analogous to a vending machine. You put in the coins (knowledge), and by automatic mechanism the correct type of drink (behavior) comes out. It hardly requires an argument to show that such a view is easily challenged by contemporary scientific knowledge, particularly in the field of psychology. However, what is required for actual transformation is much more basic and less elegant. Transformation requires us to work on the level of skills and habits, prejudice, ignorance, false assumptions; in other words, we have to get our hands dirty. We cannot teach and hope for magical transformation by vicarious engagement or via virtual reality.

The other view, which I support, holds that cognitive education is merely a partial process of learning. Not only is this process not meant to bring about real transformation, but in many instances cognitive education is destructive and goes against the best in contemporary knowledge and judgment. In my view, cognition is an instrument for the ongoing negotiation between the person and his or her environment. It is not a self-contained metaphysical reality that can be aristocratically used for intellectual joys. Instead, cognition, with its capacity for language, becomes, in John Dewey's phrase, "the tool of tools" for actual amelioration, not a transcended museum to which we can cognitively escape.

The question of education is a pragmatic one: How is the world going to be different if you choose to act in accordance with one or the other set of metaphysical assumptions?

My pedagogical position, then, rejects the notion that the mind is a subjective, unaffected, and self-contained metaphysical reality. I prefer to view the mind functionally, as an instrument for the ongoing negotiation with the environment. Such an instrument achieves its full power of growth only through dramatic situations as found in life itself. This is why *service-learning* is so important. It furnishes experience of such life situations. Service-learning requires the rejection of education as purely cognitive and passive transmission of text; it demands teaching and learning through practice and engagement.

Service-learning provides a unique opportunity to dismantle the isolating and voyeuristic apparatus of traditional classroom instruction by making the wisdom of the text consonant with the press of ordinary experience. My use of service-learning is motivated by the need to establish continuity between the ideational part of the class and the actual experience of life. Here ideas not only get informed by actual experience, but ideas help sharpen and solidify students' moral and social skills, or to use a traditional term, "character." Education, in my view, is a creative process in which ideas are used and integrated into life rather than just being talked about in class.

The result is learning and teaching in the Emersonian sense: learning takes place in students' muscles, not merely in their minds. Active learning is about creating intellectual, moral, civic and social character, skills, and habits. It follows Martin Buber's wisdom that education, like religion, will become genuine and transformative when it stops being "education" and becomes life.

Service-Learning

Our college is a national leader in a fully endowed and student-run center for service-learning. In the 2000–2001 academic year, 65 percent of our students contributed more than fifty-two thousand hours in community-related services.[1] Members of the center address my students on the first day of each course, coordinate the students' preferred service organization, and arrange meetings between the students and the local coordinators. From the first moment of class, the students must communicate and relate to the community rather than just the instructor. The system immediately makes clear to them that learning is larger than the hour they spend in the class-room. The students must arrange for transportation to their assignment, which frequently develops into camaraderie and a sense of togetherness. Their service-related work becomes the focus of their activities, a unique and new venue through which to understand the subject matter.

The practice of service-learning is not restricted to the mere notion that it is good to give back to the community. Although service-learning provides such a medium, my interest is much deeper. I seek to establish an educational framework that is consistent with the press of ordinary experience. Ordinary experience is *dramatic* insofar as its results actually matter. This is

1. The Volunteers Center involves several student-run programs, one of which is the service-learning office. This office provides student-service in the following programs: Adopt a Grandfather; Boys and Girls Club; Crossroad (sexual abuse awareness); Elon Cares (HIV/AIDS awareness); Elon Homes for Children; Family Abuse Services; Junior Achievement; Kopper Top (providing therapeutic riding lessons); Mis Amigos (tutoring Spanish-speaking children); Toys for Tears (providing toys for needy children); PEACOCK (working with minority youth); S.H.A.R.E. (animal rights awareness); The Arc (developmental disability awareness); and Wildlife Sanctuary.

in contrast to the traditional notion of pedagogy as preparation, where learning is removed from the actual consequences of the act itself. For example, it is insignificant in the life of an individual student whether or not I succeed in showing that the *argument* in support of or against abortion is invalid. The students can go on with their lives regardless of the formal argument, but not when counseling young women who are pregnant. In such a situation the results actually matter; you cannot simply sleep through such a dramatic unfolding.

The availability of service-linked pedagogy allows me to overcome most of the pitfalls of traditional instruction. The course is not different from any other form of living that is familiar to the student. I also overcome the problem of "interest" in the student because ordinary experience, as difficult as it can be, is not an empty subject matter externally imposed on them.

Although my courses usually deal with relations and the social good, which naturally lends itself to volunteer work in the community, the principles and the methodology can be applied to most disciplines. The creative involvement of the instructor rests in the ability to see the connections between ideation and experience, and capitalize on those connections by promoting specific skills and habits. These skills and habits can be in problem solving, analysis, aesthetics, ethics, and politics, to name only a few.

For my course, Philosophy 115, Ethical Practice, the structure of the class is different from ordinary meetings in the classroom two or three times a week, and instead has a more open structure. There is one meeting a week to introduce the ideas in the text and to clarify them; the rest of the week is devoted to work and reflection. The students meet again during the week to discuss their reflection papers, which are due at the end of every week. The reflection paper assignment asks the students to explain the ideas that were covered in the readings and in class, then discuss the nature of their experience in their service-learning environment. Each student is asked to make connections between the ideas in class and the way those ideas are or are not manifested in the press of her or his ordinary experience. The students are also encouraged to bring their work to class or to introduce issues that were raised during their work.

Finally, a word must be said about the dynamics of such a course. From the first meeting of the semester, the students are required to form relationships in order to survive in this course. Phone calls have to be made to connect with the supervisors of the community sites, and they have to become familiar with the town they now live in. At Elon University, there is an actual seventy-year-old wall that used to surround the college, isolating it from the town. But more significantly, the students become citizen-learners and not mere transients. Because of its intensity, the course leaves very little room for spectators who like to hide in the back of the classroom. But this is precisely the first lesson the students must learn by engagement.

Some Episodes of Service-Learning from a Philosophy Course

The following examples from the course I taught are presented in the two-phase format whereby service-learning can be applied. The "ideation" is the reading, preliminary consideration and discussion of a text. The "practice" is the effort to experience, live, and test the ideas in real-life situations with other people.

EXAMPLE ONE — IDEATION

The course began with a discussion of Daniel Quinn's short novel *Ishmael.* The novel makes the simple and challenging claim that Western society is enacting a false story about the nature of existence. The continuous enactment of this story is going to result in self-destruction. The claim opens the course to a discourse about the nature of culture, its assumptions, and the reason for their formation. The students are encouraged to inquire about their "story" and locate the foundations of their beliefs.

PRACTICE

Each student is asked to go and meet with individuals in the service site and start listening to people's "stories" in order to examine Ishmael's claim. According to Ishmael, Western individuals are captive in a more substantial way than the "lower animals," which are merely captive of iron cages. Whereas an animal's captivity is merely physical, human captivity is of the mind, imagination, and creativity. Notice humans' endless attempts to separate ourselves from the natural world and convince ourselves that we are not animals. Not only do our methodology and religious myths proclaim such transcendency, but even some of our "scientific" claims cannot avoid such prejudice. Ask an ordinary person to explain Darwin's theory of evolution, and you will find that many believe that evolution ended with the appearance of humans, that from now on it is merely a matter of perfecting the end result.

By engaging with the elderly and young children in their service activities, the students are immediately able to examine the story firsthand. It is reflected in the hopes of the elderly that life is not just about living and dying, but that life has a special purpose for humans. The children, in contrast, reflect the early struggle between their natural tendency towards egalitarianism and the demands of society to remove themselves from the ordinary nature of physical existence.

EXAMPLE TWO — IDEATION

Using Plato's "Ship of Fools" argument in the *Republic,* I present the problems Plato associated with democracy, i.e., that it is an unjust form of government. It is unjust because it allows the least-qualified individuals to become our guardians. The reason, of course, is rooted in the fact that the uneducated masses vote out of ignorance because they know nothing about running a community. The free, yet ignorant masses

> fail to understand that the Captain must devote his attention to year and season, sky and stars and wind, and all that belongs to his art, if he is really to be anything like a ruler of the ship; but that as for gaining control of the helm, with the approval of some people and the disapproval of others, neither art nor practice of this can be comprehended at the same time as the art of navigation. (Plato 1979, 256)

PRACTICE

Most students work in nonprofit organizations such as the local homeless shelter and public schools mentoring programs, where they must confront the reality of fundraising and the ongoing need in the community to beg for money. Very soon the students *physically* learn that our tax monies are somehow not sufficient for such social programs. Why aren't there enough teachers to assist the students? Why isn't there enough affordable housing for the poor or homeless? Why do people with mental disabilities live on our streets?

Prior to such an engagement, the students, who are mostly white and upper middle class, resist claims about social injustices in our democracy. Once a parent threatened to sue me if I continued to "force" his child to volunteer. These students usually fail to see intellectually the need for any revisions in health-care policy, employment security, and the like. However, with a service-learning approach to education, their minds change very quickly, as these experiences attest:

"I also found out where I came down with ringworm from. The doctor told me that I had ringworm and I could not imagine where I had contracted it. One of the students, whom I always work with one on one, was absent on Friday. I was informed that he was sent home for a week because he had such a bad case of ringworm on the back of his head. That would explain it. His family could not afford a five-dollar tube of antifungal cream. That is really depressing." (Stephanie Johnson) [2]

"I can't help but wonder what is wrong with our world today. We have kids living in such poverty with almost no way out of it. And we have people making millions, cold enough, not even considering offering any help to the less fortunate. I see kids . . . and cannot help but feel guilty for their situation . . . I am eager to do what I can to help . . . Just looking at the Boy's and Girl's Club, I have never seen a white adult in there." (Kyle Draper)

Some Reflections on a Service-Learning-Centered Course in Philosophy

With Emerson I argued that the only reason I continue to teach is because I believe that people are *convertible*. People's lives, as the universe itself, are not something that can be expressed *categorically* because they are not finished events. The universe grows by its edges, and we are the "workers from within" who determine its final shape or success. Indeed, in their final reflection papers, the students were asked to consider the question: Can improvement in the human condition be achieved by good thought alone? Here are some representative answers:

"I do not think that I can philosophically hold the view that the world will get better by 'good thought' alone. In order for the world to get better, people

2. This and the other excerpts that follow are from the class journal of students in my Ethical Practice course, Spring 2000.

have to get out there and put their good thought into action. It is the action and execution of these 'good thought' that will make the world better . . . Action gets results, not thought. This is one of the reasons that for service learning we did not sit in the classroom and think 'good thought' for 40 hours this semester, we actually went out and tried to put our 'good thought' into action and make a difference." (Adam Melchor)

"I feel that the most important thing I learned from my visits to the night shelter . . . is that actions must be taken . . . through my service learning experiences I have come to realize and really understand that everybody, rich, poor, black, or white, is a human being." (Matt Matz)

"I do not believe now that the world can get better merely by 'good thought' alone . . . I could never sit and tell anyone that this idea would ever work in our society. Good thought, as good natured as it may be would never be enough to change things." (Becca Lestner)

But How Do You Assess a Service-Learning Course?

Such a course, for obvious reasons, defies traditional evaluation and grades. The class had no required exams or any other formal testing because it is not memorization of information that I seek to teach. The students are required to write a weekly reflection paper in which they discuss the ideational claims of the course and connect those claims to their practice. This assignment allows me a continuous insight into the students' thoughts and practice.

Most significant, however, is that the instructor can no longer be a spectator in the educational process. I must visit the students in their places of work and encourage their participation by providing a model for a relational self. After such an intense interaction with the students over four months, it is very easy to evaluate the students through the quality of involvement and whether or not they were transformed by the experience.

Finally, this method of instruction cannot work in a large university class. The participants in the class, including the instructor, must become a genuine "learning-living community" for the length of the semester. In the case of our philosophy majors, it is an ongoing journey in which we join with them—for four years and, we hope, beyond.

Each ethical practice class contributes more than sixteen hundred hours of work to the community. Each student is responsible for forty hours over the period of the course. However, students in my courses contribute twice the hours that are required; they also continue to volunteer after the semester has ended. What it means educationally is not only that the students were transformed by the class, but also that the transformation is supported by actual habits, i.e., in the muscles. This ensures that the lessons will not be lost after the student completes the class or graduates. Emerson is correct! The only reason we teach is because students are convertible. A few final student reflections may illustrate the beautiful potential and transformations of service-learning in higher education:

"As a result of participating in service learning hours, I have realized that relations are significantly more important than I thought . . . I previously maintained relationships with only those I was close to, I did not attempt to form relationships outside of this circle . . . After reading the unit on Martin Buber's *I and Thou* and then interacting with the residents of the Twin Lakes Center, I discovered that I was being extremely narrow-minded. I was passing over the opportunity to know and share with so many unique individuals on a daily basis that I felt as though I was heartless . . . I learned that relationships do not have to be built up over the course of long time periods, but they can be established from a simple honest moment." (Emily Perry)

"The world is full of people who have 'good thought' and who don't back them up with action. That was the beauty of our class, ethical practice, because we were practicing the right way to treat people, by giving of our time and attention. The most significant thing I learned is that unknowingly we changed the space between others and ourselves by the way we sometimes put people off. We get so caught up in our schedules and work and things that don't really matter that we place a wedge between our fellow man and ourselves." (Jessica Courtney)

17

Nontraditional Students

Alison K. Paglia and Lisa T. Parsons

IF YOU SAY "TYPICAL COLLEGE STUDENT" to most people, what will come to mind is a single, childless, eighteen- to twenty-four-year-old, who might, but probably does not, have very clear career aspirations, who might or might not have even declared a major field of study, and who attends school full-time. But increasingly, most people would be wrong. "Traditional," rather than "typical," would be a better label for those students, because our college population is increasingly more varied. A recent survey found that nationally, 45 percent of undergraduate college enrollments were for students older than twenty-four years old working on either a bachelor's degree or a nondegree postgraduate program (Bendixen-Noe and Giebelhaus 1998). Another recent review found the fastest-growing segment of our student population to be women older than thirty-five years (Zamanou 1993).

Clearly, this "nontraditional" segment is burgeoning. Our own institution, the University of New Hampshire at Manchester, exemplifies that changing student face. At the end of the 1999–2000 academic year, some 44 percent of UNHM's student body were part-time students, and 43 percent were more than twenty-four years old. To teach effectively at institutions like UNHM, it is important for one to consider the varied life experiences of your students—both as you plan a course and as you develop a teaching strategy. Particularly pertinent should be the following questions: How do nontraditional students differ from traditional students, other than by definition? How do those differences affect nontraditional students' learning? Should the differences affect my teaching, and if so, in what ways? How can I most effectively teach nontraditional students, or classes that include both traditional and nontraditional students?

Who Are Nontraditional Students?

By most definitions, "nontraditional" students differ from "traditional" students primarily in age. That is, nontraditional students are older than twenty-four, the age by which traditional students typically have finished college. But it is not age per se that is of interest; instead, it is several other factors that correlate with age in college students: work experience, educational history, family situation, motivation, study habits. Bendixen-Noe and Giebelhaus (1998) compiled a profile of the nontraditional student: compared with traditional students, more nontraditional students are married, more have children, and many have previously done college-level work; nontraditional students tend to be more highly motivated and disciplined about attendance and studying; and their reasons for being in college are different, with financial and career incentives assuming more immediate importance. Nontraditional students more often enroll part-time than traditional students, and many more must juggle family, work, and class schedules.

In our experience, most nontraditional students are extremely dedicated and capable students who are driven toward a goal of academic success. Nontraditional students are eager for new information and experiences that go beyond the textbook. Nontraditional students are continually seeking opportunities to share their life experiences with others and are searching for links between their own lives, the course content, and applied settings.

Nationally, more than one-half of adults attending college have already earned a bachelor's degree (Nordstrom 1997). This statistic reflects nontraditional students' motivation, often work-related—to earn or maintain certification, to stay current in their field, to advance in their career. Perhaps the adult student is seeking a life transition—to gain credentials necessary for graduate school, to explore other options, to prepare for a new career. Or, the adult student might be attending college for personal enhancement—to satisfy an intellectual curiosity, to establish social connections.

How Nontraditional Students Experience the Classroom

How might all these factors affect how nontraditional students experience your course? The answer to that question depends on the individual student, but some generalizations are possible.

SOCIAL LIFE

Nontraditional students are likely to be busier and more preoccupied with family and work than are traditional students, but less preoccupied with campus social life and the dating scene. Nontraditional students are probably about as stressed as traditional students are in trying to complete their academic work, but for different reasons.

CONFIDENCE

Often, nontraditional students feel less intimidated than traditional students do by their professors and assignments, perhaps because they and their professors are closer in age and work experience or just due to the students' greater maturity and life experiences. A situation also may arise in which the nontraditional student is considerably older than the professor. In that case the student may have lived through a historic event and have a real-life perspective, whereas the young professor's perspective may be based exclusively on academic research. Whatever the reason, the result can be that nontraditional students speak more freely in class or with the professor, readily offering their views or questioning the lecture. On the other hand, some nontraditional students are less confident, because they feel out of place or feel that a great deal is riding on their performance. After all, unlike their teenaged classmates, the adult student cannot say, "It doesn't matter, I'm just here because my parents sent me. Let's party!"

RELATIONSHIPS WITH OTHER STUDENTS

On this dimension, experiences can vary dramatically. Some nontraditional students can find themselves excluded (deliberately or inadvertently) by their traditional classmates; others can find they garner special attention and respect for their insights. Some adult learners will stifle their own voices in order not to interfere with the college experience of their younger classmates. Others will talk excessively about what they consider their vast store of experience, inhibiting more useful class discussion. Either extreme is undesirable. If your class has roughly equal numbers of traditional and nontraditional students, the dynamics obviously will be different than if one group or the other is a clear majority. When the numbers are balanced, often the traditional students will socialize mainly with one another and the nontraditional students also among themselves.

On occasion, members of the groups will reach out to form a bond; a forty-something back-to-school nurse with a naïve eighteen-year-old, for example, over their shared dislike for or difficulty with course material. In the statistics in psychology class at UNHM, it is not unusual to see such relationships develop, with the older student providing the pep talks and study advice to the younger, and the younger taking down the professor's rapid-fire speech in notes for the older. The older student might take the initiative in asking the professor a question that both groups of students care about; whereas the younger student might assist the older student in navigating current instructional practices. A younger student might be more accustomed to pedagogy that includes peer editing and peer responses to journal entries than a nontraditional student. Additionally, the younger student may have had more experience utilizing technology in the classroom. A younger student may be more familiar with web-based instruction and utilizing programs such as Blackboard to facilitate the learning process and enhance the conceptualization of course material.

Teaching Strategies

In many of the cases above, how nontraditional and traditional students will experience your classroom largely depends on the personalities of the individual students involved. But it also depends on the learning environment you set up for them—that is, the way you run your class, the kinds of assignments you give, and so on. Your goal should be to maximize the benefit that nontraditional students get from your class without lessening its benefits to your traditional students (and maybe even while enhancing your own experience as a teacher).

It is essential to be aware of the attitudes and stereotypes that traditional and nontraditional students can hold about each other. Try to think ahead about how both kinds of students are likely to feel and behave in various settings. Consider how an eighteen-year-old fresh out of high school might feel having a classmate who is the same age as his parents, and conversely how an older student might feel to be taking classes with teenagers (for that matter, to being taught by a teacher the same age as her children). There are specific strategies that instructors can set up ahead of time to head off potential roadblocks to student learning. Over time, you will devise your own particular methods, but here are a few likely scenarios and generally applicable suggestions.

GRADING

Traditional students frequently will harbor resentment toward nontraditional learners, perceiving them as "average-raisers" or "curve-breakers." A simple strategy to minimize this attitude is to take the possibility into consideration when you determine your grading policy, and then make the class aware of that grading policy at the beginning of the semester. For example, rather than grading on a curve, you could offer an optional comprehensive final exam; the grade on this exam could be averaged in with a student's previous grades in order to increase the overall grade for the course. This strategy rewards students who have done well throughout the semester (because the final is optional) while allowing students who are dissatisfied with their grades to that point the opportunity to improve them.

MANAGING VOCAL STUDENTS

Make sure all your students have opportunities to contribute to and gain from class material. The nontraditional student who is stifling himself or herself in favor of the traditional classmates must be encouraged to speak up, and the traditional students should be encouraged to see the value of what he or she has to offer.

On the other hand, the nontraditional student who insists on dominating class time with stories presents a different problem. With such vocal students you must be extremely careful not to teach solely to the dominating student; obviously that would be detrimental to the less-vocal students. Consider a range of strategies for managing vocal students, choosing the strategy that is effective in your specific class. One technique is to ask the other students to react to the vocal student's comments. Another is to call on specific students to answer questions, rather than throwing out an open question for the entire class to answer. Additionally, you can change the dynamics among the students in the class; for example, you can divide them into designated discussion groups with appointed spokespersons. In dealing with this situation, given the opportunity, the other students in the class will assist you in moderating the comments of the vocal ones.

EXPERIENTIAL LEARNING

Experiential learning—learning by doing—is an extremely successful strategy for students of all ages, backgrounds, and life situations. Different students attend college for different reasons, and experiential learning can provide opportunities for them all to creatively apply course content to best fit with their individual motivation. Learning opportunities that allow them to address a current social issue or applied situation benefit many students. Experiential learning can provide the intrinsic factors that help to facilitate learning by connecting to the students' interest in their chosen field. Students are drawn to learning opportunities that they believe are pertinent to their life situation.

There are many formal and informal opportunities for students to connect course content to the practices that occur in the "real world." Traditional examples include bringing guest speakers from the field into the classroom and organizing a field experience in an applied setting. These learning opportunities help students to envision how the course material applies to their "real-world" career expectations and can even lead to internships and job offers.

A variation on the guest speaker is to assign students to research a topic related to the course, interview experts in that field, and then require the student to gain actual experience with the subject matter. In a child development or educational psychology course, for example, a student might research a topic such as attention deficit hyperactivity disorder, then ask informed questions of physicians, school counselors, or school psychologists, and conclude with observing or working with a student who has attention deficit hyperactivity disorder. In a communication or marketing course, a student could research the changing role of newspapers and radio in a society increasingly dominated by television and the Internet; then interview marketing directors, editors, and program directors; and follow up by designing a marketing plan integrating all types of media. Such experiential learning lets students customize their assignment to gain exposure in a field they are considering.

SERVICE-LEARNING

Service-learning is a form of experiential learning in which students learn course content through service in the community. Service-learning is not just volunteer work, nor simply a chance to add to one's resume. Instead, service-learning is an occasion to engage deeply with the course material and the act of learning that material. Through reflection assignments and journaling, students are prompted to think about how their understanding of the course material affects their interactions in the community, as well as how that community work impacts their understanding of what and how they are learning. (See, for example, Jacoby 1996; Kendall 1990.)

At the University of New Hampshire Manchester, service-learning has been successful in a wide range of courses including economics, math, communications, and psychology. In a recent adult development psychology course, for example, students participated in one activity per week in a geriatric residential setting. The students were male and female, full-time and part-time, and ranged in age from eighteen to seventy-plus years. They were able to customize their specific activities—ranging from Internet, e-mail, and word-processing instruction to designing book clubs and exercise programs—to their areas of interest and experience. The students willingly made time for service-learning whenever it fit with their busy schedules. For a variety of reasons, several traditional and nontraditional students decided to continue their service to the community after the semester ended.

STUDENT CHOICE OF ASSIGNMENTS

When possible, allowing students some choice in topics for assignments will help them self-direct the course material to best suit their needs and interests. Giving students opportunities to draw from their life experiences provides an opportunity for learning and application of course content that can be particularly appealling to nontraditional students. In a history class, such students will more likely engage a project researching the history of their hometown or the industry in which they currently work or the trends that created demand for the career they are preparing for. A student-initiated project may foster collaboration on a larger scale that meets the needs of the community, industry, and the academic institution.

SCHEDULING OF ASSIGNMENTS

Given that nontraditional students typically are juggling many responsibilities, it is important that you maintain a consistent scheduling in your assignments. Announcing reading assignments, exam dates, presentation dates, and paper deadlines at the start of the semester helps those students to organize their work, family, and community responsibilities and thus succeed academically. Your being realistic about their time constraints can really aid in retention of nontraditional students. For example, your nontraditional students might accommodate your course on Tuesdays and Thursdays by working longer days on Tuesday and Thursday, or a longer day on Wednesday, to make up. A well-thought-out, organized syllabus would schedule larger assignments on Thursdays rather than Tuesdays to give such students the weekend for schoolwork and the flexibility they need to balance work, family, and school.

A STEADY WORKLOAD

Flexibility in assignments and due dates is another way to enhance student learning and increase your effectiveness. The "typical" college course, aimed at traditional students, is end-loaded, with all its exams and larger assignments due at the end of the semester. Instead of end-loading, consider spreading the assignments throughout the semester to provide more balance to all your students in managing multiple courses and responsibilities. One alternative to having all the students in your class complete a research paper and oral presentation at the end of the semester would be to make papers and presentations due during the units they pertain to. In many ways, this option enhances the course material for all students, because it can be more logical and useful for the other students to hear a presentation timed to review material just presented by the professor rather than two months later. Additionally, making assignments and deadlines flexible gives students some input in balancing the intensity of their course-related assignments. A less important—but nice—benefit is that this type of plan spreads out your grading and assessment burden throughout the semester.

Conclusion

Like their traditional classmates, nontraditional students expect to receive a quality education that prepares them for the realities of life and career. Nontraditional learners typically are motivated learners and view their educational experience as paramount. It is important to have your course requirements and methods of assessments clearly articulated. If you use some form of experiential learning in the course, it is essential for the students that you incorporate their experiences with the course content.

Nontraditional learners are quite willing to work for their grade and educational experience, especially if they can see the material having practical applications. They do not want you to make exceptions for them to accommodate their specific situations. For them—as for students of all ages, background experiences, life situations, and reasons for attending college—your task is to design courses that draw out their strengths.

18

Taking Turns
Collaborative Teaching

David Smukler

THIS CHAPTER CONSIDERS "collaborative teaching" broadly, to include any teaching situation that involves more than one instructor. Many variations of the model are possible. Two (or more) professors may co-teach one course or combine two compatible courses, or a single instructor may use one or more assistants to carry out some parts of the instruction.

To write this chapter I draw on my experience co-teaching a graduate course for the past several years, as well as multiple experiences working on other instructional teams. I have found ways to collaborate that are successful for me. However, my purpose here is less to promote a particular model than it is to present a range of instructional ideas that involve collaboration and the implications of each for the faculty members who create the courses and the students who take them. What I write, then, is based not on research by others but on the individual and collective teaching experience of my teammates and me. Specifically, I consider both benefits and challenges of embracing collaboration as a structure for teaching college courses. I suggest some strategies that have been helpful to me. And I spend some time musing on pedagogical issues related to different ways instruction can be provided collaboratively.

Whenever people agree to share a task, questions are bound to arise about the division of responsibilities, and accountability for getting things done inevitably becomes more complex. To be successful, collaborative teaching requires instructors who share values and interact well with each other. Although a teammate can relieve you of certain tasks, collaborative teaching is generally not a highly efficient approach; the work involved in communication adds significantly to the overall task of planning and implementing instruction. Nevertheless, taking turns teaching offers both students and instructors opportunities that noncollaborative formats do not.

Whether there is one instructor or more than one, all classroom learning inevitably involves interaction and collaboration. But when we team-teach, our practice becomes a reflection of the underlying belief that learning is itself a process of constructing meaning collaboratively. Courses in which we collaborate in a deliberate and visible fashion encourage our students to see, hear, and participate in shared learning experiences.

Ultimately, we choose to teach with another person because we find the experience rewarding. For myself, as an instructor in a teacher-preparation program, my hope is that by modeling the synergy created by collaboration, my teammates and I offer our students a structure they can carry with them into their own future teaching situations. Similarly, my goal in writing this chapter is to inspire you to consider ways that collaboration may enrich your own teaching experience and that of your students.

Benefits of Collaboration

VARYING THE STIMULUS

A noteworthy by-product of taking turns teaching is that differences in teaching style add variety to what happens during class time. My co-instructor's quality of voice, timing, choices of examples, and ways of engaging students are necessarily different from mine. No matter how enthralling the activities I have planned, no matter how scintillating my presentation on a given day, sooner or later students become habituated to me and benefit from interaction with someone else.

If you do not have the luxury of collaborating (or even if you do), you probably already give considerable thought to how you vary the stimulus that students receive in your course. Perhaps you use different teaching formats or add videos and guest speakers, all with the object of maintaining your students' engagement and alert interest. Collaboration simply builds more of this variety into the structure of the course.

ENRICHED POSSIBILITIES FOR CONTENT

Clearly, more voices offer the potential for richer content. What and how we teach is always influenced by those with whom we have studied in the past, projects of which we have been a part, and our previous teaching experiences. In a team-teaching situation, each teammate draws on his or her unique well of knowledge, skill, and teaching experience. Perhaps one of you will have relevant parenting experiences to draw on, or facility with creating computer presentations. One of you may have helpful community connections, the other a useful understanding of the politics of your institution. The history of your subject area may be a particular interest to you, while your teammate is more focused on recent developments in the field. Collaboration creates overlapping constellations of influence and proficiency that are certain to create a richer experience for students.

RESPONSIVENESS TO STUDENTS

In a large class, having two teachers doubles the chance that a student will be heard. More important, team-teaching also makes it more likely that a student will feel that there is a good "fit" with one of you. College students are an increasingly diverse group, and we should use any way we can to increase our capacity to respond effectively and helpfully to the range of students we encounter. Different instructors' interaction styles inevitably will vary, and it is natural that any given student may be more comfortable with one style or another.

Students also learn more when they get a greater variety of feedback and response from their instructors. One of you may be better at remembering to frame feedback in a positive way. Or it may be that your teammate points out a need that you might have let slide. One of you may focus on course content in a very direct way, while the other focuses on students' ability to express course-related ideas in writing. As in families where children are raised by more than one caregiver, team-teaching can allow for guidance of a sort that a single instructor simply cannot provide as effectively.

Another important advantage of team-teaching is that it ultimately allows for less capriciousness in how we treat our students. Having you and your teammate look over each other's shoulders provides a check that your grading practices will be fair and thoughtfully applied and that no student will be penalized because he or she happens to be someone with whom one of you is uncomfortable.

SHARING TASKS

Students stand to benefit from collaboration in many ways, but what's in it for you? Collaborating on a course will not cut your workload in half, unfortunately; but it can offer great flexibility to you and your teammate around workload. Whether or not the class is mostly lecture, having two or more instructors share the responsibility of delivering instruction allows each to come at his or her share of the task with fresh energy. Furthermore, although you usually will want to be in class, team-teaching means it is no longer essential that you be present 100 percent of the time. In the event of unforeseen scheduling dilemmas, for example, there is more flexibility in covering a class.

Sharing the task of grading and providing feedback to students also can be an enormous boon, allowing each collaborator to respond to students' assignments more thoughtfully and in greater depth. We all appreciate the time we gain when the pile of ungraded papers is half as thick, and our students benefit from more meaningful feedback from more responsive instructors.

POSSIBILITIES FOR PROFESSIONAL GROWTH

I find the opportunity to learn from my teammate's pedagogy one of the most fulfilling aspects of team-teaching. None of us can help but learn from watching another teach. Even when the content is familiar, we are exposed to new ways of presenting it. We absorb the other's strategies for how to plan lessons, create memorable lessons, use technology, and so on. We also learn from seeing another instructor struggle at times—or from having our teammate see us struggle. If you and your collaborator have a strong, positive relationship, the feedback you provide each other can be extraordinarily thoughtful, as you both will have contended with similar classroom issues and types of content. While it sometimes can be intimidating to teach with a colleague present (especially at first), it certainly helps in eliminating complacency!

By their very nature, cooperative efforts have enormous value for all who participate in them. Working with others yields a richness of experience that working in isolation simply cannot match. More ideas are generated, and evaluation of those ideas is more thorough. One of the chief rewards of collaborative teaching may be that it multiplies the ways in which teaching involves learning.

Challenges of Collaboration

A collegial relationship, like any other, requires work to be successful. You should approach collaborative teaching with your eyes open to the potential challenges of working closely with another on tasks of importance. What you give up in order to gain the many benefits of sharing a teaching enterprise is a measure of your independence. Instead of moving directly and single-mindedly toward your goal, now you must accommodate the other instructor's perspective as well as your own.

DIFFERENT PRIORITIES

Teammates may have different priorities with regard to any number of pedagogical issues. Most important to sort out are those related to the purpose of the course. Any course is defined by a particular focus: on a topic, on particular content, on theory, on certain perspectives. When teammates do not share a vision of what their course is about, friction is inevitable.

If you have worked with the same teammate before on the same course, you may not need as much planning time up front. Those who choose to continue to work together over time probably have come to share values and priorities about their work. Indeed, such values and priorities are often constructed—or at least clarified—through the act of collaboration. Modifying some aspect of how you work together with a familiar colleague is easier than creating a new collaboration. Therefore, new teammates in particular are likely to benefit from lots of talking time to start sorting out values and perspectives about the course they teach together. Start by considering the context: What do you know about the course topic, and what does your teammate know? What do either of you know about the students you are likely to be teaching? Does the course stand alone, or is it part of a sequence?

You and your teammate may have different priorities about content or about students. Do you agree on questions such as how much your students should read, and how closely? what kinds of participation should be required of them? or what types of assignments are appropriate? To compromise on some issues may be essential. In my experience, most teammates are very willing to compromise and consensus is not difficult to reach if you communicate explicitly about such issues.

DEFINING ROLES (SHARING POWER AND RESPONSIBILITY)

Certain collaborative teaching situations, such as a professor employing graduate assistants to assist in teaching a course, come with an assumed hierarchical division of power. These models have the advantage of clarity—that is, the teammates generally see the course as "belonging to" the professor with the assistant role as a supporting one. But even in such a hierarchy, ownership and power are shared to some extent. The graduate assistants make some independent decisions, typically about how to respond to a student in a discussion or how to evaluate a written assignment.

In co-teaching situations between peers, ownership tends to be seen as shared more evenly, and the teammates typically work to divide responsibilities equitably. In these situations, it is important to realize that an "equitable" division of responsibility and power does not always mean *equal* shares of everything for each member. It is next to impossible to divide all tasks equally, and doing so is likely to be highly inefficient. Rather, fairness requires considering each member's strengths, interests, and areas of comfort. It can be liberating to recognize that divisions of power or responsibility are never entirely clear or perfect, and that recognition can yield an arrangement where you and your teammate are allowed to do what each of you does best. However, once again, explicit communication is key to achieving an agreeable division. Each of you must have a voice and an appropriate influence on the collaboration as a whole.

Certain roles seem to evolve easily. Leading, for example, may come naturally to one teammate or the other regarding various aspects of the class. Instructional styles in presenting to a class can vary widely; yours may be highly dramatic, your teammate's much quieter. With some colleagues I find myself taking more leadership, with other colleagues being more content in the background. You too may find yourself willing to fill different roles on different teams or perhaps to try a new role you otherwise might not have if you were teaching alone.

Because taking turns means sharing power, occasional problems are inevitable. Solving them requires balancing your wishes with those of your teammate. Teams function best when the teammates possess a positive attitude toward problems and are able to listen and work to meet everyone's needs. Remember that you are engaged in a shared enterprise; you and your teammate are on the same side!

Also consider how students may perceive your roles. Are you and your teammate seen as sharing authority equally? Be careful to avoid creating a dynamic where students think they can play one of you off the other. Although you and your teammate may not have identical expectations for the students, it is worthwhile to be reasonably consistent.

COMMUNICATION

I believe that many of us are drawn to teaching out of an interest in communicating. Teaching involves passing something on to students, be it a skill, a fund of knowledge, or a values base. Certainly the teachers I remember best are those who were most successful in communicating such things to me. Try to tap into your interest and ability in communicating as you interact with your collaborator(s).

The challenges of collaborative teaching are always best addressed by strong communication. Communication about values creates a framework for the enterprise of sharing instruction. Regular communication is critical for smooth and effective planning. Communication is vital in determining course content, even in a course with a rigidly predetermined curriculum, in order to modify how topics will be presented for a particular group of students. Communication is also a key component both in assessing your own practice and in evaluating and grading students.

Of course, acknowledging the importance of communication in theory is much easier than doing the ongoing work of connecting with another person. During those times I have found team-teaching a challenge, the strategies below have been helpful.

Effective Strategies

PLAN THE COURSE TOGETHER

The work of planning a course is easier when you have a vision of what the course will be about. Do you have a particular perspective on the material that you should acknowledge? What material do you need to cover over the semester? What sort of activity will occur during class time? What will you have students read? How will you evaluate them?

Planning a course with someone else requires asking these same questions, but doing so together in order to develop a shared vision. Working on this process as a team even offers an advantage, in that one of you may think to ask a question the other might have forgotten. The process of articulating your vision with another person can clarify issues in a way that is hard to equal in the solitude of your study. Talking through a course together often stimulates thinking that is richer and more interesting.

Another set of questions is unique to the co-teaching situation: How will tasks be divided? What ongoing structures for planning do you want to put in place? For example, will you and your teammate plan all lessons in common, or divide some or all of them between you? Once the semester begins, how regularly will you meet for planning, and how long will those meetings be? How will you handle grading responsibilities?

My advice is to meet as often as is needed to answer both sets of questions. Do not begrudge this time you spend with your teammate before the first class. The time you invest is well worth the result, because the semester will proceed more smoothly and the course will bear the imprint of each contributor.

MEET REGULARLY ONCE CLASSES BEGIN

Building regular opportunities for communication between teammates can mean the difference between a successful and an unsuccessful collaboration. Create a regular planning time both to hash out challenges and to congratulate each other on teaching that is going well.

In my experience such meetings quickly become routine, and as long as the course is running more or less as planned they are not a large drain on your time. Resist the temptation to skip meetings, as they are amazingly effective at keeping communication channels open and functioning well. Even co-instructors who have worked together for a long time benefit from checking in on a regular basis. And while e-mail is wonderful, it is no substitute for time spent face-to-face.

How frequently you and your teammate decide to meet will be determined by the logistics of your personal situations, and that frequency may change over the semester depending on individual circumstances. My experience has been that meeting weekly is generally appropriate for collaborative planning of a college course.

ALLOCATE TASKS CREATIVELY, PLAYING TO STRENGTHS

In many ways, the great advantage of taking turns over teaching alone is that you no longer must "do it all." Which of you is more dramatic? Which of you likes creating useful charts and other visual supports for students? Is one of you more of a long-range thinker and the other better on his or her feet? When you consider how to divide responsibilities, recognize your differences and use them effectively—the result will be a stronger course than either of you could provide on your own.

At the same time, though, neither of you should get typecast into always playing the same role or of playing only those roles that come most naturally. Indeed, watching your teammate in action can inspire you to take risks and try something unfamiliar or uncomfortable, and in this way your teaching repertoire will be broadened.

Obviously, playing to each person's strengths should never mean that one teammate ends up saddled with all the onerous chores. When there are tasks neither of you finds desirable, principles of collaboration dictate that they be shared.

TRY DIFFERENT CLASSROOM STRUCTURES

There are many ways to use more than one instructor in a college classroom. Experiment with various formats to see what works well for your team; no doubt you will come up with other useful methods as well.

Strict turn taking

One instructor lectures or leads the class activity while the other sits out. Leadership can rotate between class sessions or within a class session. Typically the leader would take sole responsibility for planning that portion of instruction.

One teaches, the other assists

There are many ways the second instructor can support the instructor who is leading. For example, the assistant can take notes on a flipchart, blackboard, or screen (the notes can later be e-mailed to all students). The assistant instructor can rotate among small groups to facilitate or evaluate discussion. The assistant can lead a subactivity, pulling one or two students out at a time to do something while the lead instructor continues with the larger group. The second instructor can contribute ideas and model active participation for students; teammates who have worked together often support each other simply by speaking up to ensure that important points are made.

"Duet" teaching to the whole group [1]

Using two voices can be helpful for teaching certain content, especially when information breaks down naturally in two categories. Teammates can read an exchange of letters or otherwise model two points of view. Consider using this strategy to prompt organized classroom debates on controversies relevant to course content. One instructor can demonstrate a skill while the other narrates the demonstration. Or teammates might ask each other questions during lecture to flesh out a topic or tap each other's special area of interest.

Parallel teaching to half-groups

Two or more instructors can teach the same lesson, each to a portion of the group. In this format, students receive more individual instructor attention. The strategy is especially helpful for lessons that emphasize student participation because it is more efficient of time.

Team management of small-group activity

When small-group activities are planned, having more than one instructor available to roam is useful for keeping the groups on task. More than one

1. I am indebted to Dr. Paula Kluth and Dr. Diana Straut, professors of education at Syracuse University, for this descriptive term.

instructor also allows for more thorough checking in on the discussions or products for which each group is responsible.

TAKE CARE OF EACH OTHER

Productive relationships should be nurtured among collaborators on a project as important as education. Understanding that you and your teammate share common goals and interests often leads (and appropriately so) to warm, positive feelings about each other. This is natural and valuable; foster their development when possible.

At heart, your relationship with a teammate is a working one, and it need not necessarily reach the level of personal friendship. But it is useful to have some sense of the other person's life outside of your collaboration because this knowledge can help you put his or her work behavior into context. Short of invading your teammate's privacy, ask about feelings or outside stresses (somehow, those are always there); be available and open to their response. And conversely, be open to an approach yourself. Spending some time getting to know each other as whole persons can result in a stronger work relationship overall. Personal growth through interaction with others is one of the things collaboration can offer us all.

There Are Many Ways to Take Turns

STUDENTS AS COLLABORATORS

Giving students, either individually or in teams, responsibility for teaching a small piece of your course ensures their engagement and adds variety and interest to class time. It reinforces that underlying message that we are all collaborators in the learning enterprise. In the students-as-teachers model, you would fill in where students' teaching or planning abilities fell short.

Such collaboration demonstrates that no one person is the keeper of all knowledge. A constructivist perspective of education respects the knowledge and competencies of all students and does not regard them as empty vessels awaiting filling by us. When you create opportunities for students to use and build on their existing skills and knowledge, it is good educational practice.

GUESTS AS COLLABORATORS

Inviting a guest speaker or panel of speakers into your class can add drama and immediacy to the material. Giving your students the opportunity to meet and interact with a person possessing special expertise creates a classroom experience that your regular instruction may be hard-pressed to match. Consider inviting an author whose work is relevant to the course or a colleague from another department. Someone with an underrepresented viewpoint or esoteric interest may especially appreciate having his or her voice heard by your class.

Think of guest speakers not as time off from teaching for you but as a form of collaboration that offers additional educative opportunities. Much of your role during a visit by a guest speaker is to model productive interaction. Practice active listening, and prepare some questions to ask the guest after the presentation. After the guest leaves, be prepared to debrief the experience to put the visit into a framework consistent with your goals and visions for that class session.

Visitors offer an opportunity for you to model other traits, as well. Make sure you and your students recognize the effort guests put into preparing for and presenting to the class. Show your appreciation for how much they have to offer students. As well as being unstinting with your thanks, see whether funds exist that you can tap to either pay guests for their time or send them a thank-you gift.

In my education courses, visitors have included guest professors, in-service teachers working in innovative programs, parents, so-called "at-risk" high school students, and persons with particular disabilities. In their evaluations of my courses, students often remark on the importance of the guest speakers; for many students, the speakers create the most memorable experiences of the semester.

GRADUATE ASSISTANTS AS COLLABORATORS

As mentioned earlier, a collaboration between professor and graduate assistant(s) is necessarily a hierarchical one, with a greater degree of responsibility for and "ownership" of the course lying with the professor. Even within this hierarchical relationship, there is still significant give-and-take, and meaningful collaboration is always a part of the best such relationships.

Ideally, a mentoring relationship exists between the professor and graduate assistants, through which the assistants have opportunities to build competencies both with course content and with teaching. For their part, graduate assistants often are capable of assuming significant responsibility for many aspects of a course. They may also contribute energy and fresh ideas that the professor finds revitalizing. Oftentimes professors and their graduate assistants become colleagues in the teaching enterprise and enjoy truly collegial relationships. Remember, for example, that being overworked is a problem that both graduate assistants and professor generally share, and sympathy for your teammate's situation is always helpful.

COLLEAGUES OUTSIDE YOUR DISCIPLINE AS COLLABORATORS

Two instructors may work well together because they share similar interests, and developing a course within a shared discipline is very natural. Communication is fostered because the instructors already speak much of the same language. They will be comfortable with the content and are likely to be excited about each other's insights.

However, collaboration between instructors with different areas of expertise offers a sort of cross-fertilization that is also well worth exploring. Interdisciplinary work is often the most intellectually creative and interesting, and many disciplines combine well. Consider combining arts and sciences courses that deal with similar periods of history or areas of the world, for example. Or education courses that focus on different populations. A focus in teacher preparation at my own university on inclusive education has led to some creative combining of special education and general education courses. Research courses offer many opportunities for interdisciplinary work, as do courses in areas such as women's studies, African American studies, and disability studies, which are already interdisciplinary by nature.

Degrees of Collaboration

What opportunities you may have for collaboration will depend on your individual and institutional circumstances. But it is worthwhile to be open to opportunities in whatever form they present themselves. Consider all the ways of collaboratively teaching that I outlined above. If institutional barriers make it impossible for you to collaborate as extensively as you want, look for smaller opportunities such as your guest lecturing for a colleague. Often beginning with small efforts allows for further development of meaningful collaboration over time. Being open to the possibilities of collaboration can lead you into ways of teaching you might not have predicted.

One outstanding collaborative effort at my own institution was the result of two newly hired instructors being given consecutive class times in the same classroom with a single cohort of students in our teacher-preparation program. Dr. Diana Straut was teaching a methods course for elementary school social studies, and Dr. Paula Kluth taught a course in differentiating instruction for elementary school students with disabilities. They began by sharing a few class sessions on related topics and eventually chose to team-teach both courses in a highly integrated fashion.

That collaboration allowed them to model for students how inclusive practices could be made integral to how lessons are planned and implemented rather than being afterthoughts. Their collaborative practice also taught students strategies for teamwork that the students could carry with them into their future work situations, as many were preparing to be part of teams in inclusive education programs.

Kluth and Straut wrote up their experience in "Do as I Say *and* as I Do!"[2] They recommend doing the following in collaborative teaching situations:

• Purposefully model a variety of collaborations to your students.
• Make collaborations transparent to them.
• Model the good, the bad, and the ugly of your collaborative work.
• Think "out of the collaborative box" (i.e., collaborate in any way that logistics allow).
• Seek institutional support.
• Study your experiences.

Part of my hope for this chapter was to show that most of us already use forms of collaboration in small or informal ways in our teaching. By thinking of more extensive collaborative practices as extensions of what we already do, rather than as something altogether new and different, perhaps we will see possibilities that would have otherwise been invisible to us. I know that many of my most fulfilling teaching experiences have occurred when working with others rather than flying solo. I hope that I have inspired you to become excited about opportunities to collaborate with others.

2. Paula Kluth and Diana Straut, "Do as I Say *and* as I Do," *Journal of Teacher Education* (forthcoming).

19

Mentoring and Its Assessment

Peter J. Gray and W. Brad Johnson

ALTHOUGH EXCELLENCE IN THE PROFESSOR ROLE has typically been defined almost exclusively in terms of teaching and research, faculty search committees are increasingly interested in a candidate's credentials as a mentor. Mentored students tend to be considerably more satisfied with their educational program, the larger institution, and their subsequent careers. Furthermore, mentored students often go on to mentor others themselves. For all of these reasons, developing strong mentor relationships with certain students is becoming an increasingly important dimension of successful university teaching. The purpose of this chapter is to highlight the essentials of mentorship in university settings as well as to describe issues and approaches related to the assessment of mentoring.

The Contours of Mentoring

Mentorships can be distinguished from other important faculty roles (e.g., teaching, supervising, professional service, faculty governance and other committee work, counseling, and advising) in that mentoring requires a more dynamic, engaged, long-term and multidimensional relationship between mentor and student (protégé). Mentorships provide the opportunities to pass on one's professional legacy and experience. Mentoring involves an active and very personal concern for the short- and long-term welfare of the protégé. Mentoring in universities generates a number of unique benefits both to students and professors. For the student (protégé), such things as professional skill development, enhanced confidence and professional identity, increased scholarly productivity, dissertation success, and greater satisfaction with both graduate school and one's subsequent career may all be acquired from the experience (Johnson 2002).

In a mentorship, the faculty member acts as a guide, role model, and patron of a less experienced (and often younger) college or graduate student (Johnson 2002). Mentorships often begin informally as a result of common interests, mutual validation (mutual expressions of positive regard and admiration), and reciprocity (sharing of one's feelings and experiences), and grow with increasing trust and successful collaboration (Johnson and Huwe 2002).

Once a mentorship has formed between professor and student, it often progresses through predictable phases in which the mentor offers the protégé several important "functions" (Jacobi 1991; Kram 1985). When you offer protégés *career functions,* you are helping them to "learn the ropes" of the profession. You are furnishing them with the challenging assignments that will stimulate their growth in a scholarly direction. You are coaching and encouraging them to define and establish themselves in the particular academic field. You are guiding them into suitable professional forums and networks. Equally important are *psychosocial functions.* Such functions are intended to engender in the protégé a sense of competence, identity, and effectiveness in the professional role. When you offer a student protégé acceptance and confirmation, counseling, and friendship, you are performing crucial psychosocial functions. In addition, role-modeling allows the mentor to offer a deliberate and personal illustration of what it's like to be a professional in his or her field.

Mentoring requires a strong commitment to achieving an identity transformation in your protégé. You must be resolved to do everything it takes to turn an insecure student and novice professional into an accomplished and confident colleague. This is a process that often takes at least several years. Thus, mentoring is not only resource-intensive, but also time-extensive. Generous commitment of resource and time is necessary in *any* mentorship. But what are the characteristics of *excellent* mentorship?

The Elements of Excellent Mentoring

Outstanding mentors are typically very confident and competent professors who show a vital and authentic interest in both the personal and professional development of their protégés. They possess fundamental cognitive abilities, emotional abilities (e.g., personal balance, emotional self-awareness, and receptivity), and relational abilities (e.g., interpersonal skills, empathy, and ability to generate trust in others). But outstanding mentoring involves more than this. Excellent mentors consistently employ several strategies as described below.

BEING SELECTIVE

No college or university instructor can successfully mentor all students. Not only would any attempt lead to burnout, strained relationships, and poor mentoring outcomes, it would also violate assumptions about the nature of mentoring. A mentorship is a unique and special relationship with a well-matched and particularly promising student. To employ your time and resources most efficiently, it is important to restrict the number of students you mentor. Not surprisingly, successful mentors often select students with talents similar to their own. We tend to migrate to those students in whom we see glimmers of talent and great potential. In turn, protégés often seek mentors who seem to recognize and appreciate their talents and potential. The most productive and enjoyable mentorships tend to develop between well-matched pairs, where there is mutuality of intellectual talent. When mentors and protégés admire each other and share important personality traits, professional interests, or career interests, it is reasonable to expect better outcomes (Johnson and Huwe 2002).

STRUCTURING THE RELATIONSHIP

At the outset, it is essential that mentors clarify expectations about the relationship: frequency of meetings, expected duration of the mentorship, short- and long-term academic/career goals of the protégé. It should be made clear at the beginning whether mentors expect assistance with courses or protégé participation in their research projects. In addition, successful mentors are careful to discuss their own availability to protégés. Preferably, mentors will schedule formal meetings with protégés early on in the mentorship. As the mentorship unfolds and the protégé becomes increasingly competent and confident, meetings may become more informal and ad hoc. Moreover, the meetings may become more collaborative and collegial. The important thing is to clarify expectations at the beginning and to recognize changes in the protégé as the relationship evolves.

AFFIRMING AND SUPPORTING

Excellent mentors understand that most protégés are initially inexperienced, relatively insecure, and sometimes suffer from the "imposter syndrome"—the fear that they gained admission to the program or attracted your attention undeservedly and that this fact will soon be detected. This feeling may make them hypersensitive to criticism. When a mentor takes the time to learn about; understand; and then support, affirm, and encourage a protégé, the effects (in terms of confidence, professional identity, and performance) can be striking. Fine mentors are especially careful to help the protégé conceive and articulate a professional "dream" or "vision," which the mentor then strongly affirms and supports. This is a crucial aspect of mentoring and, therefore, it is important for the mentor to be liberal with affirmation, especially early in the protégé's development.

CHALLENGING, COACHING, AND SPONSORING

Of course, it is not enough to lend emotional support to protégés; excellent mentors are active and deliberate teachers, coaches, and sponsors. They find opportunities for protégés: graduate assistantships, postdoctoral and professional positions, participation in professional organizations, and chances to present work at conferences or submit it for publication. They also challenge them to venture bold professional actions and assume greater responsibility, and then coach them through any developmental trials that ensue. An excellent mentor often pushes an undergraduate student to run for office or be involved in departmental committees; to submit a paper for presentation at a student conference; or to prepare for admission to a competitive graduate program. Graduate students may be encouraged to submit proposals for professional disciplinary conferences, lead departmental graduate student organizations, and write scholarly publications and reports. At times, the excellent mentor will steer protégés clear of bad professional decisions or department politics. The outstanding mentor will offer guidance and an "insider" perspective, and serve as an advocate for the protégé within the department.

OFFERING INTENTIONAL MODELING

Excellent mentors invite their protégés to participate with them in a wide range of professional activities. This may include co-teaching, co-presenting at conferences, co-leading meetings, and co-authoring scholarly work. These activities provide the opportunity for effective modeling. In fact, for those protégés most likely to follow your own career path, there are very few daily professional activities they would not benefit from watching you perform. Protégés may initially serve as observers but should be encouraged to assume increasingly active roles in each of the activities modeled by the mentor. Needless to say, inviting your protégés to participate with you in this way instills confidence and implicit affirmation, interest, and commitment to their development.

MAINTAINING BOUNDARIES

Mentorships are complex, emotionally intimate, and long-term relationships characterized by mutuality and multiple overlapping roles (e.g., teacher, adviser, colleague, supervisor, and friend). As multiple-role relationships, mentorships require the mentor to diligently guard against harmful professional boundary violations (Blevins-Knabe 1992). Specifically, mentors must avoid romantic/sexual relationships, business relationships, or even unduly intimate friendships with those they mentor.

ATTENDING TO EVIDENCE OF DYSFUNCTION

Excellent mentors appreciate the fact that all relationships are vulnerable to dysfunction. They watch for evidence of disturbance (e.g., conflict, distance/withdrawal, or distress related to the mentorship) and then intervene promptly to diagnose the source of dysfunction, take corrective action, and, if necessary, terminate the mentorship. They are careful to identify and correct their own possible contributions to dysfunction (e.g., relational incompetence, exploitation of a protégé, protégé neglect or abandonment, and personal problems). When signs of dysfunction appear, it may be advisable to introduce a third party (e.g., trusted colleague or department chair) for the sake of an objective perspective, and to help investigate the source of dysfunction and explore possible remedies.

Assessing Your Mentoring

As with the assessment of teaching and learning generally, the purpose of the assessment of mentoring should be improvement of the experience for both teacher and learner, mentor and protégé. Mentoring assessment must begin with the goals that the mentor and protégé have enunciated. Typically, one of these goals is career development (Kram 1985). A mentor-protégé pair may also share the psychosocial goal of enhancing the protégé's sense of competence, identity, and work-role effectiveness.

ASSESSING INITIAL PHASE

Assessment activities may involve a variety of qualitative and quantitative evaluation methods designed to gather data to inform the mentoring process and to evaluate its success. At the selection and orientation (initiation) stage, a predominantly quantitative instrument may be developed to observe whether behavior is intelligent, caring, appropriately humorous, flexible, empathic, patient, interpersonally supportive, encouraging, poised, ethical, psychologically well-adjusted, kind, and professionally competent. Mentors who exhibit these characteristics usually prove very effective (Johnson 2002). As we have seen, these characteristics can be grouped into three categories: cognitive abilities, emotional abilities, and relational abilities.

Quantitative and qualitative assessment concerned with these essential mentoring abilities may be used by administrators and department chairs to make decisions about the assignment of mentors. For example, prospective mentor candidates could be asked to rate the extent to which they are comfortable with activities such as sponsorship, coaching, provision of challenging assignments, and transmission of applied professional ethics (Johnson 2002), as well as role-modeling and counseling (Kram 1985). It is particularly important for new faculty to receive preliminary feedback regarding cognitive, emotional, and relational abilities. New faculty members themselves should reflect on their performance to identify any inadequacies in the three areas.

ASSESSING THE WORKING-RELATIONSHIP PHASE

Mentors and protégés may consider using a formal or informal "contract" (Johnson and Huwe 2002) that describes expectations, understandings, and agreements regarding the focus of the relationship, expected outcomes, anticipated meeting frequency, and duration of the mentorship; specific mentor functions desired by the protégé; and expectations for assistance with classes/projects on the part of the mentor. At various points in the development of the mentorship, this "contract" can be consulted to judge whether the relationship is proceeding successfully—and to identify areas where improvements may be needed. A face-to-face "briefing," based on the "contract," once a semester is an effective way to keep the mentorship on track.

In order to assess a professor's competence as a mentor, it is appropriate to evaluate him or her throughout the working-relationship phase. Simple quantitative rating scales may be used to measure student development and awareness of mentor functions. A qualitative approach may be employed to check whether the professor demonstrates the ability to (a) determine which functions a protégé most requires at specific stages of development; (b) understand how to structure mentorships at the outset; (c) manage boundaries and avert the development of harmful relations; (d) recognize and respond to dysfunctional or ineffective mentorships; and (e) handle cross-gender and cross-race mentorships appropriately. Interviews and journals may be used to provide evidence of these abilities.

We recommend that those responsible for mentoring programs at the departmental or institutional level ask students to complete anonymous annual mentor competency evaluations composed of both quantitative ratings and open-ended questions about the mentor's abilities and the nature of the mentoring relationship. This information may be used to guide the mentoring program and to give feedback to mentors. If problems are indicated, further investigation and dialogue with students and faculty should take place to better understand the causes of problems and their possible solutions. In this way, mentor evaluations can function like the best teaching evaluations.

At the end of the working-phase of the mentoring relationship some tangible student success outcomes may be assessed; for example, time to degree, number and type of leadership roles within the department or institution, frequency of co-authorship on presentations and publications, quality and prestige of conferences and publications, growth in self-confidence, and expectations for future achievement. Post-graduation indicators of success might include initial position and salary and level of satisfaction; further graduate study or postdoctoral positions; and, within the first three years, quality of professional presentations and publications, funded research grants, promotions and salary increases, self-reported confidence in the professional role, and number of protégés mentored. This information may be gathered as part of an institution-wide or departmental alumni follow-up process that might involve a combination of telephone interviews and web-based surveys. While none of these outcomes can be attributed solely to mentoring, they are correlates of good mentoring and—along with other information about the success of the mentoring process gathered during and at the termination of the mentorship—they can shed light on the efficacy of the mentorship program and guide its improvement.

Final Thoughts

In contrast to teaching and advising functions that typically have shorter durations and less depth, mentorships are generally long-term and complex relationships that seldom have a clearly defined terminus. Therefore, the creation and implementation of sound mentoring relationships and the assessment of mentoring success require deliberate planning and a longitudinal study design. By a careful consideration of the elements of excellent mentoring and the aid of a well-thought-out assessment process, a successful mentoring program can be realized for the benefit of faculty, students, departments, and institutions.

20

Playing a Role in Preparing a Diverse Faculty for the America of Tomorrow

Orlando L. Taylor and Kimarie Engerman

THE CHALLENGE OF CREATING racial and ethnic diversity in higher education has been discussed widely in recent years. Supporters of this type of diversity typically cite such benefits as fulfilling the American ideal, meeting future national workforce needs, and creating an effective learning environment for all students. Several recent statements by such august bodies as the Association of American Universities and the Council of Graduate Schools typify the views of the supporters of diversity. In 1997, for example, the prestigious Association of American Universities made the following case in speaking to the need for affirmative action in admissions:

> We speak first and foremost as educators. We believe that our students benefit significantly from education that takes place within a diverse setting. In the course of their university education, our students encounter and learn from others who have backgrounds and characteristics very different from their own. As we seek to prepare students for life in the twenty-first century, the educational value of such encounters will become more important, not less, than in the past. (Association of American Universities, 1997)

A very substantial portion of our curriculum is enhanced by the discourse made possible by the heterogeneous backgrounds of our students. Equally, a significant part of education in our institutions takes place outside the classroom, in extracurricular activities where students learn how to work together, as well as (how) to compete; how to exercise leadership, as well as (how) to build consensus. If our institutional capacity to bring together a genuinely diverse group of students is removed—or severely reduced—then the quality and texture of the education we provide will be significantly diminished (Association of American Universities, 1997).

In the same year, 1997, the Council of Graduate Schools asserted the following: "Broadening the talent pool from which graduate students are chosen enhances the educational and scholarly activities of all students and faculty and is good academic policy. Graduate education establishes an atmosphere of intellectual collegiality in which interaction among people with differing points of view is essential to learning" (Council of Graduate Schools 1997, 1).

While the discussion of the diversity topic has centered primarily on the topic of diversity within student bodies, far too little conversation has focused on the topics of faculty diversity and on preparing future faculty members to teach our nation's increasingly diverse student bodies. Turner speaks directly to the issue of faculty diversity. According to Turner (2002), the argument for faculty diversity is just as compelling as the argument for student diversity. Faculty diversity makes a direct contribution to educational quality because a diverse faculty leads to better educational outcomes for all students. At every level of college teaching and governance, multiple and diverse perspectives are needed to serve current and future student populations. Students are more likely to be exposed to a wider range of scholarly perspectives and to ideas drawn from a variety of life experiences when college and university faculty are diverse. Intellectual stimulation for both students and faculty alike are created because diverse faculty bring new research questions and fresh perspectives to the academic enterprise.

Turner may be included within a growing number of higher education leaders who assert that faculty diversity, in many ways, is where we must focus our efforts if we are to make institutional diversity a reality in the long run. Simply stated, they claim that without significant diversity of the faculty other institutional diversity goals will likely fall short (Boyd, 2004; Villalpando, 2002).

Why would one make such a bold statement? The reasons are many. First of all, faculty members teach their classes within a framework of their own cultural backgrounds. Truth is rarely a *fixed* concept in most disciplines. It is most often a reflection of the perspectives, theoretical orientations, and values of those who perceive—and teach—that truth. All of these traits come, at least in part, from one's cultural orientation.

Faculty members also determine the research priorities and research methodologies within their academic units and these, too, are often reflective of cultural orientations. This point is easily made by observing the significant changes in many disciplines over the past three decades as a result of more women and more people of color on college and university faculties. The rise of such interdisciplinary academic programs as women's studies and various forms of ethnic studies documents this point. Similar changes have occurred in the physical and life sciences. It might be argued that the significant increase in research—and ultimate knowledge—in the area of women's health is directly related to the presence of significantly more women in the biomedical academic and research communities who might have differently prioritized research questions or differently preferred research paradigms than those of men.

Also, faculty members from diverse groups can serve as role models and inspire students from underrepresented groups who aspire to high achievement in the academic world—including acquiring an advanced degree and possibly becoming a faculty member. They also can inform the *overrepresented* white student majority on most campuses that the search for truth is universal and that as they learn more about others' perceptions of truth, they too become more informed and better prepared to function effectively in multicultural America and the global community. In other words, the presence of diverse faculty is also a benefit to majority students.

To better serve new students and to prepare all students for an increasingly diverse world, it is important that instructors and administrators not only diversify their curricula but also examine *how* teaching is being done. Evidence suggests that college exposure to a diverse faculty, along with exposure to culturally inclusive curricula and teaching methods, produces students who are more complex thinkers, more confident in negotiating cultural differences, and more likely to seek remedies for inequities after graduation (Antonio, 2003; Hurtado, Milem, and Clayton, 1999; Smith, Wolf, and Busenberg, 1996). Because faculty of color frequently take scholarship and teaching in new directions, their presence on campuses makes the goal of enhanced learning outcomes easier to attain. In fact, faculty of color surpasses their white colleagues in using teaching techniques associated with student-centered pedagogy (Turner 2002). O'Banion (1997) has offered a helpful prescription for such pedagogy. It is argued that learning colleges exemplify six principles. They (1) create substantive change in in-

dividual learners; (2) engage learners in the learning process as full partners, assuming primary responsibility for their own choices; (3) create and
offer as many options for learning as possible; (4) assist learners to form and
participate in collaborative learning activities; (5) define the roles of learning facilitators by the needs of the learners; and (6) measure success of facilitators only insofar as improved and expanded learning can be documented
for the learners (O'Banion 1997, 15).

In striving for more faculty members from diverse groups, particularly
from currently underrepresented groups, the point must not be lost that *all*
new faculty members from *all* racial/ethnic groups, regardless of gender,
need to understand the issues, pedagogies, challenges, and sensitivities
required to teach in the increasingly diverse American college classroom.
Turner (2002) cites the following statistics to make the case for the growing
diversity of the American college and university classroom:

> America's colleges and universities are educating a larger and more diverse
> group of students than ever before. According to a recent study conducted
> by the Educational Testing Service, an even greater transformation in the
> student body will occur over the next decade. By 2015, for example, 80 per-
> cent of the anticipated 2.6 million new college students will be African Amer-
> ican, Hispanic, Asian/Pacific Islander, or American Indian. Nationwide, the
> number of undergraduate minority students enrolled in colleges and uni-
> versities will increase from 29.4 percent to 37.2 percent. The number of mi-
> nority students in the District of Columbia, California, Hawaii, and New
> Mexico will exceed the number of white students. In Texas, the campus pop-
> ulation of minorities will be nearly 50 percent, and in New York, Maryland,
> Florida, New Jersey, Louisiana, and Mississippi, minority student enrollment
> is expected to exceed 40 percent of the total undergraduate population. (1)

Already fully 20 percent of American college and university students are
members of racial and ethnic minority groups, representing the fastest-
growing group of postsecondary students in graduate education. While
these students continue to be underrepresented in student bodies—not to
mention on faculties—they come from the fastest-growing segment of the
American population. In the 2000 census, they represented nearly 30 percent of the American people and some demographers project that they will
comprise the *majority* of the American people by the year 2050.

These statistics, taken in isolation, may mean little. Indeed, one might say that the changing demographics of college and university classrooms actually mean that nothing needs to change. Others might say that various groups may reflect differences in learning styles, curricular interests, motivational factors, persistence tendencies, etc. Thus, faculty members must be well prepared to address these and other issues if they are to enhance learning outcomes for *all* students. Because one size is not likely to fit all students, current doctoral students and faculty members of all "stripes" need to be prepared to teach, mentor, conduct research, and provide public service in a multicultural environment.

So How Are We Doing in Diversifying the Professoriate?

Assuming that most leaders in American higher education espouse the view that faculty diversity is a good thing, let us take stock of how good intentions have met reality. Clearly, there have been intensified efforts over the past three decades to attract more individuals from underrepresented minority groups into the college and university professoriate. However, after about thirty years of affirmative action, African Americans, Hispanics, Native Americans, and individuals from other underrepresented groups still only comprise an embarrassingly small percentage of our faculties.

Citing U.S. Department of Education data, William Harvey (2002) of the American Council on Education presents a somewhat encouraging trend with respect to diversity among the more than 570,000 full-time faculty members in American colleges and universities. In the ACE Nineteenth Annual Status Report of *Minorities in Higher Education,* Harvey reports that from 1991 through 1999, the number of faculty of color increased by more than 28 percent, with women of color increasing by nearly 47 percent compared to an increase for men of color by slightly more than 18 percent. Moreover, the proportional representation for faculty of color increased from 12.3 percent during this same period to 14.4 percent.

Yet further inspection of the data reveals a continuing pattern of low representation of African Americans and Hispanics on college and university faculties. While these two groups combined comprise more than 25 percent of the American people, African Americans comprised only 5.1 percent and Hispanics 2.9 percent of the American professoriate in 1999, the latest year for which data are available. Moreover, it is estimated that approximately 50 percent of full-time African American faculty members are hired in the nation's 105 or so Historically Black Colleges and Universities (HBCUs). This fact means that Traditionally White Institutions (TWIs) still employ fewer than 6 percent of their faculty members from the nation's two largest groups of color.

The conclusion that we draw is that, despite the aforementioned gains in faculty diversity cited above, the problem of underrepresentation of persons of color on college and university faculties—even with affirmative action— is real. One shudders to think what would happen if affirmative action strategies are attenuated or eliminated. Yet, with upwards of one-half of the current professoriate expected to retire by 2020, the nation has many opportunities to make changes in college and university faculty a reality— especially if it can increase its Ph.D. production of underrepresented minorities and women.

Meeting the Challenges of Faculty Diversity

Perhaps a major first step for the nation in achieving greater faculty diversity is to increase the number of underrepresented minorities receiving the Ph.D. degree, the usual academic degree requirement for faculty appointments. Despite the proclaimed benefits of diversity in graduate education, numerous challenges have emerged in recent years that threaten the realization of the goal of achieving equality of access for all students in graduate education. The most daunting of these challenges is increased opposition to affirmative-action policies and practices in university admissions and the awarding of financial aid. *Hopwood v. Texas* in the 5th Circuit Court of Appeals, Proposition 209 in California, and Initiative 200 in the state of Washington suggest that a substantial portion of the American public is resistant to many of the strategies that have been employed to achieve racial and ethnic diversity in higher education. The emergence of what might be called an "anti-affirmative action" environment threatens to mitigate the modest gains in racial and ethnic inclusiveness in graduate education that have been achieved in the past three decades.

Whatever the reasons, one of the impediments to faculty diversity is the continuing problem of low productivity of doctoral degree recipients among underrepresented groups of color. According to the most recent statistics reported by the National Science Foundation (October 26, 2002, Internet), nearly 43,000 individuals received doctoral degrees in 1998. African

Americans received approximately 1,500 of these degrees (3.5 percent), while Hispanics received approximately 1,300 (3.0 percent), and Native Americans approximately 200 (0.05 percent). Asian Americans, who are *not* underrepresented in relation to their total presence in the U.S. population, received about 2,700 Ph.D. degrees (6.3 percent) but received relatively few doctorates in the social sciences and humanities.

These statistics mean that the nation's two largest minority groups— African Americans and Hispanics, which represent close to one-quarter of the American people—are only receiving approximately 6.5 percent of all Ph.D.s awarded annually. The numbers are even more disturbing in many disciplines. For example, only 16 of the approximately 1,100 (1.5 percent) doctorates awarded in mathematics in 2000 were awarded to African Americans and non-U.S. black students with Permanent Visas. At this paltry rate, it means that it will take more than 200 years for each of America's 3,500 or so colleges and universities to hire one new African American doctoral recipient in mathematics—provided, of course, no one dies or chooses to work outside the academy! Absurdities aside, it is clear that, at the current rate of doctoral degree productivity in many fields, full faculty diversity is a literal impossibility within our lifetime.

Fixing the Problem

As either a teaching assistant or early-career faculty member, you have the opportunity to play a significant role in determining whether institutions of higher education will be able to meet these challenges. First, there is a major need to improve our mentoring of students of color—both undergraduate and graduate—on the joys of academic careers and the range of choices that are available to them. Far too many students have stereotypical notions about the professoriate and the various campus cultures that exist within American higher education. This is a problem for more than just students of color.

Second, we must mentor students of color on the need to participate in faculty-preparation programs, especially those that exist on their campuses. Even if we increase the number of students of color with Ph.D.s, they will find all too often that they are not as competitive as they otherwise might have been if they had participated in such formal preparation programs.

Third, doctoral-granting institutions must find new and creative ways to assure inclusiveness in their graduate student bodies that are acceptable in the contemporary legal environment and the court of public opinion that are increasingly challenging traditional affirmative-action strategies. This means, among other things, that we must redefine criteria for determining "merit" in admissions and financial aid decisions that are fairer and less dependent upon standardized tests. It also means that we must place greater emphasis on attenuating the factors that lead to academic and social isolation on campuses—factors that rank very highly in leading to attrition and in determining time to degree for graduate students of color.

Fourth, as was stated earlier, *all* new faculty members from *all* racial/ ethnic groups, regardless of gender, need to understand the issues, pedagogies, challenges, and sensitivities required to teach in the increasingly diverse American college classroom. Today's American college classroom is composed of more students of color, older, part-time, international students, women, as well as students with a range of sexual orientations and various disabilities (Adams and Marchesani 1999). It is understandably difficult for faculty who are socialized within another historical and cultural situation to know how to best facilitate student learning within a diverse context. Therefore, to make learning possible, it is proposed that all faculty members should receive training in the following three elements: (1) didactic course on cultural issues impacting the professoriate, (2) supervised experience in teaching culturally diverse students, and (3) research experience that focuses on teaching and learning issues that impact diverse students.

All graduate students preparing for careers in the professoriate, regardless of their race, ethnicity or gender, need to be prepared to teach in the most culturally diverse classroom—and cyberspace environment—that has ever been known before to humanity. In the United States, it is projected that upwards of 50 percent of the American people will be people of color by 2050. Already, more than 20 percent of all college students come from these same groups—and they represent the fastest-growing segment of American higher education.

In addition, the rapid globalization of economies, businesses, and education, bundled together in a technology-based environment, has ensured that professors of the future, if not the present, must be able to teach students to function in a world of diverse people. Moreover, they will increasingly teach such knowledge and skills in a distance-learning environment in which their students will be connected to one another electronically. It is readily apparent, therefore, that the professor of the future must be prepared to work in a vastly different environment than those in previous generations. In short, while diversification of the professoriate in terms of people is important, diversification of the intellect and outlook are equally important.

If one accepts this picture, a question naturally arises: "What can I do?" You may then begin to wonder what type of preparation you need to be prepared to teach in the type of academic environment described above. We would submit that such preparation must involve, at minimum, didactic and hands-on experiences. One must make a deliberate effort to acquire wide and varied experience, whether attending workshops or seeking diverse groups and individuals with whom to interact.

Rich didactic experiences can often be gained from workshops or sections of formal courses for graduate students on teaching and learning for diverse students; these workshops are usually followed by a set of focused and supervised experiences in which students have opportunities to teach a critical mass of students from cultures different from their own. Alternatively, if not additionally, they may seek a short-term teaching appointment at an institution composed of individuals traditionally underrepresented in higher education, e.g., a Historically Black College or University (HBCU), a Hispanic Serving Institution (HSI), or a Tribal College. The workshop or course might focus on such topics as:

- demographic trends in the United States;
- world demographic trends;
- demographic profiles of Aamerican college students by race, gender, and discipline;
- learning styles characteristic of specified racial/ethnic groups and genders;
- academic and research topics of particular interest to selected racial/ethnic groups and genders;
- special challenges faced by selected racial/ethnic groups and genders in American higher education;
- hidden vestiges of discrimination in American colleges and universities—for example, standardized tests, monocultural curriculum offerings, and the devaluation of diversity efforts in the promotion and tenuring of faculty.

The personal experience component of this preparation can involve teaching a course or giving guest lectures in an ethnic studies or women's studies course, participating in a service-learning project in a culture different from one's own, or teaching a course or guest lecturing in a Minority Serving Institution (MSI).

Graduate students of color will need to have particular mentoring on the challenges they might well face in the professoriate, particularly if they are employed at a non-Minority Serving Institution. Such factors as questioning authenticity by majority students; lack of interest in ethnic-based research topics or research paradigms; disregard for participation in racial/ethnic/gender programs in the merit pay, promotion, and tenuring process; and often dealing with social isolation and disconnectivity with one's own cultural community. The Doctoral Scholars Program provides an outstanding training program in the form of a three-day workshop that addresses these issues on a yearly basis.

With regard to supervised experience in teaching diverse students, *all* teaching assistants and future faculty members should look for opportunities to teach groups of students whose culture differs from their own. Difference in culture can be defined in terms such as language, gender, and ethnicity/race. For instance, a white doctoral student might try a supervised experience of teaching in a classroom that consists primarily of students of color. As Hilliard (1989) has pointed out, this experience is essential because in a classroom, cultural style is a dynamic that cannot be ignored. Cultural style is the "personality" of the group; when cultural style is ignored, misunderstandings arise.

A misunderstanding of cultural style may lead a faculty member to make mistakes in estimating the intellectual potential of a student or a cultural group, misread achievement in academic subjects such as creative expression, misjudge students' language abilities, and contribute to difficulty in establishing rapport and effective communication in the classroom. Therefore, the opportunity for graduate students to teach with supervision in a culturally diverse environment allows them *all* to receive guidance in facilitating the needs of diverse students. In this process, future faculty members are provided an opportunity to become more sensitive to cultural differences and learning styles, thereby reducing the probability of cross-cultural missteps and misunderstandings from occurring in their own classrooms.

Debunking Myths Regarding the Hiring of Faculty of Color

As a graduate student or new faculty member, you are likely to get the opportunity to sit on search committees for new hires. As you participate in this process, it would be helpful to be aware of some misconceptions and problems that often affect it. According to Lopez (1997), the processes that exist now are not effective in that the selection of faculty of color from the applicant pool is limited. To rectify this problem and improve diversity, institutions—and you, as a contributing member—must overcome the mythologies that exist, employ and assist effective recruitment strategies, re-move barriers that discourage faculty members of color from remaining at institutions, and groom promising students of color for careers in academia.

Smith, Wolf, and Busenberg (1996) have provided well-documented evi-dence to show that many institutions and their faculty search committees often operate based on several "myths" about the hiring of faculty members of color that compromise their effectiveness in achieving faculty diversity goals—and that the myths are contradicted by the reality experienced by the study participants. According to Smith, Wolf, and Busenberg, hiring institu-tions must debunk these myths; and they must encourage a broader percep-tion of and respect for the variety of institutions that award doctoral degrees (HBCUs, for example), avoid hidden factors that discourage minority appli-cants (e.g., presuming a primary interest in minority topics), and include factors in job descriptions that might be particularly attractive to persons of color. According to their study, the six myths are:

1. Too many institutions mean too few applicants. However, the reality was that only 11 percent of the participants in the study by Smith, Wolf, and Busenberg were actively recruited for a faculty position.

2. Few applicants mean high demand for these applicants. Yet, 54 per-cent of the scientists in the study who had pursued postdoctoral positions were not recruited for faculty positions. Additionally, because they were un-able to find faculty positions, other scientists left academia for industry.

3. Graduates from prestigious institutions desire to work only at presti-gious institutions. On the contrary, faculty members of color expressed a wide variety of preferences; for instance, study participants chose institu-tions based on their academic environment, similarity of the institution's mission with their professional goals, or their desire to teach a diverse stu-dent body.

4. Ordinary institutions lack adequate resources for hiring faculty of color. The reality was quite the opposite, because financial packages and prestige were not among the reasons that faculty members of color gave for leaving an institution. In most instances, faculty members of color left an institution because of questions of appropriate fit, dual career choices, and unresolved issues with the institution.

5. Lucrative offers come only from government and industry. In reality, decisions by study participants to leave resulted from problems inside academia, not from irresistible offers elsewhere. These problems in academia included a need to establish a career before the age of forty, feeling unappreciated due to the search processes, and job market difficulties.

6. Heterosexual white males are unsuccessful at securing jobs in institutions seeking to diversify. In actuality, the white males in the study had a good experience in the labor market and were indeed successful. The only white males who had difficulty in finding a faculty appointment were those whose field specialties had virtually no openings.

We would posit a seventh myth, one not stated by Smith, Wolf, and Busenberg—the belief possibly held by some in academia that the Ph.D. degrees awarded by HBCUs and other minority-serving institutions to people of color are not equal in quality of education to those awarded by TWIs. If that myth persists, then another major problem will need to be addressed, because HBCUs produce about 14 percent of all Ph.D. recipients. Howard University, for example, is the highest producer of African American Ph.D. graduates; for the academic year 1999–2000, Howard produced eighty African American Ph.D. graduates, whereas Harvard University produced twenty-eight and Yale University produced only one (Borden 2002).

African American graduates from HBCUs do equally well in post-college activities and employment as those from other institutions (Redd 2000). For instance, graduates of HBCUs are just as likely as their peers from non-HBCUs to be employed full-time and be satisfied with their pay, job challenges, and promotion opportunities. Therefore, considering these and other factors, if HBCUs continue to play a leading role in producing Ph.D. graduates, then HBCUs must be viewed as a valuable asset in contributing to diverse faculty.

Moreover, some faculty search committees might perceive the academic curriculum at prestigious TWIs as being more academically rigorous than the academic curriculum at HBCUs. As a result, only graduates of color from TWIs—not those from HBCUs—would be hired for faculty positions. If this possible myth that discredits the quality of doctoral education at HBCUs continues to exist, the likelihood of achieving diversity will be diminished, because graduates from HBCUs might not be selected from the applicant pool for faculty positions.

Only by addressing these myths—and any others that might exist—will institutions be able to match their performances in faculty hiring with their marketing and rhetoric about diversity. A firm commitment to diversity requires executive leadership and planning. This commitment must begin with the presidents and other senior leadership of higher education institutions.

The Power of Mentoring and Other Tools

Even if the possible barriers mentioned above are removed, the number of Ph.D. recipients per year needs to be increased to have a diverse faculty. Because immediate action needs to be taken, an ideal way to achieve diversity would be to groom promising doctoral students of color for a career in academia. This can be done through mentoring. The goal of mentoring relationships should be to advance the educational and personal growth of doctoral students (*Advisor* 1997). According to Peyton (2001), doctoral students' goals are difficult to attain without the guidance of someone with experience. Furthermore, findings from a study by Kelly and Schweitzer (1999) indicate that students of color have better outcomes when they are mentored than do white students.

Through effective mentoring relationships, faculty mentors can encourage students of color to pursue careers in academia. Wright and Wright (1987) found that higher productivity both before and after attaining the doctoral degree was the result of collaboration with mentors. For this reason, faculty mentors should be responsible for helping doctoral students of color become aware of career opportunities in academia. Also, faculty mentors should provide the resources needed to assist the students in their quest for employment. These resources could include the following: (1) postings about job openings and recruitment fairs; (2) assistance with preparation of the curriculum vitae and application packet; (3) hosting mock face-to-face and telephone interviews; (4) hosting seminars on issues related to the professoriate, such as ethics and tenure; and (5) sponsoring alumni lectures by recent graduates now in academic positions to talk about their experiences and current positions ("Graduate Studies" 2002).

By fostering the implementation of graduate school pipeline programs, people of color can be positioned to join the professoriate. Roach (1999) stated that minorities participating in these programs reportedly have higher retention rates and complete their degrees in shorter periods than do the general population of doctoral students. These programs help prepare students for the daunting number of responsibilities of a faculty position. According to LaPidus (1997), these responsibilities include teaching advanced courses, doing research, and advising and mentoring graduate students.

However, to maintain diversity, resources should be devoted to retaining faculty members of color, too. New faculty members of color should be oriented to the campus and surrounding community. They should also be included in the decision-making process of the institution—but not be "the minority representative" on every committee. Their teaching assignments should be mainstreamed. More important, not only should the faculty be diverse but the administration, staff, and the student body should be diverse as well.

As the United States becomes increasingly diverse with respect to its racial and ethnic composition, colleges and universities must expand their pools of individuals to be considered—*and hired*—for faculty positions. If nothing else, the demographics of the future workforce will require a widening and deepening of the pool of candidates and hires; otherwise, these institutions will face increasing difficulties in replacing their aging faculties. Moreover, graduate schools must prepare *all* students who wish to pursue faculty careers to acquire competence in teaching and mentoring culturally and linguistically diverse students. They must also prepare them to be knowledgeable of diverse views on the perpetual question within the academy, namely, "What is truth?" In this chapter, an effort has been made to provide perspectives on these topics.

21

The Adjunct Instructor

Kristi Andersen and Ryan Petersen

MANY GRADUATE STUDENTS find themselves, at some point before completing their dissertations, teaching a course or two at a neighboring college or university as a temporary part-time, or "adjunct," instructor. Sometimes those with fully credentialed Ph.D.s find themselves in similar situations, for a variety of reasons both personal and career-related. In this chapter, we describe briefly the role of adjunct teaching in institutions of higher education nationwide and in Central New York. But our principal focus is the advantages and disadvantages of adjunct teaching for advanced graduate students.

Teaching in Today's Academy

By some accounts, almost one-half of all faculty occupy part-time positions. In general, the proportion of teaching faculty who are tenured or on the tenure track is on the decline, and the number of part-time faculty has increased (Mathews 2000). This fact is a result in part of the growing enrollments in community colleges, where part-time employment is most common, and in part of the financial pressures on colleges and universities in the 1980s and 1990s, which created incentives to shrink the number of tenure-track faculty and increase the number of nontenure-track and part-time employees. These trends raise a number of thorny issues about the structure of the academy, the role of tenure, academic freedom, and the quality of undergraduate education (see, for example, Hickman 1998; Leatherman 1997; Schneider 1999; Wilson 1998). Here, though, we are primarily concerned about part-time or adjunct teaching from the point of view of Ph.D. students who might take on these jobs to support themselves while they write their dissertations or while they look for full-time, permanent jobs.

We asked department chairs at sixteen Central New York colleges and universities about their use of adjunct instructors: how frequently they use adjuncts, the qualifications they look for, how satisfied they generally were with adjuncts' teaching, and how they thought Ph.D. students could best prepare themselves to take advantage of such positions. We believe their responses are broadly representative of the ways adjuncts are used in many places.

Adjuncts are used most often to fill in for permanent faculty members on leave, to staff courses while faculty searches are being conducted, or sometimes to respond to unexpected increases in student enrollment or demand in some areas. Perhaps unlike some larger universities, the departments we heard from "do not build adjuncts into [their] regular staffing plans," preferring to hire full-time replacements for people on leave. Nonetheless, what with unexpected leaves, over-enrollments, and such, most chairs we asked said that each year they employ at least one adjunct.

The minimum qualifications sought by the hiring departments are ABD status and relevant teaching experience. One chair described the department's process: "We advertise or call around to the major universities in the area. At a minimum, we seek students working on their dissertations who have had coursework or dissertation topics in the areas in which they [would] be teaching. Typically, we hire adjuncts to teach introductory (100 level) courses. Ideally, we look for students who have experience teaching courses similar to the ones we want them to teach."

Hiring institutions almost always want to talk with the student's adviser or department chair; some want to see letters of recommendation or teaching evaluations. But hiring is usually done by the department chair, with no formal search process. Once adjuncts are hired, their teaching performance is evaluated in a variety of ways—sometimes by the department chair's review of the standard student course evaluation, sometimes via classroom observation, often through informal input from the undergraduates in the adjunct's classes. For the most part, the department chairs we contacted have been quite happy with the work of adjunct instructors.

Opportunities

There is certainly no shortage of articles documenting the often-difficult plight of adjunct instructors. Horror stories abound: adjuncts relegated to trailers on the edge of campus, adjunct instructors teaching full course loads for less than one-half the salary of a full-time faculty member, and even a documentary film comparing adjunct instructors to migrant agricultural workers (see, for example, "Footnotes" 1999; Scarff 2000; Wolliver 2000). Because most articles deal with the problems faced by reluctant adjuncts—usually academics who have completed their graduate work and are actively seeking full-time positions—few mention that adjunct jobs can be positive opportunities, particularly for graduate students. True, most Ph.D. students in the arts and sciences eventually hope to secure a permanent, tenure-track post. But without a completed dissertation in hand you are unlikely to be offered one; and given the demands of completing a dissertation, you wouldn't want to be also teaching full time, anyway. Thus a part-time position as an adjunct instructor can be a valuable opportunity for such individuals.

SURVIVAL

Given that the average completion time for the Ph.D. is somewhere just over seven years and most departments only fund graduate students for four or five years, the most obvious benefit of adjunct teaching is the income to keep a roof over your head and food on your plate while you complete your dissertation. The current job market is, in many ways, quite good for the ABD in need of short-term employment. Certainly, there are other ways to fund your last few years as a Ph.D. candidate, including fellowships, grants, and nonacademic jobs. But fellowships and grants large enough to support a graduate student for even a single academic year are few and far between (not to mention extremely competitive). A nonacademic job might pay the bills, but long hours and inflexible schedules are not conducive to finishing your dissertation.

In contrast, as an adjunct instructor, your supervisor (likely the department chair) and faculty colleagues, having been through graduate school themselves, are more likely to be both sympathetic to your situation and concerned about your academic progress. With nonacademic jobs, particularly off campus, you risk becoming too far removed from your field of study. Staying current in your discipline is hard enough under ideal circumstances; but if you are not regularly exposed to other people who are "doing what you are doing," it becomes more difficult to keep up-to-date and, more important, to stay focused on your dissertation. Teaching as an adjunct instructor keeps you plugged into your discipline.

JOB SECURITY

It might seem strange to use the terms "job security" and "adjunct instructor" in the same sentence, but from the unique perspective of the graduate student, adjunct teaching does provide a certain kind of security. Teaching as an adjunct at an institution other than where you pursue your graduate degree has the benefit of your job not being tied to your coursework or dissertation progress. Typically graduate students undergo periodic review that, in part, determines whether or not their department continues its financial support, whether in the form of an assistantship, fellowship, or part-time teaching post. Teaching as an adjunct at another institution gives you a certain degree of freedom from the effects of that process. Poor performance in a single graduate course or delays in completing your dissertation will not end up costing you your job.

JOB SATISFACTION AND PROFESSIONAL RESPECT

As an adjunct faculty member, you are responsible for teaching your own course, dealing with student problems, writing and grading exams, thinking up assignments, and so on. Because you are their instructor, not "just a graduate student," your credibility with the students in your classes could be greater than at your home institution. That can be very satisfying, as can seemingly little things such as getting a faculty rather than a student parking permit, for example. Other satisfactions are not so little: being treated like a colleague by other faculty in the department and being accorded faculty privileges by campus media support personnel, librarians, and other staff.

TEACHING EXPERIENCE

Increasingly, departments in all kinds of institutions look for solid teaching experience from applicants for tenure-track faculty positions. Though neither as lucrative nor probably as valuable as one or two years experience in a full-time position, adjunct teaching is still evidence of your teaching experience. A Syracuse University Ph.D. (now finishing his third year of a tenure-track job) who "adjuncted" at many area colleges, said, "If you have multiple teaching jobs, if you can show any 'upward' trend in them (e.g., two courses at a good school one year, full-time adjunct at a better school the next . . .), then that can make you more marketable, increase your informal rating among faculty. 'Informal' means the grapevine of faculty calling each other about potential faculty hires."

Along with having instrumental value on your vita, teaching you do in an adjunct position can provide valuable additions to your pedagogical repertoire. At minimum, you will have one or several course preparations under your belt that you can later use and modify. But adjunct teaching also offers a special opportunity to "test" your teaching. Because an institution rarely hires its adjuncts in permanent jobs, you should feel less pressure to fit in or be pedagogically conservative and thus more free to experiment with different teaching styles, activities, exercises, and lectures.

Teaching elsewhere also can offer you exposure to a wider range of students, and thus different teaching challenges, than you have at your home institution (presumably a research university). Here we quote extensively from a Ph.D. student who has taught several courses at a community college:

> Because the range of student quality was [broader], it was much harder to balance the need to challenge the brightest, hardest-working students with the need to not go too far over the heads of those at the bottom. . . . One example in this regard: My first Federalist Papers reading assignment imploded because many of the students couldn't follow the argument. Many of them just gave up, without pressing to understand it. The next time we went through the argument in class, broke it down, and discussed it. I think a lot of [those] students came away with the view that Madison, Hamilton, and Jay were not indecipherable after all.
>
> The other thing I had to get used to was the very different demographic makeup of students. The students in my first class . . . were much more ethnically and economically diverse than my students at Syracuse University. Many of the women were single mothers . . . There were also several nontraditional (older) students in the class. . . . The racial mix was very different from the four-year institution. . . . There was also a tremendous economic mix.

Challenges

Your faculty advisers will almost certainly tell you that a year of fellowship support or research supported by a faculty member's grant will more likely produce a finished dissertation than will a year of teaching courses at several nearby colleges. In fact, perhaps the biggest drawback to adjunct teaching is that it can be such a time sink and distraction from dissertation work. This is especially true if you are teaching more than a couple of courses. Said one ABD currently living and teaching in Canada:

> Teaching a course for the first time was far more time consuming than I'd anticipated. . . . [E]very class prep took as much time as writing a paper, plus making up homework assignments, plus making up and grading exams, and their one paper for the course, plus meeting with students who needed extra help. . . . I'm embarrassed to admit how little progress I made on my dissertation that fall.

Another adjunct pointed out that, though your new employer will say "we want you to get your thesis done," in reality "it gets TOUGH to do so during the heavy teaching times in the academic year. . . . I lost (easily) two years on completion by teaching."

In addition to the obvious time problems, there are other pitfalls.

LOW PAY, NO BENEFITS

Most adjunct teaching jobs pay only a couple of thousand dollars per course, meaning you will probably have to teach at least two classes every semester just to make a salary equivalent to a teaching assistant's. To earn an amount even close to a full faculty salary would require an extremely heavy teaching load. Moreover, whereas most teaching assistantships now include some sort of health insurance, few part-time adjunct positions offer any medical benefits. This can leave the part-timer facing a difficult choice: try to get by for a couple of years without health insurance (not advisable) or pay for private insurance (which, in light of your salary, might be nearly impossible). Between the low pay and the lack of benefits, surviving as an adjunct for more than a year or two can be a difficult proposition.

SHORT-TERM AND LAST-MINUTE

Another problem adjunct instructors face stems from the very reasons a department decides to hire an adjunct. Because most adjuncts are part-time, temporary employees hired to fill a short-term need due to a faculty sabbatical, leave of absence, or last-minute departure, most institutions make adjunct hiring decisions late in the year and for one semester at a time. Thus, you typically have very little advance notice before the job begins and rarely can anticipate what or even where you might be teaching next semester, let alone the following year.

One consequence of this last-minute process is you get little time to prepare for a course. Putting together a college-level class in a week can be a difficult task for an experienced professor under ideal conditions; for a novice (maybe even first-time) instructor, the lack of prep time can be downright frightening.

LOGISTICAL DIFFICULTIES

If low pay, no benefits, and short-term contracts don't deter you, consider that adjunct teaching involves logistical difficulties that most full-time faculty members and even teaching assistants do not have to deal with. A long commute to your job is a distinct possibility, but what if you are teaching multiple classes at more than one institution? Driving forty-five minutes to campus might be acceptable, but what if one institution is west of your home and the other is east? Suddenly you find yourself driving three hours in a single day. Hours of teaching, office hours, and long drives make working on your dissertation only that much more difficult.

An adjunct instructor also faces logistical problems on campus. Office space will likely be at a premium, and you could be sharing space with other adjuncts or even the department's filing cabinets. Maybe you have no permanent desk or shelf space of your own, requiring you to carry all of your materials to and from work each class. As a part-timer, you might get fewer resources than you were accustomed to at your home institution. Fairly simple things that you took for granted as a graduate student (e.g., photocopying large reading packets, making overheads, or just finding markers and chalk) are no longer simple and certainly cannot be left to the last minute.

Some Concluding Advice

How can graduate students best prepare themselves not only to take advantage of the job market for adjuncts but also—perhaps more important—to take maximum advantage of the opportunities thus presented? First, since institutions rarely want to hire adjuncts who lack substantial teaching experience, try to make sure you get extensive, broad, and successful experience as a teaching assistant. If you can gain experience preparing and teaching your own course at your home institution, so much the better.

Second, even if you will not undergo a formal search process, you will undoubtedly have one or two conversations with the department chair before being hired. Prepare yourself for these conversations by being able to describe cogently and enthusiastically your previous teaching experiences and your career goals. You should also have thought about and be prepared to talk about courses you could teach—how you would structure them, readings you might assign, and so on. You should also be prepared to give the department chair the name of a faculty member who can talk knowledgeably about your previous teaching experience.

Once hired, how can you get the most out of the job? Although part of the appeal of adjunct status is freedom from committee assignments and other departmental and institutional responsibilities, it can be to your advantage to spend a bit more than the minimal time at your new campus. A department chair at a liberal arts college commented that adjuncts should try to set up their schedules

> so that they can spend the better part of the day here a couple of days a week, teaching and holding office hours. . . . By spending several hours here on the days that they teach, the adjuncts get a better sense of what life at the institution is like, as well as what the students are like. They also have a much better chance of meeting and getting to know the full-time members of the department.

Here we would like to elaborate on two implications of that advice. First, use your adjunct teaching as a way to get a picture of life as a professor at particular kinds of institutions that you might not be familiar with. Talk with students. Get to know the faculty members along with the operant expectations about teaching, advising, research, and service. Ask yourself what it would be like to be a full-time faculty member there. Talk with the administrative and clerical staff, always a good source of information. Maybe you can attend department meetings or participate in some other department-wide activities. If your schedule permits, talk to other faculty members about their teaching or ask to visit their classes: tap into both their specific insights about engaging their particular students and their general advice about teaching.

Second, think of your colleagues at your adjunct institution as part of your growing network of professional colleagues. A Syracuse Ph.D. now teaching in Kentucky shared this good advice: "Networking [is an advantage]. You broaden the [range of] folks who have seen you in action, the coin of the realm when asking for references and other assistance with jobs. And you can mine those [contacts] later on."

Particularly if you teach a number of courses, the department chair might be willing to write a letter of support for your placement file. Identify colleagues who share research interests with you. One recent Ph.D. ended up asking a colleague at his adjunct institution to serve on his dissertation committee, and they have remained in contact now that he is in a tenure-track job in California.

Finally, it is extremely important to keep in mind your primary job: being a student. Indeed, the teaching you do (at least at this point in your career) is a means to an end; that is, a way to make money while you finish your graduate education. This can seem obvious now, but it is all too easy to take on more teaching responsibility than is advisable, particularly if you are passionate about teaching. If you find teaching more enjoyable than working on your dissertation, it can be tempting to repeatedly put aside your research and writing. Even if you are not so passionate or ambitious about teaching, the need to make money or the desire to gain experience can still lead you to take on more classes than you should. After you've acquired a certain level of teaching experience, you can find yourself in demand as a part-time instructor. But you must practice saying no. It is both flattering and tempting to be offered several courses in one semester, but you will probably be better off in the long run if you turn down some offers. Be realistic about how much you can teach and still make progress on your dissertation.

Here's your take-home message: Don't lose sight of your ultimate goal: completing your degree and securing a permanent, full-time job.

22

Balancing Multiple Responsibilities

Heather Frasier Chabot and Le'Ann Milinder

MAYBE YOU ARE JUST STARTING graduate school and find yourself with a teaching assistantship. Maybe you are a fresh Ph.D. in your first faculty position. And maybe you are wondering what this teaching life is all about. Where will you find the time and energy to meet all the new demands in your life? What effect will your new responsibilities have on your personal life? Having looked back on our own journey, we are ready to offer some reflections of our own.

Juggling Issues in the Academic Arena

Whether you are a graduate student or a professor, you will find there will always be multiple tugs at your academic regalia. As a new graduate TA, you'll find you have three important roles to play: student, researcher/scholar, and teaching assistant. The roles, however, shift for professors to teaching, research/scholarship, and service. So, no matter how you look at it, it is not possible to focus on only one role in academia. For a detailed review of juggling professorial roles, we suggest Crepeau, Thibodaux, and Parham's "Academic Juggling Act: Beginning and Sustaining an Academic Career" (1999). In this chapter, we will address the responsibilities of the graduate student.

THE STUDENT ROLE

For first-year graduate students, what's important is getting acclimated to your new surroundings and a feel for the culture of your program and school. Make friends with your peers, but don't shy away from the more senior students. Those folks are great resources—they have made it in your program! Your classmates are good study and commiserating partners in dealing with your immediate experiences; more senior students can give you many tips for making it all the way.

Perhaps the most important person to get to know is your adviser or mentor. Try to find one with whom you feel well-matched. Some advisers like to wield the power in your relationship; they will tell you what research to do and how to teach. Other advisers will share their power and will let you make your own choices. In making a good match, it is easier if you know such information beforehand, as well as how much control you want to have. Another factor to consider is that your adviser will have some opinion as to where and how you should focus your time among the three graduate student roles. In their own professorial role, some advisers focus on research, others on teaching or service. Better to spend some time your first year shopping around than to find you and your adviser are not compatible years later during your thesis crunch.

If you are typical, you probably intend to be a model student and are used to getting good grades. However, the reality is there is more to fulfilling your student role than getting all A's. In fact, coursework is only part of what's necessary for a graduate degree. Most programs have a research component; some require service or internships. Furthermore, you miss out on many important opportunities for learning if you focus just on the grades that go on your transcript. There's a nifty little quotation that emphasizes this point: "B equals Ph.D." In other words, you still get the degree if you don't get all A's. Maybe you will gain some important insights from that B, or instead of studying you will do something that at the time is even more important, such as teach your first course or write your thesis. Don't get us wrong: Grades are important, and you could be dismissed if they are too low. Just don't be a slave to your coursework.

THE RESEARCHER ROLE

Many master's and all doctorates are research degrees; in other words, competency in conducting research is a requirement for most graduate degrees. How involved you must get in that research varies. Some programs require a short project, others a lengthy work. Again, give this factor some thought, and select your program and adviser accordingly. If research is your love, you will be happiest in a program that allows you to spend every waking hour in the lab. If your focus is teaching, then it would be wise to select a research topic that examines issues associated with teaching and its scholarship. Keep in mind that your research choices, more so than your coursework, will determine your postgraduate career options. If you do minimal research, then you will not be competitive for an assistant professorship at a research-oriented institution.

As with coursework, research is a requirement for your degree but it also offers a wonderful opportunity for learning. The techniques of most research approaches are based in critical thinking. Conducting research develops your ability to formulate and answer questions and your skills of evaluation. Such skills and abilities are important to being a good teacher, as are the presentation skills you will practice if you get to present your research at professional and scholarly meetings. Conducting research independently or in collaboration with faculty members can open the opportunity to attend such conferences, which are important learning and networking occasions for both your education and your career.

What if you choose an adviser with whom you are compatible, except she or he is doing less research than you would like? Look for other faculty members with whom you could collaborate. No law states that all your research must be conducted with your adviser. It is common for a student to work with multiple researchers. To find a collaboration opportunity, watch for advertisements from researchers needing assistants or approach specific researchers to offer your time. It is always best to read up on their research before you approach them; they will be more eager to talk with you and will appreciate that you did your homework.

THE TA ROLE

Fulfilling your teaching or research assistantship obligation is the third role in the academic arena. Assistantships can take many forms. Try to gain as much information about your options and duties beforehand. Sometimes you have a choice between a teaching or research position. If you know that you want to focus on enhancing your skills as a teacher, you should opt for a TA; but if you want to spend your energies conducting research, try to get an RA. Selecting an assistantship (if you get the choice) is almost as important as selecting your adviser. Try to get to know the various faculty members for whom you could be working. Some faculty assign very light duties, some are more rigid, and some are wonderful mentors who will help develop your teaching skills.

After four years of undergraduate tuition, an offer of a teaching assistantship and its tuition waiver and/or stipend might have enticed you to choose a given school, but it probably is not going to be the factor that keeps you there. In most cases, an assistantship is a wonderful opportunity, but you should not let your assistantship run your life. Most assistantships are for a designated number of hours per week, usually twenty hours. Find out how many hours you are expected to work, then keep track of your time. If you find you are greatly exceeding the expectation, then talk with the faculty member(s) with whom you are working. The professor might have some tips to offer about working more efficiently, which could prove useful throughout your academic career. If your faculty member is not helpful, seek assistance from the chair of your department or your dean.

Keep in mind that the TA-professor relationship should be a mutually beneficial one. You should gain experience and knowledge (in addition to your stipend), and the faculty member should benefit from your assistance in the class or lab section. What if you find that your assistantship is meeting only your financial needs? You might want to reconsider your options. Perhaps you could obtain a different assistantship, or find a higher-paying job elsewhere that would leave you more time to spend on your roles as student and researcher. Yet another option is to forego working altogether and get a student loan so you can dedicate more time to your studies. As with the student and researcher roles, you must decide what your priorities are and devise the best plan to meet them.

OTHER ANCILLARY ROLES

While it can seem that being a student, a researcher, and a TA is more than enough, you could find it beneficial to expand your knowledge beyond the four walls of your program by attending workshops or conferences or by offering service on campus (membership on committees or task forces) or in the local community. If you are interested in taking this step, talk with other students and your adviser about the time commitment required. Keep in mind that such service would be in addition to your other roles, and it will not substitute for any of them (unless you can work out an arrangement by which the service fulfills some departmental assistantship obligations). Service takes away some of your free time, but you could find that this type of giving has distinct advantages. Serving on a university committee, for example, expands your view of your university or college, teaches you how to interact with others, and gives you the opportunity to meet graduate students outside your discipline. You might even locate individuals outside your department to serve on your dissertation committee!

THE TAKE-HOME MESSAGES

In closing this section, we would like to reiterate some important messages regarding juggling issues in the academic arena. First, know thyself. Specifically, be aware of your needs and desires regarding teaching, research, and what you want to get out of your graduate experience. In other words, follow Dr. Suess's (1990) excellent advice in *Oh, the Places You'll Go:* You be the guy who decides where you will go.

Second, take your time in selecting an assistantship and an adviser with whom you are compatible. The choices you make there are crucial. The quality of your graduate experience will depend on your being in the right place and working with the right people.

Third, prioritize your time to meet your needs. If you have not already honed your time-management skills, now is the time! Some people find setting aside a specific number of hours a week or day for each responsibility works, while others work best by limiting themselves to a day for each task. Determine how you work best. It could also be useful to seek out advice on how to become a more efficient reader, grader, or writer; ask your adviser, other faculty members, and fellow students. There are lots of methods and tricks to improve your skills! As a graduate student, you should have some say in how much time you dedicate to your coursework, research, and assistantship duties. Assuming you meet the minimum requirements for each, you should be free to spend more time in the area that most interests or benefits you.

Fourth, keep the lines of communication open. If you have a concern or issue, discuss it with your adviser, professor, or chair in a reasonable manner. Speak your mind and express your thoughts and feelings, but do not ridicule others who have different viewpoints and approaches. Learn to agree to disagree without feeling hurt. Being exposed to differing viewpoints and experiences, as suggested by Matsumoto (2000), will only enhance your ability to interact with a variety of people. In other words, try to stay open-minded. Recall that who you meet, what you do, and who you work with in graduate school will play a part when the time comes to obtain that coveted first job. Try not to burn any bridges—you never know who you might need to ask for a letter of recommendation.

Fifth, verify that you like what you are doing. If this is the first time you have questioned whether you can—or even want to—wear the multiple hats of academe, think hard. Which specific three roles you must balance changes, but balancing and prioritizing roles is not going to get easier if you opt for a full-time tenure-track academic position. Most faculty members say it only gets harder! Your graduate student experience is a training ground for what is to come. Think of graduate school as a microcosm of academic life. If you realize that this life is not for you, talk with those around you regarding your options. Don't feel like a failure if you decide you do not want to complete your degree or work in academia. Many graduate students who begin a program never complete their degree and less than half of all degree recipients are employed in academia.

Juggling Issues in the Personal Arena

As you should have gathered by now, meeting the responsibilities of your three roles as a graduate student, and later as a faculty member, can expand to fill whatever time you have available. Thus, it is easy to lose your personal life. If that vision appeals to you, then you can probably skip this section (but we urge you not to!). But if you hope to strike a balance between a personal and a professional life, then learning to juggle is part of what you can learn in graduate school.

What is the stereotypic advice for juggling personal and professional responsibilities? *Don't have a personal life.* But that just is not possible if you bring with you to graduate school the intense personal responsibilities of marriage, children, and the like. There is no question that your personal life will be a high priority. Even if you have few responsibilities now, be aware that it is not unusual for graduate students to marry, start families, buy homes, help out family members—all while still in school.

But even if circumstances would not prevent you from devoting your life to your work twenty-four/seven, we believe there are many reasons why you should make time for a personal life:

• Working all the time can be counterproductive (Hollenback and Morfei, 1996).

• You'll be fresher and more productive if you take time off when you really need it.

• The quality of your work and overall graduate experience will be enhanced.

• When your worklife hits the inevitable rough spots, your outside friends and interests will help you keep perspective and give you opportunities for positive experiences.

• You will be a better teacher and mentor to your students, most of whom are themselves not exclusively devoted to the academic life.

When you add your personal life to everything else you have to juggle in graduate school, knowing yourself and seeking support become critical. Next, we offer some general advice along those lines, and discuss three occasions where maintaining balance can be especially challenging.

KNOW THYSELF

No one can do everything and do everything well. The academic life requires you to continually choose among competing tasks and demands. To make good decisions you need to know what is most important to you, both professionally and personally. We have already discussed some of the competing academic demands, but the personal questions are just as important to ask yourself. *Do I want to have children soon? What do my partner and I need to keep our relationship strong? What friendships and family connections do I want to maintain? How much money will I need to lead a reasonable life?* If you have a spouse or partner, you are probably negotiating the answers to these questions.

These are big questions, and giving them some serious thought is well worth the effort. The clearer you are about what's important to you, the more effective you will be at setting goals for your time in graduate school and establishing the day-to-day priorities that will help you meet those goals. Even if you are not ready to answer some questions yet (*Will I focus on teaching or research?*), you can set goals that will help you make the decision later (*I'll do some teaching early on to see how much I like it*).

Every day you will be faced with choices that reflect conflicting priorities. *Which is more important to be working on right now, the revision of my paper or plan-*

ning for my next research project? Should I go home at five and have dinner with my partner, or stay until ten and get this task done on time? Do I grade these papers, or have a conversation with my friend visiting from the East? During the semester break, should I do research, or travel to grandfather's now that he's out of the hospital? How you will answer depends on what best serves your goals. No answer will be perfect, and you might have to sacrifice to stick with what's most important to you—whether that means giving up that A grade, extra publication, perfect teaching evaluation, or special closeness with your old friends. It will, however, be easier if you know *why* you are doing it.

Sticking to your goals also means not letting other people's priorities become yours. It's easy to take on too much or take on the wrong things. One way to avoid that is to be firm in setting limits. Say no to optional tasks that do not meet your needs, but say yes enthusiastically to the tasks that do. Again, the better you know yourself and your goals, the clearer the value of each task will be.

SEEK SUPPORT

Juggling graduate school and your personal life can yield frustration, conflict, and change—the very elements that define a stressful situation. But you can cope! It's well documented that one of the most important things you can do for yourself to handle stress is develop a strong network of social support (Cohen 1988; Sarason, Pierce, and Sarason 1994).

First, talk with the faculty in your program about your goals. Once they know what you are trying to accomplish, they can help you use your time most efficiently. They and your adviser can alert you to opportunities and resources that really fit your needs, both in the academic arena (e.g., guidance in applying for grants, or which faculty members will help you learn the most as a TA) and in the personal one (e.g., the best daycare centers, or a reliable mechanic). Conversely, they can steer you away from things that won't benefit you (e.g., service activities where you don't meet people or develop new skills). Because faculty have been juggling their own priorities for years, their advice about how they manage their own balancing act will be some of the most helpful you can get.

Use the faculty, but also stay connected with your peers. They, more than your family and friends, can empathize with the conflicts you face. They will commiserate with you on the bad days and celebrate with you on the good ones. Those who have been around for a while also will have tips about the program, the faculty, and the community that can help you cope more effectively. If the graduate students in your department are competitive or reluctant to be friendly, seek out graduate students from other departments with whom you don't compete. Find out whether there is a graduate student organization on campus or special events for graduate students.

Keep up with some people outside the program, as well. While they might not understand all the ins and outs of your academic experiences, maybe they know your personal challenges quite well. Or perhaps they share your passion for hobbies or activities that you find rejuvenating or relaxing. And they will have the energy to be there for you when all your graduate student friends are worn out by the same exams, deadlines, and demands that exhausted you.

MAJOR CHALLENGES

Finances

As you make financial plans, consider all possible sources of income: assistantships, research work on a faculty member's grant, adjunct teaching at another institution, outside consulting (e.g., using skills from a previous job or skills developed in graduate school), grants (e.g., for research, travel to conferences, special awards), savings, financial aid, and loans. Check with your department or dean's office whether your assistantship or other awards come with any limitations on your ability to work. Find out from your adviser and other faculty members what money might be available from the department, the institution, government programs, and professional associations. Taking the time to apply for funding can pay off in many ways. It could allow you to enhance your research, pay research assistants, meet your living expenses, reduce future debt, gain valuable experience writing proposals, enhance professional experience, or win awards to add to your curriculum vitae.

Whether or not you need to seek alternative sources of income depends on what trade-offs you are willing to make. Obviously, the less money you need to survive, the more flexibility you have in choosing activities that meet your long-term goals. But be realistic about what sort of lifestyle you are willing to tolerate. Getting the one-room studio apartment far from campus to save money might sound like a great idea—until the commuting and cramped quarters drive you crazy. If you have a family, amenities that give you more time together (e.g., onsite laundry facilities, playground) could be well worth getting an extra loan or support from your parents. Again, our advice is to know yourself, your family, and what you really need to be comfortable.

If you are already an experienced bargain hunter, you are well prepared for getting by on the typical graduate student budget. No matter what your needs and goals, thinking creatively about how to spend less will let you do more. For example, some students manage to live in big, well-appointed surroundings by house-sitting for faculty members who are on leave. Also keep your eyes open for the free or inexpensive activities, as well as the plethora of second-hand stores and cheap eats typical in college towns and big cities. If low-budget has not been your strength before, seek ideas from your thriftier peers and check out web sites generated by searching the Internet under "cheapskate."

Families

When you have a family, "know thyself" means also knowing your partner and children. When you start graduate school, they need to understand what changes will be expected of them and how those changes fit into the whole family's plans for the future. You, your partner, and your children should talk about how priorities and schedules will be established.

At the start of each semester, discuss the likely ups and downs of the coming weeks. When you set your day-to-day schedule, consider the patterns of work that generate the best fit between your competing responsibilities. Maybe you would be most effective working furiously for ten hours with no break, followed by an evening of undivided attention to your family. Or maybe working in small, sporadic chunks of time would allow you the flexibility to run errands, attend the kid's soccer game, or nurse a baby. With good communication, your family will let you know when they really need you and when they can get along without you. Do not assume you know their needs without asking. Some parents find that weekly family meetings, where everyone can share their expectations and plans for the week, keep the communication flowing.

Another benefit of good communication is that it allows you to acknowledge your feelings and expectations and to make sure that you are comfortable with the priorities you have chosen. Few things are more painful than devoting yourself to your work when you feel it comes at the expense of your child. Conversely, the frustration of not being able to get work done can be enormous. Thus, it might be helpful to map out a realistic trajectory through graduate school for yourself. You don't have to be on a mommy or parent track, but a fast-paced worklife if you have children means you have to be especially good at identifying critical tasks and focusing your effort. Again, keeping yourself focused could mean getting rid of anything extraneous that does not serve your goals, whether it's personal or professional.

If you become a parent for the first time during graduate school, you will face many adjustments, as do all new parents. Don't underestimate the stamina and support you will need to keep up with a new baby. But know that other graduate students have done it before you, and you can do it too! Departments vary widely in their flexibility and responsiveness on family issues. If you can anticipate parenthood, you might want to explore the possibility with the program's other graduate students, faculty, and administrators before you enroll, to make sure the program matches your personal goals. In general, the more you can plan ahead (e.g., finding good childcare, adjusting your work responsibilities), the better your overall experience will be. Seek out other parents as much as you can, even if it is just a few minutes for coffee or a walk. Their reassurance and experience could help you persist on those inevitable days of too many deadlines and not enough sleep. Hanging out with parents of older children can help you look ahead to times when parenting does get easier.

Consider also that some graduate students take time off completely when a child is born or during other times of transition or need. You will feel less frazzled and more satisfied if you can focus completely on your family during important times. If you do take time off, be confident that even if graduate school takes you longer to complete, you still can build the knowledge, skills, and record to get the job you want.

Crises

The more demanding your personal life is, the greater your probability of experiencing a crisis that makes you unable to meet your academic and personal responsibilities simultaneously. Fortunately, some crises can be avoided with advance planning. *How can I help care for Dad when he's older when I'm so far away? How will we meet our expenses if she quits her job to go to graduate school too?* Perhaps your adviser and other faculty members can assist you in planning ahead for any major changes or conflicts you can anticipate. There could be departmental policies or precedents relevant to your situation. Or you might need to consult with others, such as the dean or the faculty committee responsible for graduate students. With forethought, diligence, and creativity, often you can find solutions to seemingly intractable differences between your personal life's demands and your program's requirements. Take a proactive approach, and look ahead with the help of more experienced eyes.

Unfortunately, we can't always see a crisis coming. If you are faced with an emergency, let your adviser and department chair know right away. They will help you make arrangements to cover your academic responsibilities while you are away. This is also a time to draw on your peer network: Can a colleague teach your class? Conduct your experiments? Watch your kids? Plus, your university probably has some sort of counseling center that can provide confidential, free help. Often such centers also help with ongoing problems and can provide referrals to a wide variety of services.

Think through what you need, both for the moment and the future. Time off? Reduced responsibilities? Flexibility in deadlines? Resources? A shoulder to cry on? Ask for what you really need, not just the minimum you can get by on for now. If you are not sure what you need, talk to your adviser or trusted faculty members and benefit from their experience. Consider the likely course of the problem—caring for a sick family member, for example, can be a long-term commitment. It will be easier for everyone to help with arrangements if they know the whole picture, rather than dealing with your piecemeal requests. As you weather the storm, regular communication with your adviser about your program's requirements and your own is critical to keeping you on track with your career.

The academy is an environment with high standards for productivity. You might feel that once your immediate emergency is over, everyone expects you to just "get back to work." Some people do find it therapeutic to immerse themselves in work, but if you are not one of them, seek out people in your social network who understand other ways to cope. As always, know thyself. Be confident that only you know best what you need to meet your responsibilities and take care of yourself.

But what if you find yourself in a perpetual state of crisis? Consider whether you need to make some larger changes in your life. *Am I taking on more than I can handle? Is there a bad fit between me and my program? Are my family circumstances too demanding or complicated to also focus on graduate school?* Step back from your life, and take a hard look at what is and isn't working for you. Talk to people who know you well. Perhaps the discussions could lead you to reevaluate your priorities or make much-needed changes.

Having It All

You can finish graduate school, launch an academic career, and have a full personal life! The issues we raised here might seem daunting, but we encourage you to try your hand at this juggling act. Everyone gets overwhelmed at times, but a satisfying balance is possible. The independence and discovery you find in the classroom, the stimulating communities in which you live and raise your family, and the opportunity to make lasting contributions on which others can build all will be rich rewards for the intense demands placed upon you.

23

Reflective Practice

Merylann J. Schuttloffel

BEGINNING K-12 TEACHERS ARRIVE in their classrooms shaped by formal teacher preparation, and often, by their personal educational experiences. By comparison, novice collegiate instructors lack the benefits of formal preparation and often simply rely on their images of typical professoriate behavior formed by experience and popular culture. They soon discover that collegiate teaching is a solitary life and must learn for themselves how to manage students and, ultimately, how to teach. Reflective practice is a process that assists novice teachers to think about the decision-making that leads to their individual teaching practice.

The purpose of this chapter is to describe major characteristics and processes of reflective practice. First, I will briefly introduce the roots of reflective practice within educational settings. Second, I will present a fictitious case study to provide a common ground of experience for my discussion. Third, I will describe a model of reflective practice, then apply that model to various dilemmas posed in the case study. Next, I will introduce the role of action research in reflective practice. And last, I will summarize the significance of reflective practice as a process for professional development.

What Is Reflective Practice?

THE BEGINNINGS

The modern roots of reflective practice are found in the works of philosopher John Dewey (1933), who believed that reflective practice was a tool capable of initiating professional development in teachers. More recently, Schön clarified the use of reflective practice for teachers (1983, 1987,

1991). Within the current educational environment of accountability and technical sophistication in teaching, we might well ask, "How does reflective practice contribute to teaching and learning?" Let's begin to answer that question with an excursion into teaching practice.

Teaching is composed of hundreds of decisions made during the course of a lesson's development, delivery, and evaluation (Ross, Bondy, and Kyle 1993; Zumwalt 1989). By examining the elements of reflective practice and demonstrating their application within an instructor's daily practice, we can see the value of reflective practice in its capacity to enhance that decision-making. As a novice, you might require some clarification of reflective practice as it relates to teaching before the concept becomes useful to you. But, we would hope, ultimately you will recognize the relationship between reflective practice and your own growth and development as a professional.

REFLECTIVE PRACTICE FOR INSTRUCTORS

Reflective practice is closely related to the concept of *metacognition,* which is the process of examining one's own thinking and decision-making prior to taking action (Flavel 1977). For example: *I am a novice professor trying to decide on an appropriate midterm examination for my undergraduate students. I choose to give an open-book take-home exam. I begin to question why I made that choice.* When we begin to question why we chose a particular methodological procedure, the reflection on our own thinking demonstrates metacognitive behavior. Metacognition assists novice instructors in their most difficult task: learning to think like teachers.

CASE STUDY: BECKY, THE TEACHING ASSISTANT

When Becky arrived at Midwestern University, she had completed a successful undergraduate program at Lakeland State College. Her major in political science allowed her to take many courses in history—so many that she was just shy of a double major. Now she was beginning graduate studies in American history at Midwestern. With her strong academic background in the discipline, Becky was immediately singled out by the chair of the History Department to teach a section of the undergraduate core course requirement. Becky's duties included teaching the required text, grading papers, and giving exams. The History Department gave her a box of lecture notes that previous teaching assistants had used and a key to a file cabinet. Like the department's other TAs, she was directed to use the course exams locked in the file cabinet. Becky was assured that all she had to do was "follow the paper trail" her predecessors had created.

But Becky found her teaching situation problematic from two perspectives. First, because her undergraduate history studies had not been at Midwestern, she was not familiar with the content of the core course she was teaching. Second, Becky had not been prepared as a teacher, so she was not secure in her own philosophy of teaching. Fearing she would lose her assistantship, she lacked confidence to approach the chair or any professor in the department about her dilemma.

Seeking advice on how to approach the situation, Becky confided in her mother, an experienced classroom teacher. Her mother advised Becky to teach like those professors she admired at Lakeland. Soon Becky began to create her own lessons for her section, which differed from the lecture notes she had been given. These changes became public when a group of her students pointed out to the department chair that their assignments differed from assignments in other sections of the same course. Now Becky was asked by the History Department to explain what was going on in her class. What was she going to say?

One Model of Reflective Practice

There are numerous approaches to reflective practice, but Van Manen's (1977) framework has been successfully used in teacher-preparation programs (Valli 1992). By clarifying an instructor's thinking process, Van Manen also illuminates for novices how to think like a teacher. Van Manen's model of reflective practice comprises three levels: the critical, the interpretive, and the technical. In this chapter, my discussion of Becky's case presents the three levels individually, but in reflective practice the levels are more accurately described as three dynamic elements of a single process. Their interrelatedness and interactivity give the reflective process its synergism.

THE CRITICAL LEVEL OF REFLECTION

The *critical* level of reflective practice refers to the first, or highest, level of reflection. The critical level of reflection asks the question *why?* At the organizational level, what is the philosophy of the program, department, or university? What is the purpose of the course? Why does the department value this course? At the individual level, the novice instructor must examine his or her own purpose for becoming a teacher; what beliefs and values does the instructor hold? By responding to questions such as these, novice instructors begin to discover sources of their classroom decision-making.

THE INTERPRETIVE LEVEL OF REFLECTION

The second level is the *interpretive* level of reflection. This level relates to the critical level by communicating beliefs and values through symbols and inferences. The interpretive level responds to the question *what?* What messages are sent by the teacher's decisions? What is the shared meaning of knowledge or learning that the faculty as a whole attempts to develop in order to build a cohesive community of inquiry? Students and other members of the educational community constantly are "reading" what is going on. Interpretive reflection reminds us that actions carry messages and create meaning. Through metacognitive behavior, novice teachers not only learn to think like a teacher but also learn to interpret like a mindful teacher.

THE TECHNICAL LEVEL OF REFLECTION

Technical reflection is the third level. Reflection at the technical level answers the question *how?* When we attempt to solve a pedagogical problem, our technical skills of teaching provide the tools to implement a solution plan. Although the technical level could be considered the lowest level of reflective practice, the need for technical knowledge and skills should not be underestimated. Nor should they be our sole focus. The power of reflective practice resides in implementing technical choices made with a clear purpose.

A Reflective Analysis of Becky's Case

Critical reflection (level one) requires Becky to clarify to members of the History Department *why* she chose to teach the way she did. Becky needs to explain her understanding of the department's philosophy of teaching or its underpinning framework that guides curricular decision-making by the department. Becky also needs to identify those departmental beliefs and values that are consistent with her beliefs about teaching.

Becky's likely explanation describes beliefs and values rooted in her family, where her mother is a teacher. Becky's mother encouraged her to read current research on best practices in teaching practices and recent findings in cognitive theory. These readings helped to shape Becky's teaching beliefs and values and her practice. Becky also relates experiences with history teachers she considered effective and how she attempts to model them. She shares her values through her descriptions of "good classrooms," "good teachers," and "good students."

Becky's critical reflection points to her motivation for a teaching style that differs from the technical-survival approach her fellow teaching assistants chose. Becky's values and beliefs expose why the department's expectations raise a moral dilemma for Becky. She confronts a choice between what she believes "good teaching" means and the minimum requirements necessary to maintain her role as a TA.

The description of Becky's moral dilemma at the critical level of reflection defines Becky's interpretations of her teaching experiences. At the interpretive (second) level, Becky creates her own meaning of a "good classroom." She sends messages to students that support her beliefs about teaching and learning. The dilemma emerges when Becky discovers that some students recognize a lack of consistency with the messages they are hearing from other instructors in the History Department. Becky's behavior calls into question the department's current culture of teaching assistants. Other TAs also might question what a change in culture would mean for expectations about their teaching. How much control is the department going to exert on Becky? Will she be able to resolve this dilemma so she can remain true to her beliefs about teaching and learning?

Technically (third level), Becky demonstrates behaviors particular to certain beliefs about teachers and students. Becky's responses to the department's questions illustrate the ability of her methodology to meet curricular requirements while remaining consistent with her beliefs about teaching and learning. Becky recognizes that through her pedagogical actions, students not only learn content but also interpret those behaviors to create a particular meaning for history learning. Becky's dilemma marks a point where the History Department must decide whether methodology is to be controlled, or student learning might have various acceptable processes. Becky must be able to explain the relationship between the classroom management decisions she makes, the methodological choices she makes, and her critical rationale. Her choices are unacceptable if they represent merely a preference she holds. Her technical reflection also includes an examination of her students' performance. The evaluation of student performance will no doubt raise other critical and interpretive questions.

Reflective practice requires Becky and the History Department to analyze thoughtfully decisions of curricular, methodological, and classroom management. Reflective practice challenges university teachers to seek a substantive framework for decision-making that supports the values and beliefs of their program. The History Department's challenge for Becky to explain her actions provides her an opportunity for further reflective practice. Becky has the opportunity to point out that her choices had a purposeful *why*, and that *what* students have interpreted and experienced is *how* she chose to implement the meaningful learning experiences her actions demonstrate.

PROBLEM SOLVING AS A REFLECTIVE PRACTITIONER

The process of reflective practice has the potential to assist us in decision-making for problem solving. This process can be applied to a variety of issues, from minor practical problems to grave moral dilemmas. Becky's dilemma with the History Department provides her an opportunity for *action research*, meaning research conducted by a teacher to solve problems that emerge within his or her own practice (Kemmis and McTaggart 1982). Action research is closely identified with reflective practice, where such research serves as a tool to create professional knowledge that leads to professional development. A reflective-practice approach to problem solving is outlined in the following list of steps (Kemmis and McTaggart 1982, as adapted in Schuttloffel 1999, 38), which can then be applied to Becky's dilemma.

1. *Identify the dilemma:* Find the root issue. Don't be misled by symptoms.

2. *Search for multiple solutions:* Who gains or loses from each plan? Why?

3. *Test and evaluate the solutions:* Consider various scenarios from the plans.

4. *Choose the best solution:* Look for the plan with the most positive results.

5. *Formulate a plan of action:* Lay out the details of the plan step by step.

6. *Implement the plan of action:* Inform key players and begin the plan.

7. *As events unfold, evaluate the results and adjust as necessary:* Are you moving toward the intended results? If not, modify the plan and continue.

According to this approach, the first step in a reflective-practice approach to problem solving is to identify the dilemma. Sometimes it is difficult for us to separate the fundamental dilemma from the problem symptoms, and to state clearly what the core issue really is. Cuban (1992) distinguishes that *problems* propose a potential solution, while "*dilemmas* are conflict-ridden situations that require choices because competing, highly prized values cannot be fully satisfied" (6, emphasis added). Becky's case study, for example, presents control, curricular, and societal dilemmas (Berlak and Berlak 1981, 135–75). The control dilemma involves the History Department's control over Becky's teaching practice. The curricular dilemma flows from her individual choice of materials and exam questions. And finally, the societal dilemma emerges from the possibility that the department's students who are taught by other TAs would receive an educational opportunity of lower quality. These three dilemmas require prioritization.

The second step requires a search for multiple solutions. Before the department and Becky can act, reflective practice requires that they test and evaluate potential solutions (step three). Then, having thought things through more carefully, the next step is to pick what appears to be the best solution (step four). The History Department might determine that the best possible solution is to allow Becky to continue to teach according to her lesson plans. Step five requires that the solution translate into a coherent plan-of-action. The implementation of the plan takes time (step six), all the while observing the results and determining whether the department, the students, and Becky are satisfied with the solution.

By taking time to evaluate the effects of their actions, the department and Becky build a knowledge base for dealing with this type of dilemma should it recur in the future (step seven). The department benefits, as this action research creates professional knowledge that responds to a problem that emerged directly from daily teaching practice within the department. Becky herself also grows through the action research, because she observes mindfully the results of her teaching decisions.

Reflective Practice as a Means of Professional Development

Dewey's vision of reflective practice as a means of professional development is best realized through action research that challenges instructors to change and improve. When offered, professional development too often consists of one-shot workshops that focus on technical skills of teaching without referencing rationale for one's pedagogical choices. Action research, as part of reflective practice, supports you in progressing from your initial stage of development, with all its dilemmas, to higher performance levels. The goal becomes to think like a "master" teacher (Seifert 1999).

Many universities assume too much about the individual development of their instructors. Institutions offer few formal supports or rewards for those who desire to improve. Informally, a mentor or a critical friend might serve as a potential source of encouragement for professional growth. Reflective practice engages introspection, responsibility to person and profession, and open-mindedness to lifelong learning (Ross, Bondy, and Kyle 1993, 24). These characteristics foster Dewey's concept of professional development. Reflective practice showcases the complexity of teaching and learning by revealing those dilemmas that emerge from human interaction. By uncovering root values and beliefs, teachers begin to understand why classroom dilemmas evolve and how to resolve them. Reflection challenges teachers to seek coherence in their practice. Reflective practice does not promise to remove dilemmas from our practice; instead, reflection proposes a shift toward metacognitive thinking that leads to a mature focus on lifelong learning. Students and faculty, as well as the university, ultimately benefit from that shift.

24

The Teaching Portfolio

Harry Richards, Lee Seidel, and Michael Lee

OVER THE PAST DECADE, the portfolio movement has taken root in the college teaching profession. The term "portfolio," once associated with the fine arts, has now become so familiar throughout the academy that anyone contemplating a career in higher education should seriously consider developing one. In the first edition of this guide, Leo Lambert presented an informative overview of the professional portfolio, with a focus on why and how university faculty should engage in the process of building one (Lambert 1996). In this edition, the focus shifts to the development of a "teaching portfolio" as a process that should prove helpful both to graduate students ready to embark upon academic careers and to teaching faculty who want to reflect upon and improve their teaching effectiveness via the portfolio-building process.

The Portfolio Movement—A Brief History

> One roadblock to change has been that it was more difficult to document teaching than to compile evidence for [scholarly] accomplishments. Teaching portfolios appear to offer a mechanism for providing such documentation.
>
> —*C. K. Knapper*

The teaching portfolio movement began in Canada with an initiative of the Canadian Association of University Teachers (CAUT) in the early 1970s (Knapper 1995). Then as now, faculty were evaluated on the basis of "teaching effectiveness, scholarly work, and service" (1995, 46), with teaching effectiveness being measured primarily by student evaluations and by hearsay.

The association established a Professional Orientation Committee, chaired by Christopher Knapper, which reported in 1972 that "evaluation procedures had to have strong faculty involvement to be effective" (46). The committee "urged colleagues to be much more proactive in gathering evidence about their own teaching performance" (46). In 1973, Knapper's successor as chair of the committee, Bruce Shore, of McGill University, introduced the idea of a "portfolio of evidence" to build a case for teaching effectiveness and set upon a course of developing an approach to the documentation and evaluation of teaching. In 1980, a *Guide to the Teaching Dossier: Its Preparation and Use* was published and distributed widely across Canada (Knapper 1995, 47).

Also in 1980, Peter Seldin's book *Successful Faculty Evaluation Programs* included a section on the teaching portfolio and acknowledged Canadian origins of the idea (Seldin 1980). In the early 1990s, several authors including Seldin (1993) were championing the use of portfolios as a way to promote better teaching and to document teaching effectiveness (e.g., Edgerton, Hutchings, and Quinlan 1991). In 1995, the *Journal on Excellence in College Teaching* devoted a special issue to teaching portfolios. The movement continues to grow, with as many as 1,500 colleges and universities in the United States and Canada using or experimenting with portfolios (Seldin 2000).

Today, graduate schools and faculty-development programs routinely encourage the use of portfolios as a means to improve the teaching of current and future faculty. As society demands more accountability from its institutions of higher education, teaching effectiveness remains a central issue. Graduate students and new faculty need to consider the central importance of teaching effectiveness in their career development and should seriously consider the use of teaching portfolios to document and assess their teaching.

"Teaching Effectiveness" and "Effective Teaching"

The words fit so naturally, the phrases come so easily. Perhaps too naturally, too easily, to promote clear thinking about what they mean. The fact is, throughout your teaching career you will be asking yourself the question (and in different ways and for different reasons others will be asking it of you): "Am I (or *Are you*) an effective teacher?" How you answer that question, and how others answer it about you, depends, of course, upon the meaning of "effective" teaching. One major contribution of the portfolio movement to the ongoing conversation about college teaching is that it forces members of the profession to address that question a priori. One major benefit you, as an individual instructor, will derive from the portfolio-building process is that it forces you to make explicit your own ways of answering the question. Because the implied thesis of every teaching portfolio is "I am an effective teacher," everyone building a portfolio should be addressing the question of what that means.

What Is a Teaching Portfolio and What Purpose Does It Serve?

Typically, the teaching portfolio is a relatively short (six to eight pages of narrative, plus appendices) collection of materials you select to document, summarize, and highlight your growth, your experiences, and your strengths as a teacher. When you first enter the job market, having a portfolio can help set you apart from other candidates. Once hired, a faculty member's portfolio provides concrete evidence of teaching effectiveness to offer promotion and tenure committees. For adjuncts—and for anyone else who teaches—it can become part of a formal process of reflecting on one's practice and developing one's strengths as a teacher.

While you can certainly provide evidence of teaching experience through such traditional means as the "classes taught" list in your curriculum vitae, the portfolio presents this information in a more useful, more compelling manner. Not only can you note *that* you have taught, you can also show *how* you teach and *why* you teach as you do.

Because teaching is such a complex, multidimensional activity, the portfolio has as a primary strength the ability to integrate information from several areas rather than relying on a single measure. The portfolio allows teaching and learning to be considered in their appropriate context—a context that changes by field and discipline and by class size and level. Because teaching is such a creative activity, there is no expectation that all faculty will teach alike. Thus, portfolios will vary, each one mirroring the unique attributes and styles of the person who created it.

Just as teaching approaches vary, so too is student learning individually and aggregately differentiated by many factors, including teaching approaches. While faculty must teach in accordance with expectations set within a discipline and shaped by the curricular objectives of a specific course, knowledge of the best professional practices based upon available scholarship in the field of college teaching should foster teaching that best facilitates student learning. To make this connection explicit, your teaching portfolio should highlight and explain your specific strategies and approaches to prioritizing, enhancing, and assessing the student learning that results from your teaching.

The term "portfolio" is not used loosely. An effective teaching portfolio is neither a "file cabinet" nor a "highlights film," but rather *a thematic collection of materials selected to "define" your teaching and to demonstrate the effectiveness of your approaches and the quality of your outcomes*. Think of your teaching portfolio as artists and designers think of theirs: as a collection of your best work presented systematically and thoughtfully for your own self-improvement and for others to learn about your solutions to the problem of teaching in the contemporary college or university.

What Should Be Included in a Teaching Portfolio?

> What we have looked for, but not seen, in advice for developing portfolios is advice on how to go about a concurrent process to understand and express what constitutes excellent teaching in the academic unit in a way that reflects actual teaching practice.
>
> —*L. Richlin (1995)*

No hard and fast rules govern what you may or may not include. However, there is a consensus among experts in the field of college teaching as to the professional values most directly associated with "best practice" (see, for example, Angelo 1993 and Bass 1999). Thus, if you want your portfolio to make the case that you are an effective teacher, you should be sure that it demonstrates a set of specific competencies that reflect those professional values. These "core competencies," outlined and discussed below, are founded upon professional values such as these: "Having an understanding of how students learn. Having a concern for students' intellectual development. Being committed to the scholarship of pedagogy. Wanting to work with and learn from colleagues. Reflecting continually on one's own professional practice. Being aware of the importance of 'student culture' to the learning process."

Best Practice and Core Competencies

The teaching portfolio represents a dual opportunity. It allows you to articulate the beliefs and values you hold about teaching, and it allows you to demonstrate your mastery of the competencies that make up your "best practice." While some studies of effective teaching list as many as twenty-seven "competencies required for good teachers" (Smith and Simpson 1995), a teaching portfolio should be centered on a more focused set of "core competencies." To this end, the University of New Hampshire teaching portfolio handbook, for example, stipulates that graduate students *must* provide evidence that in their teaching they can effectively accomplish each of the following tasks:

1. Articulate appropriate course goals and objectives that are (a) tied to specific learning outcomes consistent with existing scholarship about how students learn; and (b) explained clearly to students—perhaps in a syllabus—to allow them to use these goals and objectives to assess their own progress and learning.

2. Organize and design courses with those goals and objectives in mind. This includes but is not limited to designing formal assignments and examinations appropriate to the learning goals/outcomes of the course; using multiple approaches to instruction, such as multimedia technologies, computer-based materials, and writing to enhance students' understanding of course material; designing and applying appropriate assessment techniques to ensure student learning by getting useful feedback from them.

3. Present material effectively and communicate with students in a variety of settings, including large classes and small groups. Effective communication with students has two dimensions that can be addressed in the portfolio: stimulating students' interest in and engagement with the course material by making it relevant to their lives, and facilitating students' participation in classroom activities that provoke their interest and appropriately challenge them.

4. Provide feedback to students to give them clear messages about their performance in ways that will help them improve before the semester is over. The portfolio should demonstrate that an individual can (a) give students frequent, timely, and constructive feedback; and (b) use fair and consistent grading methods, with criteria that are clearly conveyed to students.

5. Employ varied teaching methods that appeal to the various learning styles and "intelligences" of today's diverse student population. Examples include lecturing to convey information and concepts clearly, using forms of group learning and collaborative learning, and introducing service-learning where appropriate to the discipline and the course content. Other

examples include running effective discussions and using cases when appropriate to course content.

6. Apply knowledge of undergraduate student culture to specific features of one's course design.

7. Incorporate the latest field or discipline scholarship into a course.

How best to demonstrate these competencies in the portfolio will vary from individual to individual, from discipline to discipline. What is important is that you consciously attempt to do so, both in the selection of materials to include in your portfolio and in your explanations of why and how those materials were used in your teaching. The following list offers an idea of the kinds of materials you might choose from to accomplish those ends:

- A statement of philosophy of teaching and learning
- A statement of teaching competency
- Course syllabi
- Methods used to assess student learning
- Analysis of samples of student work related to course objectives
- Analysis of student evaluations
- A statement of teaching goals

THE IMPORTANCE OF A STATEMENT
OF TEACHING PHILOSOPHY

With teaching portfolios constructed as arguments, faculty members who may resist assembling a portfolio from a potentially bewildering array of items will be more inclined to make a case for their teaching because every college teacher knows how to construct an argument—and knows the value of building a case and having it evaluated by others (Lang and Bain 1997, 1).

An essential part of any teaching portfolio is a short (one to two pages), concise, and cogent expression of your beliefs, attitudes, and values regarding teaching and learning. Your statement should include commentary on your teaching goals, both long- and short-term. Because much of the actual content of the portfolio will be a logical extension and concrete demonstration of the principles you present in this statement, keep in mind that what you say there must be supported by materials you choose for inclusion later on. Also remember that your strengths as a teacher are really an expression of your values regarding the teaching profession, some of which could be implied in your classroom approaches. This part of the portfolio forces you to make those values explicit—to yourself as well as to others.

Creating a portfolio is a reflexive as well as a reflective process. Thus, you will probably rewrite your philosophy of teaching statement a number of times as you fill in other sections of the portfolio. Just as your statement will help you decide what to include elsewhere, some of those choices will help you rethink and refine how you articulate your approach to teaching. Think of the statement as an abstract to a scholarly article. Writing the abstract first is a way of focusing the main points of the paper, even though you know that after you write the paper you will have to go back and rewrite the abstract.

STATEMENT OF TEACHING COMPETENCY

This section of the portfolio serves as a bridge between your teaching philosophy statement and the syllabi and other course-related teaching materials you provide in the portfolio's appendices. Here you solidify your argument that you have attained the "core competencies," making direct reference to the items in the appendices that illustrate that attainment. The objective is to provide a context for anyone examining the materials you are using as evidence. In a sense, you are answering the unspoken question, "What does this syllabus, this assignment, this example of student work, etc. provide evidence *of*?" The answer is your way of linking your stated beliefs about how students learn (teaching philosophy) and your own practice.

One of the hallmarks of effective teachers is their ability to reflect upon their classroom experiences—both positive and negative—and to grow from those experiences. The statement section of the portfolio shows that you have done so. In essence, it's a "lessons learned" statement, with an eye to using those lessons as a means of self-improvement. In this section, you can be open about approaches you have tried without complete success; you can admit that you—like all teachers—have run up against problems you could not solve the first time around. Indicating ways in which you have *responded* to challenging situations shows you to be a responsible teacher, one who has learned from mistakes to become a better teacher.

TEACHING GOALS

Here you can discuss the specific areas and ways in which you would like to improve your teaching. Keep your list limited to two or three goals, each of which you can address in a single paragraph. Each goal should be accompanied by a plan—specific ways of achieving that particular goal.

A rule of thumb is *Nothing speaks for itself.* Your materials "speak" through the selection process, through the contextualizing discussions in previous sections of the portfolio, and through the "transparent" organization of the portfolio. For example, including student evaluations makes sense if you provide your own evaluative statement of those student evaluations. So, too, sample assignments or examples of student work should be linked directly to a statement about how the assignment enhances or assesses understanding, or what the student work tells us about that student's learning in your course. If you include graded student papers, you might choose one very good paper and one poor one, both annotated to show why you judged them as you did.

Keep in mind that there should be a three-way link from philosophy to design to execution. A well-constructed portfolio makes the linkage clear with each of the materials chosen for inclusion.

The Portfolio and Evaluation: Formative or Summative?

At different points in your career, a teaching portfolio will serve different purposes. For someone preparing for tenure or promotion review, or being considered for a teaching award, the portfolio can be part of a "summative" evaluation. As such, constructing the portfolio is an essentially retrospective process, the intent of which is to document your teaching achievements. While your professional development is never complete, at this point in your career you will be able to offer evidence of where your professional journey has taken you to date and what you have accomplished along the way.

As a graduate student you should see your teaching portfolio as part of a more developmental, "formative" process. In many ways, the portfolio can be seen as a "map" of where you intend to go in your teaching career, with the emphasis, of course, on your proven ability to get where you want to go. This map should serve you well as your portfolio evolves into a professional portfolio that reflects the research and service dimensions of your career as well as your teaching accomplishments. Your portfolio will be a concrete reminder to you individually, as the portfolio movement does to the academy at large, that the central mission of any academic institution is to meet the learning needs of the students it serves.

Further Readings/Resources

Anderson, Erin, ed. 1993. *Campus Use of the Teaching Portfolio: Twenty-Five Profiles.* Washington, D.C.: American Association for Higher Education.

Bernstein, David. 1998. "Putting the Focus on Student Learning." In *The Course Portfolio,* edited by P. Hutchings, 77–83. Washington, D.C.: American Association for Higher Education.

Hutchings, Pat. 1998. "How to Develop a Course Portfolio." In *The Course Portfolio,* edited by P. Hutchings, 47–55. Washington, D.C.: American Association for Higher Education.

Millis, Barbara J. 1991. "Putting the Teaching Portfolio in Context." *To Improve the Academy* 10: 215–29.

Murray, John P. 1995. *Successful Faculty Development and Evaluation: The Complete Teaching Portfolio.* ASHE-ERIC Higher Education Reports, no. 8. Washington, D.C.: Graduate School of Education and Human Development, George Washington Univ.

Seldin, Peter, Linda Annis, and John Zubizarreta. 1995. "Answers to Common Questions About the Teaching Portfolio." *Journal on Teaching Excellence* 6, no. 1: 57–64.

Web Sites

http://www.libfind.unl.edu/teaching/tchport.html
http://english.ttu.edu/Rickly/teachingport.html
http://www.wisc.edu/MOO/tfolio.evidence.html
http://www.sci.wsu.edu/cos/portfolio.html
http://www.utep.edu/cetal/portfoli/index.html
http://www1.umn.edu/ohr/pff/portfolio.html
http://www.psu.edu/celt/portfolio.html
http://depts.washington.edu/cidrweb/TeachingPortfolioIntro.html

25

Finding an Institution
That "Fits" You

Leo M. Lambert

WHAT SORT OF ACADEMIC CAREER do you envision for yourself? Are you spending your time conducting research at the cutting edge of scholarship in your discipline? Teaching talented undergraduates in small classes and seminars? Mentoring graduate students? Do you imagine yourself on the faculty at a select, private institution? Do you envision teaching at an open-enrollment institution, such as a community college, attended by first-generation college students? Or is your ideal simply an institution just like your alma mater, the inspiration for your joining the professoriate in the first place?

Your answer is important, because the institutional environment in which you choose to pursue your career will shape it to a very large extent. The purpose of this introductory chapter, then, is to help you understand and accommodate the academic reality that the traditional professorial roles of teaching, research, and service are interpreted and valued very differently across various types of institutions. The academic job market is such that you may not secure employment in a setting that meets your absolute ideal. But I believe strongly that the very process of defining clear professional goals and expectations for yourself will increase your chances of landing at an institution where you can find professional fulfillment—or, perhaps, where you even may be able to help shape the institution's future direction to make it more compatible and sympathetic to your scholarly interests.

Recognizing Variety in Institutional Mission

The more than 4,000 colleges and universities in the United States represent the broadest array of higher education institutions found anywhere in the world. If you are like most new Ph.D.s or postdocs searching for their first academic position, you probably are freshly familiar with the nature and mission of the research or doctoral university. And certainly the classic American liberal arts college is a familiar model to most everyone. But by far the greatest number of higher education institutions in the United States, and hence most academic openings, fall outside the typologies of elite research university (Harvard, Yale, Stanford, Chicago, etc.) and classic liberal arts college (Swarthmore, Williams, Davidson, etc.).

One such institutional type is a group of hybrid institutions called "associated new American colleges"[1]—private; principally undergraduate, but with selected graduate and professional programs; comprehensive; and dedicated to the integration of liberal arts and professional studies. But they are only one innovative example among all the institutions outside of the research university and liberal arts college models. That still leaves hundreds of master's universities and regional colleges, public and private, two- and four-year, selective and nonselective, church-related or not, prosperous or struggling, each with its own unique institutional culture.

Further, huge variation in institutional culture, values, and traditions exists *within* any institutional type. On this point, findings from the National Survey of Student Engagement are illustrative. According to that data, while undergraduate students' engagement with faculties and academic programs did generally decrease as institutional size increased,[2] large variations in engagement existed among similar institutions, to the extent that some large research universities did a better job of engaging, supporting, and providing academic challenge to their undergraduate students than did some small liberal arts colleges. This is an excellent example of the variance in the nature and quality of the experiences to be found by both students and faculty members within groups of like institutions.

1. Linda A. McMillin and William G. Berberet, eds., *New Academic Compact: Revisioning the Relationship Between Faculty and Their Institutions* (Bolton, Mass.: Anker, 2002).

2. National Survey of Student Engagement, *Improving the College Experience: National Benchmarks of Effective Educational Practice* (Bloomington: Indiana Univ. Center for Postsecondary Research and Planning, 2001).

Teaching: Finding a Pedagogical Fit

I recently spent a number of days visiting several fine colleges and universities with my oldest daughter, who soon will be applying for admission. On the campus of one highly selective liberal arts college, the intimately sized classrooms, many with chairs around a single table, reflected the nine-to-one student-faculty ratio. On another, larger, university campus, the student tour guide took us into a 200-seat amphitheatre and, with remarkable candor, told us this was the largest lecture hall on campus, but that when she had a freshman history course in that very room, the faculty member had recognized her face when she approached the instructor for help with a paper. Both are excellent institutions, but they conveyed two very different impressions of the student academic experience.

In investigating a prospective institution during your job search, your look into its teaching culture will necessarily extend much deeper than a two-hour undergraduate admissions tour. Based upon my experience as a dean, provost, and president at three very different universities, I have constructed a list of questions for you to think about that may aid you in evaluating the potential for a good fit between your professional goals and that institution's mission, priorities, and values regarding teaching.

QUESTIONS RELATED TO TEACHING

• What evidence is presented to you, or can you discern, that undergraduate teaching is valued by the institution? (Faculty members will give you an honest assessment about how seriously undergraduate teaching is weighted in personnel decisions.)

• What evidence of excellence in teaching does the institution expect you to present for promotion and tenure? Does the institution expect more than satisfactory student ratings?

• Does the institution value and reward efforts to use technology in the teaching/learning environment?

• What types of faculty-development support exist? Who provides such support? A teaching and learning center? The dean?

• Does the institutional environment support experimentation and innovation in teaching? For example, if you were to seek support to redesign a class to incorporate community-service experiences, does such support exist? More important, would your pedagogical creativity be valued or rejected by that institution's culture?

• Does the institution value and reward efforts to mentor and teach outside of traditional classroom contexts, such as advising undergraduate research experiences?

• Do faculty colleagues regularly have serious and scholarly conversations about teaching? Are institutional forums held regularly to discuss aspects of teaching?

• How often do students and faculty interact outside of the classroom, and in what contexts: International study trips? Open in-person access to faculty in their offices? Via e-mail?

• What are expectations regarding your doing academic advising?

Research: Evaluating Support for Inquiry

Most faculty members are committed to maintaining a program of research scholarship and intellectual inquiry, but with varying priority. If you view such research as your principal professional activity, you should seek out an institutional environment that expects and supports cutting-edge discovery by faculty. Some institutions place primary emphasis on teaching while still highly valuing and indeed demanding high-quality research scholarship. Still others require very heavy teaching loads but also have some expectation for scholarly research or creative effort.

Understanding the nature and level of an institution's expectations for research scholarship is one of your most important tasks in determining whether its professional priorities align with yours. Another task is making a judgment about whether you can be successful in meeting those expectations given the level of research support (start-up funds, research space, summer support, sabbaticals, released or reassigned time, etc.) that the institution is willing to provide.

QUESTIONS RELATED TO RESEARCH

• What constitutes "scholarship" at that institution? Does it apply Boyer's paradigm[3] (which values equally the scholarships of teaching, inte-

---

3. Ernest L. Boyer, *Scholarship Reconsidered: Priorities of the Professoriate* (Princeton, N.J.: The Carnegie Foundation for the Advancement of Teaching, 1990).

gration, application, and discovery), or does it value research (discovery) most? This topic merits serious discussion with your prospective department chair, dean, and colleagues.

• Does the institution view teaching and research as *competing* demands, or does it support a culture where research scholarship and creative activity energize teaching and vice versa? For an example of the latter written for prospective faculty candidates and new faculty to introduce them to a specific institutional culture, read *The Elon Teacher-Scholar.*[4]

• Is there tangible support for research scholarship, such as institutionally funded grants, sabbaticals, and travel support for conferences? Is summer support available?

• Can the institution's physical plant infrastructure and technology support the requirements of your research?

• Are the research expectations appropriate given the demands of your other professional responsibilities, especially teaching?

• Are there colleagues at the institution to offer advice, feedback, and criticism about your research scholarship or will you have access to such assistance elsewhere?

• Are library resources adequate or available nearby?

• If the institution demands a heavy teaching load, can your teaching schedule be adjusted to allow for some concentrated periods to focus on research activity?

Service: Responsibilities of Institutional Citizenship

Being a good and contributing citizen in your academic community is an important part of professional life. Effective shared governance and good decision-making at many levels of the institution are dependent on faculty participation. At many colleges and universities, a strong sense of community emerges from a common commitment to serve the institution and work toward its betterment.

Unfortunately, one of the traps that junior faculty can fall into easily is to overcommit themselves to such service responsibilities. Opportunities for committee service abound (from departmental search committees, to a college-wide curriculum committee, to specialized task forces), and usually the

4. www.elon.edu/academics/teasch.asp

reward for effective service is to be asked to serve again! But you should be cautious and take on service roles judiciously, perhaps with the advice of your department chair. As an early-career faculty member, you need to commit yourself foremost to teaching and research scholarship, opting for only a limited number of meaningful service responsibilities that will introduce you to the workings of the institution and orient you for future leadership opportunities.

QUESTIONS RELATED TO SERVICE

• Are service opportunities assigned meaningfully, taking a faculty member's expertise, interest, and career stage into account?
• What advice does your department chair offer regarding service roles?
• Are service expectations reasonable, especially for junior faculty? Or are too many service responsibilities foisted off on them?

Investigating Institutional Context

Determining the fit between your professional aspirations and the culture and context of a potential employing institution requires careful investigation on a range of issues. What resources the institution has at its disposal, for example, very well may determine the availability of the support you will need to attain your professional goals. Thorough preparation on your part will aid you in asking more serious and probing questions, which will help you in your decision-making as well as demonstrate to your prospective colleagues your depth of insight. Much of this information is easily available online.

BACKGROUND RESEARCH

Prior to even applying for a position, and certainly before an interview, the following background reading about an institution is recommended:
• Strategic plan: Where does the institution want to go?
• Mission statement: Is the statement distinctive and compelling, or routine boilerplate? What values does it project?
• Admissions website: How does the institution pitch itself to prospective students and parents?

• Department's web site, including faculty biographies and course syllabi: In the department you would join, what proportion of the faculty are active in both teaching and research scholarship? What can you discern about the teaching environment? Who will be your colleagues?

• Faculty handbook: What information is available about personnel processes, such as promotion and tenure review?

• General catalogs and financial statements: What resources does the institution have (academic support endowments, library holdings, numbers of faculty members, etc.) that may be critical to supporting your work?

• Published statements about scholarship: Has the institution issued any formal statement about the types of scholarship it values?

CRITICAL FACE-TO-FACE CONVERSATIONS

When you have the opportunity to visit a campus for a formal interview, bear in mind that the interview is two-way: The interviewers will be making a close examination of your personality, disposition, talents, and achievements; but you also will have the opportunity to size up prospective colleagues and determine whether the institution can provide an environment compatible with your professional objectives. From interviewing prospective faculty members myself, I can tell you that candidates obtain a great advantage when they ask challenging questions about institutional values and culture, demonstrate interest in the institution beyond the hiring department, and show that they not only are knowledgeable about but also can help advance an institution-wide program (such as undergraduate research).

Key individuals can provide tremendous insights about the characteristics of the institutional environment: the perspective of the *department chair* is especially important. Chairs are usually of senior rank, are experienced faculty members themselves, and have an administrative perspective on vital issues such as standards for promotion and tenure. A good department chair is an invaluable resource for an early-career faculty member. You should expect the *dean* to be frank and candid about expectations for success, to have a knowledgeable perspective on the institution's major academic directions and priorities, and to offer clear answers about resources and support the institution is willing to offer.

Before accepting an offer for a faculty position, speak to a *prospective colleague* who is a few years ahead of you in the tenure cycle. Has the institution met that person's expectations; if not, what specific elements have been disappointing? Finally, *students* can usually be counted on to give an unvarnished view of academic life, including faculty accessibility, the level of academic challenge, and satisfaction with life both in and out of the classroom.

Gaining insights from each of these perspectives will help you make a better judgment about whether or not a particular institution will provide you with the right setting for a satisfying and productive academic career.

Works Cited

Index

Works Cited

Abraham, Ansley. 2000. "The Compact for Faculty Diversity: The SREB Model." In *Leadership Summit on Diversity in Doctoral Education: Creating Greater Opportunities in the New Millennium*, 47–57. Washington, D.C.: U.S. Department of Education and Howard Univ.

Adams, Dennis, and Mary Hamm. 1994. *New Designs for Teaching and Learning: Promoting Active Learning in Tomorrow's Schools*. San Francisco: Jossey-Bass.

Adams, Maurianne, and Linda S. Marchesani. 1999. *A Multidimensional Approach to Faculty Development: Understanding the Teaching-Learning Process*. http://www.diversityweb.org/Digest/W99/multidimensional.html.

American Association of University Professors. 1990. *Policy Documents and Reports*. Washington, D.C.: AAUP.

Angelo, Thomas A. 1993. "A Teacher's Dozen: Fourteen General, Research-Based Principles for Improving Higher Learning in Our Classrooms." *AAHE Bulletin* 45, no. 8 (April): 3–7.

Angelo, Thomas A., and K. P. Cross. 1993. *Classroom Assessment Techniques: A Handbook for College Teachers*. San Francisco: Jossey-Bass.

Antonio, Anthony Lising. 2003. "Diverse Student Bodies, Diverse Faculties." *Academe* 89, no. 6, 14–17.

Association of American Universities. 1997. *AAU Diversity Statement on the Importance of Diversity in University Admissions*. Retrieved October 26, 2002, from http://www.aau.edu/issues/Diversity4.14.97.html.

Bandura, Albert. 1982. "Self-Efficacy Mechanism in Human Agency." *American Psychologist* 37, no. 2: 122–47.

Barton, Angela Calabrese. 1998. *Feminist Science Education*. New York: Teacher's College Press.

Bass, Randy. 1999. "The Scholarship of Teaching: What's the Problem?" *Inventio* 1, no. 1. http://www.doiiit.gmu.edu/Archives/feb98/randybass.htm

Bean, Christine. 1993. "Universal Precautions in the Laboratory Setting." Chapter 4 in *Bloodborne Pathogens,* National Safety Council. Sudbury, Mass.: Jones and Bartlett.

————. 1998. *Safety Manual of the University of New Hampshire.* Durham: Univ. of New Hampshire.

Bean, John C. 1996. *Engaging Ideas. The Professor's Guide to Integrating Writing, Critical Thinking, and Active Learning in the Classroom.* San Francisco: Jossey-Bass.

Bendixen-Noe, Mary K., and Carmen Giebelhaus. 1998. "Nontraditional Students in Higher Education: Meeting Their Needs as Learners." *Mid-Western Educational Researcher* 11: 27–31.

Berlak, Ann, and Harold Berlak. 1981. *Dilemmas of Schooling: Teaching and Social Change.* London: Methuen.

Berlyne, Daniel E. 1960. *Conflict, Arousal, and Curiosity.* New York: McGraw-Hill.

Billson, Janet Mancini. 1994. "Group Process in the College Classroom: Building Relationships for Learning." In *Collaborative Learning: A Sourcebook for Higher Education,* vol. 2, edited by Stephanie Kadel and Julia A. Keehner. University Park, Pa.: National Center on Postsecondary Teaching, Learning, & Assessment (NCTLA), Pennsylvania State Univ. Press.

Blevins-Knabe, Belinda. 1992. "The Ethics of Dual Relationships in Higher Education." *Ethics and Behavior* 2: 151–63.

Borden, Victor M. H. 2002. "The Top 100: Interpreting the Data." *Black Issues in Higher Education* 19, no. 9: 40–43.

Boulton, Andrew, and Debra Panizzon. 1998. "The Knowledge Expansion in Science Education: Balancing Practical and Theoretical Knowledge." *Journal of Research in Science Teaching* 35: 475–81.

Boyd, Eulas. 2004. "Placing Diversity at the Core of Institutional Excellence." *Black Issues in Higher Education* 21, no. 1: 82.

Brophy, Jere. 1987. "Synthesis of Research on Strategies for Motivating Students to Learn." *Educational Leadership* 45, no. 2 (October): 40–48.

————. 1998. *Motivating Students to Learn.* Boston: McGraw-Hill.

Brown, David, ed. 2000. *Interactive Learning: Vignettes from America's Most Wired Campuses.* Bolton, Mass.: Anker.

Browne, M. Neil, and Stuart Keeley. 1997. *Striving for Excellence in College: Tips for Active Learning.* Upper Saddle River, N.J.: Prentice Hall.

Buber, Martin. 1988. *Eclipse of God.* Translated by Walter Kaufmann. Trenton, N.J.: Humanities Press International.

————. 1996. *I and Thou.* New York: Touchstone Press.

Cannell, Stephen J. 1999. "A Dyslexic Writer's Story." *Newsweek,* November 22, 78.

Cohen, Sheldon. 1988. "Psychosocial Models of the Role of Social Support in the Etiology of Physical Disease." *Health Psychology* 7: 269–97.

Colby, Anita, and Elizabeth Foote. 1995. *Creating and Maintaining a Diverse Faculty.* ERIC Document Reproduction Service no. ED386 261, Los Angeles.

Council of Graduate Schools. 1997. "Building an Inclusive Graduate Community: A Statement of Principles." *Communicator* 30, no. 5 (June): 40–43.

Crepeau, Elizabeth, Louise Thibodaux, and Diane Parham. 1999. "Academic Juggling Act: Beginning and Sustaining an Academic Career." *American Journal of Occupational Therapy* 53: 25–30.

Cross, K. Patricia. 1983. "On College Teaching." *Journal of Engineering Education* 72 (January): 9–14.

———. 1990. "Classroom Research: Helping Professors Learn More About Teaching and Learning." In *How Administrators Can Improve Teaching,* edited by P. Seldin et al., 122–42. San Francisco: Jossey-Bass.

Csikszentmihalyi, Mihaly. 1997. "Intrinsic Motivation and Effective Teaching: A Flow Analysis." In *Teaching Well and Liking It,* edited by J. L. Bess, 72–89. Baltimore, Md.: Johns Hopkins.

Cuban, Larry. 1992. "Managing Dilemmas While Building Professional Communities." *Educational Researcher* 21, no. 1: 4–11.

Daspit, Toby, and John A. Weaver, eds. 1999. *Popular Culture and Critical Pedagogy: Reading, Constructing, Connecting.* New York: Garland.

Day, H. I. 1982. "Curiosity and the Interested Explorer." *NSPI Journal* 21, no. 4 (May): 19–22.

Deci, Edward L. 1995. *Why We Do What We Do: Understanding Self Motivation.* New York: Penguin.

Des Marchais, Jacques E. 1993. "A Student-Centered, Problem-Based Curriculum: Five Years Experience." *Canadian Medical Association Journal* 148: 1567–72.

Dewey, John. 1933. *How We Think: A Restatement of the Relationship of Reflective Thinking to the Educative Process,* 2nd rev. ed. Lexington, Mass.: D.C. Heath.

Dweck, Carol. S. 1986. "Motivational Processes Affecting Learning." *American Psychologist* 41, no. 10 (October): 1040–48.

Edgerton, Russell, Pat Hutchings, and Kathleen Quinlan. 1991. *The Teaching Portfolio: Capturing the Scholarship in Teaching.* Washington, D.C.: American Association for Higher Education.

Elbow, Peter. 1998. *Writing with Power: Techniques for Mastering the Writing Process.* New York: Oxford Univ. Press.

Feldman, Kenneth A. 1976. "The Superior College Teacher from the Students' View." *Research in Higher Education* 5: 43–88.

Flavell, John. 1977. *Cognitive Development.* Englewood Cliffs, N.J.: Prentice Hall.

"Footnotes." 1999. "Adjuncts and TAs at Las Vegas Are Relegated to Trailer." *The Chronicle of Higher Education,* January 15, A14.

Fredrickson, Scott. 1999. "Untangling a Tangled Web: An Overview of Web-based Instruction Programs." *T.H.E. Journal* 26, no. 11. http://www.thejournal.com/magazine/vault/A2087.cfm

Friere, Paulo. 1970. *Pedagogy of the Oppressed.* New York: Continuum.

Fulwiler, Toby. 1987. *Teaching with Writing.* Portsmouth, N.H.: Boynton/Cook.

Gephart, Daniel J. 2000. *Disability Compliance for Higher Education, 2000 Year Book.* Horsham, Pa.: LRP Publications.

Glendon, Kellie, and Deborah Ulrich. 1992. "Using Cooperative Learning Strategies." *Nurse Educator* 17: 37–40.

Graduate Studies Mentoring Guidelines. http://www.ku.edu/~graduate/Faculty/mentoring.shtml.

Hamilton, Edith, and Huntington Carns, eds. 1961. *The Great Dialogues of Plato.* New York: Pantheon.

Hansen, Edmund J., and James A. Stephens. 2000. "The Ethics of Learner-Centered Education: Dynamics that Impede the Process." *Change* 33, no. 5: 40–47.

Harvey, William. 2002. *Minorities in Higher Education 2001–2002: Nineteenth Annual Status Report.* Washington, D.C.: American Council on Education.

Henderson, Cathy. 1999. *1999 College Freshmen with Disabilities.* Washington, D.C.: HEATH Resource Center, American Council on Education.

Hernandez, Adriana. 1997. *Pedagogy, Democracy, and Feminism: Rethinking the Public Sphere.* Albany: State Univ. of New York Press.

Herreid, Clyde F. 1994. "Case Studies in Science: A Novel Method of Science Education." *Journal of College Science Teaching* 23: 221–29.

———. 1997/1998. "What Makes a Good Case?" *Journal of College Science Teaching* 27: 163–65.

Hickman, John N. 1998. "Adjunct U." *The New Republic,* December 7, 16.

Hilliard, Asa G. 1989. "Cultural Style in Teaching and Learning." *The Education Digest,* 55: 21–23.

Hilosky, Alexandra, Frank Sutman, and Joseph Schmuckler. 1998. "Is Laboratory-Based Instruction in Beginning College-Level Chemistry Worth the Effort and Expense?" *Journal of Chemical Education* 75: 100–04.

Himley, Margaret, et al. 1997. *Political Moments in the Classroom.* Portsmouth, N.H.: Boynton/Cook.

Hollenback, Sharon, and Milene Morfei. 1996. "Balancing Roles as Teacher, Student, and Person." In *University Teaching: A Guide for Graduate Students,* edited by Leo M. Lambert, Stacy Lane Tice, and Patricia H. Featherstone, 137–40. Syracuse, N.Y.: Syracuse Univ. Press.

Huff, Charles. 1997. "Cooperative Learning: A Model for Teaching." *Journal of Nursing Education* 36: 434–36.

Hurtado, Sylvia, Jeffrey F. Milem, and Alma Clayton-Pedersen. 1999. "Enacting Diverse Learning Environments: Improving the Climate for Racial/Ethnic Diversity in Higher Education." *ASHE ERIC Higher Education Reports,* 26, no. 8: 1–116.

Jacobi, Maryann. 1991. Mentoring and Undergraduate Academic Success: A Literature Review. *Review of Educational Research* 61: 505–32.

Jacoby, Barbara, et al. 1996. *Service-Learning in Higher Education: Concepts and Practices.* San Francisco: Jossey-Bass.

Jensen, Murray S. 1998. "Finding a Place for the Computer in the Introductory Biology Laboratory." *Journal of College Science Teaching* 27: 247–49.

Johnson, David W., Roger T. Johnson, and Karl A. Smith. 1991. *Active Learning: Cooperation in the College Classroom.* Edina, Minn.: Interaction Book Company.

———. 1998. "Cooperative Learning Returns to College: What Evidence Is There that it Works?" *Change* 30, No. 4 (July/August): 27–35.

Johnson, W. Brad. 2002. "The Intentional Mentor: Strategies and Guidelines for the Practice of Mentoring." *Professional Psychology: Research and Practice* 33: 88–96.

———. Forthcoming. "A Framework for Conceptualizing Competence to Mentor." *Ethics and Behavior.*

Johnson, W. Brad, and Jennifer M. Huwe. 2002. *Getting Mentored in Graduate School.* Washington, D.C.: American Psychological Association.

Keller, John M. 1983. "Motivational Design of Instruction." In *Instructional Design Theories and Models: An Overview of Their Current Status,* edited by C. M. Reigeluth, 383–434. Hillsdale, N.J.: Erlbaum.

———. 1987. "Strategies for Stimulating the Motivation to Learn." *Performance and Instruction* 26, no. 8 (Sept./Oct.): 1–7.

Kelly, Shalonda, and John H. Schweitzer. 1999. "Mentoring Within a Graduate School Setting." *College Student Journal* 33, no. 1: 130–48.

Kemmis, Stephen, and Robin McTaggart. 1982. *The Action Research Planner.* Victoria, Australia: Deacon Univ. Press.

Kendall, Jane, et al. 1990. *Combining Service and Learning: A Resource Book for Community and Public Service.* Raleigh, N.C.: National Society for Experiential Education.

Kleffner, J. H., and T. Dadian. 1997. "Using Cooperative Learning in Dental Education." *Journal of Dental Education* 61: 66–72.

Knapper, Christophen K. 1995. "The Origins of Teaching Portfolios." *Journal on Excellence in Teaching* 6, no. 1: 45–56.

Kram, Kathy E. 1985. *Mentoring at Work: Developmental Relationships in Organizational Life.* Glenview, Ill.: Scott Foresman.

Lamb, S. I. 1997. "The Laboratory." In *Effective Teaching and Course Management for University and College Science Teachers,* edited by Eleanor D. Siebert, Mario W. Caprio, and Carri M. Lyda, 189–202. Dubuque, Iowa: Kendall/Hunt.

Lambert, Leo M. 1996. "Building a Professional Portfolio." In *University Teaching: A Guide for Graduate Students,* edited by Leo M. Lambert, Stacey Lane Tice, and Patricia H. Featherstone, 147–55. Syracuse, N.Y.: Syracuse Univ. Press.

Lang, James, and Kenneth R. Bain. 1997. "Recasting the Teaching Portfolio." *The Teaching Professor* 11, no. 10: 1.

LaPidus, Jules B. 1997. *Doctoral Education: Preparing for the Future.* Washington, D.C.: Council of Graduate Schools.

Lazarowitz, Reuven, and Pinchas Tamir. 1994. "Research on Using Laboratory Instruction in Science." Chapter 3 in *Handbook of Research on Science and Teaching: A Project of the National Science Teachers Association,* edited by D. L. Gabel, 94–128. New York: Macmillan.

Leatherman, Courtney. 1997. "Growing Use of Part-Time Professors Prompts Debate and Calls for Action." *The Chronicle of Higher Education,* October 10, A14.

Lopez, Tom. 1997. "Several Factors Hinder the Recruitment of Minorities." *The Minnesota Daily Online,* March 11, http://www.mndaily.com/daily/1997/03/11/news/minor.

Mannara, Tracy, Salma A. Ayyash, Mary Cannella, Charles Widener, and Frederick Phelps. 1996. "The Laboratory." Chapter 5 in *University Teaching: A Guide for Graduate Students,* edited by Leo M. Lambert, Stacey Lane Tice, and Patricia H. Featherstone, 44–49. Syracuse, N.Y.: Syracuse Univ. Press.

Markie, Peter J. 1994. *A Professor's Duties: Ethical Issues in College Teaching.* Lanham, Md.: Rowman and Littlefield.

Mathews, A. Lanethea. 2000. "The Changing Structure of the Academic Job Market." *PS: Political Science and Politics* 33, no. 2 (June): 237–42.

Matsumoto, David. 2000. *Culture and Psychology: People Around the World.* Belmont, Calif.: Wadsworth/Thomson Learning.

McCabe, Donald, and Gary Pavela. 2000. "Some Good News About Academic Integrity." *Change* 33, no. 5: 32–38.

McDermott, John J., ed. 1980. *The Philosophy of John Dewey.* Chicago: Univ. of Chicago Press.

McGrory, Kathleen. 1996. "Ethics in Teaching: Putting It Together." In *Ethical Dimensions of College and University Teaching,* edited by L. Fisch, 101–7. Series *New Directions for Teaching and Learning* no. 66. San Francisco: Jossey-Bass.

Meyers, Chet, and Thomas B. Jones. 1993. *Promoting Active Learning: Strategies for the College Classroom.* San Francisco: Jossey-Bass.

Miller, John W., Leonard P. Martineau, and Robert C. Clark. 2000. "Technology Infusion and Higher Education: Changing Teaching and Learning." *Innovative Higher Education* 24, no. 3 (Spring).

Modell, Harold I., and Joel A. Michael. 1993. "Part I. Plenary Papers. Promoting Active Learning in the Life Sciences Classroom: Defining the Issues." *Annals of the New York Academy of Sciences,* edited by H. I. Modell and J. A. Michael, 1–7. New York: New York Academy of Sciences National Commission on Mathematics and Science Teaching for the 21st Century.

Mosteller, Frederick. 1989. "The Muddiest Point in the Lecture as a Feedback Device." *Teaching and Learning: The Journal of the Harvard-Danforth Center* 3: 10–21.

National Academy Press. 1997. *Advisor, Teacher, Role Model, Friend: On Being a Mentor to Students in Science and Engineering.* Washington, D.C.: National Academy Press.

National Science Foundation. 1998. *Doctorate Recipients from United States Universities: Summary Report 1998.* http://www.nsf.gov/search97cgi/vtopic.

Newton, Doug P. 1996. "Causal Situations in Science: A Model for Supporting Understanding." *Learning and Instruction* 6: 201–17.

Nickerson, Raymond S. 1995. "Chapter 1: Can Technology Help Teach for Understanding?" In *Software Goes to School: Teaching for Understanding with New Technologies,* edited by D. N. Perkins, J. L. Schwartz, M. M. West, and M. S. Wiske, 7–22. New York: Oxford Univ. Press.

Nordstrom, A. D. 1997. "Educating Adult Learners: Thinking about Providing the '40-year Diploma.' " *Marketing News,* September, 1–8.

O'Banion, Terry. 1997. *Creating More Learning-Centered Community Colleges.* Mission Viejo, Calif.: League for Innovation in Community College.

Pascarella, Ernest, and Patrick Terenzini. 1991. *How College Affects Students.* San Francisco: Jossey-Bass.

Pechenik, Jan A. 1997. *A Short Guide to Writing about Biology.* New York: Longman.

Peyton, A. Leigh, Michal Morton, Molly M. Perkins, Linda M. Dougherty. 2001. "Mentoring in Gerontology Education: New Graduate Student Perspectives." *Educational Gerontology* 27, no. 5: 347–59.

Pintrich, Paul R. 1988. "A Process-Oriented View of Student Motivation and Cognition." In *Improving Teaching and Learning Through Research,* edited by J. S. Stark and L. A. Mets, 65–79. Series *New Directions for Institutional Research,* no. 57. San Francisco: Jossey-Bass.

Plato. 1979. *Great Dialogues of Plato.* Translated by W. H. D. Rouse. New York: New American Library.

Program Assessment Consultation Team (PACT). 1999. *PACT Outcomes Assessment Handbook.* Bakersfield: California State Univ.

Redd, Kenneth. 2000. "HBCU Graduates: Employment, Earnings, and Success after College." *USA Group Foundation New Agenda Series,* vol. 2, no. 4.

Richlin, Laurie. 1995. "A Different View on Teaching Portfolios: Ensuring Safety While Honoring Practice." *Journal on Excellence in Teaching* 6, no. 1: 161–78.

Roach, Ronald. 1999. "Grooming the 21st Century Professoriate." *Black Issues in Higher Education* 16, no. 18: 20–23.

Ross, Dorene. D., Elizabeth Bondy, and Diane W. Kyle. 1993. *Reflective Teaching for Student Empowerment.* New York: Macmillan.

Rosser, Sue V. 1991. *Female Friendly Science: Applying Women's Studies Methods and Theories to Attract Students.* New York: Teacher's College Press.

Rowe, Mary B. 1986. "Wait Time: Slowing Down May Be a Way of Speeding Up!" *Journal of Teacher Education* 37, no. 1: 43–50.

Sarason, Irwin G., Gregory R. Pierce, and Barbara R. Sarason. 1994. "General and Specific Perceptions of Social Support." In *Stress and Mental Health: Contemporary*

Issues and Prospects for the Future, edited by William R. Avison and Ian H. Gotlib, 151–77. New York: Plenum.

Scarff, Michele. 2000. "The Full-Time Stress of Part-Time Professors." *Newsweek,* May 9, 10.

Schneider, Alison. 1999. "To Many Adjunct Professors, Academic Freedom Is a Myth." *The Chronicle of Higher Education,* December 10, A18.

Schön, Donald A. 1983. *The Reflective Practitioner: How Professionals Think in Action.* New York: Basic Books.

———. 1987. *Educating the Reflective Practitioner.* San Francisco: Jossey-Bass.

———, ed. 1991. *The Reflective Turn: Case Studies in and on Educational Practice.* New York: Teachers College Press.

Schuttloffel, Merylann. J. 1999. *Character and the Contemplative Principal.* Washington, D.C.: National Catholic Educational Association.

Seifert, Kelvin. L. 1999. *Reflective Thinking and Professional Development.* Boston: Houghton-Mifflin.

Seldin, Peter. 1980. *Successful Faculty Evaluation Programs.* Crugers, N.Y.: Coventry.

———. 1993. *Successful Use of Teaching Portfolios.* Bolton, Mass.: Anker.

———. 1997. *The Teaching Portfolio: A Practical Guide to Improved Performance and Promotion/Tenure Decisions,* 2nd ed. Bolton, Mass.: Anker.

———. 2000. "Teaching Portfolios: A Positive Appraisal." *Academe* 86, no. 1 (Jan./Feb.): 36–44.

Sherman, Thomas M., et al. 1987. "The Quest for Excellence in University Teaching." *Journal of Higher Education* 58, no. 1 (Jan./Feb.): 66–84.

Silberman, Melvin. 1996. *Active Learning: 101 Strategies to Teach Any Subject.* Boston: Allyn and Bacon.

Small, Ruth V., and Marilyn P. Arnone. 1998/1999. "Arousing and Sustaining Curiosity: Lessons from the ARCS Model." *Training Research Journal* 4: 103–16.

———. 2000. *Turning Kids On to Research: The Power of Motivation.* Englewood, Colo.: Libraries Unlimited.

Small, Ruth V., Martin Dodge, and Bin Jiang. 1996. "Student Perceptions of Boring and Interesting Instruction." In *Proceedings of the Annual Conference of the Association for Educational Communications and Technology,* edited by M. R. Simonson, M. Hays, and S. Hall, 712–26. Ames, Iowa: AECT.

Smith, Daryl G., Lisa E. Wolf, and Bonnie E. Busenberg. 1996. *Achieving Faculty Diversity: Debunking the Myths.* Washington, D.C.: Association of American Colleges and Universities.

Smith, Kathleen S., and Ronald D. Simpson. 1995. "Validating Teaching Competencies for Faculty Members in Higher Education: A National Study Using the Delphi Method." *Innovative Higher Education* 19: 223–34.

Stuhr, John J. 1987. *Classical American Philosophy.* New York: Oxford Univ. Press.

Tobin, Kenneth, Deborah J. Tippins, and Alejandro J. Gallard. 1994. "Research on Instructional Strategies for Teaching Science." Chapter 2 in *Handbook of Research on Science and Teaching: A Project of the National Science Teachers Association,* edited by D. L. Gabel, 45–93. New York: Macmillan.

Towns, Marcy H., and Edward R. Grant. 1997. " 'I Believe I Will Go Out of This Class Actually Knowing Something': Cooperative Learning Activities in Physical Chemistry." *Journal of Research in Science Teaching* 34: 819–35.

Turner, Caroline S. V., Samuel L. Myers, Jr., and John W. Creswell. 1999. "Exploring Underrepresentation: The Case of Faculty of Color in the Midwest." *Journal of Higher Education* 70, no. 1: 27–59.

Turner, Caroline S. V. 2002. *Diversifying the Faculty: A Guidebook for Search Committees.* Washington, D.C.: Association of American Colleges and Universities.

"The 28th Annual Survey of High Achievers." 2000. *Who's Who Among American High School Students.* http://www.eci-whoswho.com/highschool/annualsurveys/29.shtml

Valli, Linda, ed. 1992. *Reflective Teacher Education: Cases and Critiques.* Albany: State Univ. of New York Press.

Van Manen, Max. 1977. "Linking Ways of Knowing with Ways of Being Practical." *Curriculum and Inquiry* 6, no. 3: 205–28.

Villalpando, Octavio. 2002. "The Impact of Diversity and Multiculturalism on All Students: Findings from a National Study." *NASPA Journal* (online) 40, no. 1, 124–44.

Vroom, Victor H. 1964. *Work and Motivation.* New York: Wiley.

Weber, Sandra, and Claudia Mitchell. 1995. *That's Funny, You Don't Look Like a Teacher!: Interrogating Images and Identity in Popular Culture.* Philadelphia: Falmer.

Wexler, Dara H. 2003. *Shifting Pedagogies: Intersections of Computer-Supported Technologies, Education, and Power.* Ph.D. dissertation, Cultural Foundations of Education, Syracuse University, Syracuse, N.Y.

Whicher, Stephen E., ed. 1960. *Selections from Ralph Waldo Emerson.* Boston: Riverside Edition.

Wilson, Robin. 1998. "For Some Adjunct Faculty Members, the Tenure Track Holds Little Appeal." *The Chronicle of Higher Education,* July 24, A8.

Wlodkowski, Raymond J. 1993. *Enhancing Adult Motivation to Learn: A Guide to Improving Instruction and Increasing Learner Achievement.* San Francisco: Jossey-Bass.

Wlodkowski, Raymond J., and Judith H. Jaynes. 1990. "Overcoming Boredom and Indifference." In *Eager to Learn,* 85–98. San Francisco: Jossey-Bass.

Woliver, Robbie. 2000. "Adjunct Professors: Low Pay and Hard Going." *New York Times,* May 7, 14LI2.

Wright, Cheryl A., and Scott D. Wright. 1987. "The Role of Mentors in the Career Development of Young Professionals." *Family Relations* 36: 204–8.

Young, M. 1982. "Increasing Learner Participation." *Performance and Instruction* 21, no. 4 (May): 7–10.

Zamanou, Sonia. 1993. "Differences Do Make a Difference: Recruitment Strategies for the Non-Traditional Student." Paper presented at the 79th Annual Meeting of the Speech Communication Association, Miami Beach, Fla.

Zemke, Ron, and Susan Zemke. 1981. "30 Things We Know for Sure about Adult Learning." *Training* 18, no. 6 (June): 45–46, 48–49, 52.

Zinsser, William. 1998. *On Writing Well.* New York: HarperPerennial.

Index

World Wide Web: for campus-based
instruction, 123, 125, 126–28; computer-
based research, 126–28; discussion
servers, 125. *See also* web pages; web sites
Wright, Cheryl A., 237
Wright, Richard, 50
Wright, Scott D., 237
writing: every teacher as teaching, 162–63; as
learning tool, 177; process of, 180–82;
revisions and reviews, 181–82; in science
classes, 174–83; style, 179–80; writing-
intensive courses, 162–73
writing-across-the-curriculum movement,
162
writing-intensive courses, 162–73;
assignments for, 164–65, 166–68, 170–72;

defining, 163; discipline-specific
writing instruction in, 168–69;
emphasizing writing process in, 164–65;
require significant amounts of writing in,
166; variety of writing types in, 166–68;
writing to develop critical thinking in,
169–70
writing-to-communicate, 167–68
writing-to-learn, 167, 175–79
written language disorders, 97

Yale University, 236

Zinsser, William, 181